What Works When

with Children and Adolescents

A Handbook of Individual Counseling Techniques

Ann Vernon

Research Press
2612 North Mattis Avenue
Champaign, Illinois 61822
[800] 519-2707
www.researchpress.com

Copies of this book may be ordered from Research Press at the address given on
the title page.

Composition by Jeff Helgesen
Cover design by Linda Brown, Positive I.D. Graphic Design, Inc.
Printed by McNaughton & Gunn

ISBN 0-87822-438-6
Library of Congress Catalog Number 2002109730

Contents

Activities

Foreword

I enthusiastically endorse Ann Vernon's book on individual counseling interventions with children and adolescents. I think that it is easily the most comprehensive and practical book that exists on how to apply rational emotive behavior therapy (REBT) to emotionally and behaviorally troubled youngsters. Oh, yes—and, by all means, to the parents of these youngsters, too.

There have been other books that nicely apply REBT to children and adolescents, including Bill Knaus's (1974) pioneering presentation, *Rational-Emotive Education;* my 1983 anthology with Michael Bernard, *Rational-Emotive Approaches to the Problems of Childhood;* a fine book by Michael Bernard and Marie Joyce (1984), *Rational-Emotive Therapy with Children and Adolescents;* Jerry Wilde's (1992) *Rational Counseling with School-Aged Populations;* Michael Bernard's (2001) *Program Achieve;* as well as important previous programs by Ann Vernon, such as *Thinking, Feeling, Behaving: An Emotional Education Program for Children and Adolescents* (1989a, 1989b) and *The Passport Program: A Journey through Emotional, Social, Cognitive, and Self-Development* (1998a, 1998b, 1998c). None of these texts, however, covers the scope of materials that Ann Vernon herewith presents to therapists, teachers, and parents who are willing to devote themselves to aiding troubled youngsters.

First of all, Ann describes the special considerations that practitioners need to take into account as they apply REBT to young clients. As she points out, these methods are quite different in many respects from those that are used to apply individual counseling to adults, and she gives a number of suggestions that almost any kind of child counselor can effectively employ. She then clearly and accurately states the basic principles of REBT and their application to children and adolescents. Counselors who are relatively unfamiliar with REBT are efficiently introduced to it in Ann's presentation.

Following the first two chapters, Ann provides examples of special interventions for children's and adolescents' emotional problems, behavioral difficulties, and typical developmental issues. In these core chapters she not only tells counselors exactly what they can do to help clients, but also includes a considerable number of interventions that she herself has creatively invented that can be used effectively with young clients. The many REBT techniques she presents include descriptions of rational and irrational beliefs; the disputing of irrational beliefs in language that youngsters can easily understand; the use of appropriate homework assignments; the employment of rational emotive imagery, role playing, and other experiential and emotive-evocative methods; a host of special exercises, activities, games, visuals, and sentence completions; serious and humorous stories, songs, and an assortment of similar tools that counselors can use; and many other down-to-earth procedures that are common to REBTers—and, for that matter, can be employed by therapists following other kinds of therapies.

I found particularly valuable the many verbatim therapeutic transcripts that Ann has included in most of the chapters. While she was writing this book, Jerry Wilde and I were editing another book, *Case Studies in Rational Emotive Behavior Therapy with Children and Adolescents* (2001), which includes a transcript of a case by Ann. If readers want to see exactly what REBT counselors say to troubled youngsters, they can find ample illustrations of this material in this book as well as in Jerry Wilde's and my compilation of case studies.

A final note: Ann's unusually good book tends to substantiate my original hypothesis that REBT can be used effectively, in relatively few sessions, with moderately and more seriously disturbed children and adolescents. As presented by Ann and appreciably helped by her fine examples, rational emotive behavior therapy will, I predict, continue to grow in popularity through the 21st century and beyond. Thank you, Ann, for making this fine contribution to it.

Albert Ellis, Ph.D.
President
Albert Ellis Institute

Acknowledgments

For 25 years I have personally and professionally practiced rational emotive behavior therapy (REBT) to the best of my ability, acknowledging that, as a fallible human being, I have not always done it perfectly, and that, under certain circumstances, it has been more of a challenge to apply the principles to my own life than at other times. Nevertheless, this theory has, beyond a doubt, profoundly affected me in positive ways too numerous to describe.

I would like to thank Dr. Albert Ellis for creating this theory and for devoting much of his life to promulgating it through his writing and by establishing the Albert Ellis Institute, whose mission is, among other things, to train practitioners in the theory and practice of REBT. It was through my training at the Institute that I first began using this approach with children and adolescents and subsequently began publishing books and articles with the encouragement and support of other noted REBT practitioners, Drs. Virginia Waters, Richard Wessler, Dominic DiMattia, Ray DiGiuseppe, and Janet Wolfe.

I also wish to acknowledge Dr. Jennifer Naidich, former head of Children and Family Services at the Albert Ellis Institute, for her very thorough and professional critique of this manuscript. Her comments were insightful and extremely helpful, and her suggestions enhanced the end product.

Writing a book such as this takes persistence and patience, but, as I used various interventions with my child and adolescent clients during the writing process, it reaffirmed for me how important it is to have a variety of techniques to facilitate their growth. I feel privileged to be able to counsel these young people, and I thank them for sharing their lives with me. I remain strongly convinced that developing rational thinkers is the key to healthy development.

Last but not least, I would like to thank my spouse for his ability to tolerate my long hours at the computer; my editor at Research Press, David Hamburg, for tolerating my perfectionistic tendencies in the preparation of this manuscript; and Ann Wendel at Research Press, for her enthusiasm for my projects.

Introduction

A 10-year-old was referred for counseling by his mother, who was concerned about her son's quick temper and his recent anxiety about her safety. She indicated that he had been in counseling the previous year to work on his anger following her divorce. Although counseling had not been especially helpful for Shannon at that time, he was not averse to starting again with a new counselor.

When I first met with Shannon, I asked him about his expectations for counseling. "Well, last time I went to counseling, all I did was talk about my anger. At first that was good, but nothing really changed. This time I want something that really helps me get better," he explained. Although I was surprised that a 10-year-old could articulate his expectations so clearly, I definitely agreed with him. Counseling needs to do more than help clients "feel better"; it also needs to help them "get better."

This young client's seemingly simple statement showed unusual insight and intuition. In fact, he unwittingly stumbled upon the central objective of rational emotive behavior therapy (REBT), a theory developed by Dr. Albert Ellis in 1955. REBT is based on the notion that how we think largely determines our feelings and behaviors (Dryden & Ellis, 2001). By helping individuals learn to identify and challenge the dysfunctional or irrational thinking patterns that create emotional disturbance, we can empower them to deal with a wide array of problematic situations.

Early in the practice of REBT, Ellis and his colleagues began applying the theory to children and, for several reasons, found it to be a highly effective form of therapy with young people (Vernon, 1997). First, it is easily understood and is adaptable for children of most ages, cultures, and intelligence levels. Second, it is a short-term problem-solving form of therapy, which makes it particularly useful in school settings, where time for counseling sessions is limited and more traditional forms of therapy are inappropriate. The same time constraints hold true in mental health settings, where the number of sessions is limited by managed health care companies. That REBT is a brief form of therapy is also especially important for young clients because their sense of time is so immediate; they need something that will help them *now*. Additionally, this theory is widely applicable for work with children and adolescents who are in the concrete operational stage of thinking. The teachable concepts inherent in this approach offer a highly effective, concrete way of matching therapeutic style with youngsters' level of cognitive development. As young people mature into the stage of formal operational thought, the therapy can easily be adapted to incorporate more abstract concepts.

Perhaps more important, REBT empowers individuals, making it a particularly relevant form of therapy for young people, who typically have very little control over most significant life events. Children are uniquely vulnerable to the decisions the adults in their lives make. For instance, most youngsters are not consulted about the death of a family member, parental divorce or remarriage, loss of family income due to a parent's unemployment, or parental substance abuse. REBT teaches behavioral and emotional self-control by helping children to understand the connection between thoughts, feelings, and behaviors. In doing so, and in promoting psychological well-being, it helps them to deal realistically with what they can and cannot change in their lives.

REBT is applicable to a wide range of normal developmental concerns such as self-consciousness during puberty, academic pressure, friendship problems, and competition. Whether the problem is situational or developmental, this theory is more effective than many others because it immediately addresses the problem and teaches children how to think clearly and solve problems independently.

Finally, an integral part of this theory is its emphasis on teaching and prevention. In 1971, The Living School was established to help young people learn rational principles. Although The Living School no longer exists, the concepts introduced in that setting have been applied to children and adolescents across the United States and abroad through several emotional education programs. These programs, which promote emotional and behavioral health, are designed to help them apply rational thinking skills to the problems they face in their daily lives (Bernard, 2001; Knaus, 1974; Vernon, 1989a, 1989b, 1998a, 1998b, 1998c; Waters, 1979, 1980). These programs teach children the skills necessary for dealing with current problems and also enable them to acquire techniques they can use to prevent or minimize problems that arise in the future. The self-help emphasis that results from teaching these REBT concepts can facilitate problem resolution independent of regularly scheduled counseling sessions; this factor is especially beneficial for children and adolescents.

The purpose of this book, then, is to describe specific applications of REBT that help practitioners understand "what works when with children and adolescents." Chapter 1 discusses developmental considerations in working with younger clients and how REBT so aptly addresses developmental limitations that are characteristic of children and adolescents. The chapter includes strategies for establishing a therapeutic relationship with young clients, who are often referred by others and are therefore apprehensive or opposed to counseling. Chapter 2 outlines the basic REBT schema and elaborates on the theory, putting major emphasis on the assessment process and problem conceptualization as it applies to young clients. Chapters 3 and 4 describe specific cognitive, emotive, and behavioral interventions for internalizing and externalizing problems of childhood and adolescence. These two chapters are designed to help practitioners deal with problems concerning self-downing, anxiety, perfectionism, guilt, depression, anger, acting out, procrastination, and underachievement. Included are selected case examples that illustrate various techniques. Chapter 5 identifies typical developmental problems and also provides examples of REBT interventions. Chapter 6 describes the various applications of these principles for parents and teachers.

Designed for counselors, social workers, and psychologists in school and mental health settings, this practical handbook offers creative, useful interventions for problems children and adolescents commonly experience. It includes games, art and music activities, role plays, and other strategies designed to motivate young clients to participate in their own therapy.

A few of these interventions involve the use of a game board or game cards. The point of using the game board is not to finish first or determine a winner, but to encourage the client's self-disclosure and involvement within the familiar, comfortable context of playing a table game. You may create your own game boards, or you may photocopy the generic game board included in the Appendix, glue or tape it to an open manila folder or a large sheet of tagboard, then decorate it however you wish. The game board in the Appendix is a continuous loop, with no finish line: You can play the game as long as you find it helpful and stop any time. Dot stickers of different colors are sometimes needed to color-code the game board and game cards. For some activities, you will need dice; coins or buttons can serve as game markers. When an activity calls for the use of game cards, you will need to photocopy the page on which they appear, cut the items apart, and affix them to index cards or card-sized strips of tagboard. If you wish, you can also create your own game cards to fit your particular client and circumstances.

Many of the interventions include stories, songs, and poems that bring REBT principles to life by showing how other children and adolescents think, feel, and behave in various situations. You may read these materials aloud to clients, give them to clients to read, or read aloud while your clients read silently—whatever best suits the particular individual. Pages you may photocopy and give to your clients are included for all but the briefest of these items.

Additional materials accompanying the interventions in this handbook include photocopiable worksheets, checklists, and illustrations. If hands-on materials like balloons or art supplies are called for in an activity, these are specified.

Although many of the strategies presented here can be adapted for use in small-group counseling or classroom settings, they are designed specifically for use in individual counseling and are based on my extensive experience applying REBT to children and adolescents. Practitioners using this book should find that this theory helps young clients *get* better, not just *feel* better. REBT will strengthen their "emotional muscle" and equip them to deal more effectively with the normal challenges of growing up as well as more serious problems. Consequently, these young clients will be better able to take charge of their lives and avoid self-defeating behaviors that are likely to have serious negative implications.

CHAPTER 1

Considerations in Working with Young Clients

Twelve-year-old Lisa sat silently across from her counselor, staring at the floor. Attempts to get this young client to talk had failed. In desperation, the counselor continued asking questions, hoping for some response. With each question, Lisa withdrew even further, causing greater frustration for her counselor.

This scenario may sound familiar. For a variety of reasons, attempts to get young clients to open up are often met with resistance. These youngsters may not understand what the process of counseling entails, and they may be frightened or confused when a parent tells them they are going to see a counselor. This lack of understanding contributes to the fear that many children have that they are "crazy" or "bad" or that something is seriously wrong with them if they need professional help. Adolescents in particular resent being labeled "the problem," especially when they don't think anything is wrong with them. This same dynamic operates when an adolescent is a juvenile offender and is ordered by the court to receive counseling. Furthermore, many youngsters enter therapy without being told why by the adults who referred them. All of these factors can initially have a negative impact on the client-counselor therapeutic alliance.

Another factor contributing to these youngsters' reluctance to communicate is that they may not be adept at describing how they feel or what has occurred, so what seems like resistance is simply a matter of their not knowing what to say. Younger children in particular like to please adults, and it may be safer for them not to say much if they are not sure how to express themselves. One can imagine being in their shoes—being 8 years old and not having any idea what a counselor does: One day your mother announces that you are going to see Dr. Vernon, who will help you with your sad feelings. A week or so later, Mom loads you in the car and takes you to a strange office, where you sit in a waiting room with people staring at you. Finally, someone you have never seen before comes to get you, and you have to go all by yourself into another room. You really do not know what to say, and you want to avoid sounding dumb, so you just sit there. Should it surprise counselors that some young clients may initially give them the silent treatment?

During the past 30 years, helping professionals have gradually recognized that, in many respects, counseling children and adolescents is quite different from counseling adults. Fortunately, practitioners are now incorporating more child-oriented approaches into their work with young clients. In the field of rational emotive behavior therapy (REBT), however, there is a paucity of work that specifically addresses important developmental considerations and individual counseling interventions with children and adolescents. This book was written to fill that void.

DEVELOPMENTAL CONSIDERATIONS

Early Childhood

For 4- and 5-year-olds, the world is a fascinating place. These children are curious, energetic, and eager. With the help of their imaginations, anything is possible. As a result, it is often difficult for them to distinguish between real and make-believe, which is why the "monsters" under the bed seem so real (Vernon & Al-Mabuk, 1995). Preoperational thinking characterizes their cognitive development and limits the degree to which they can think logically or understand abstract concepts (Berk, 2001; McDevitt & Ormrod, 2002). By nature, preschoolers are egocentric; they assume that everyone thinks and feels the same way they do. Consequently, it is difficult, if not impossible, for them to see things from another's perspective. During this period of development, their self-esteem is quite high (McDevitt & Ormrod, 2002), and they tend to overestimate their abilities, thinking that they can do anything. Because they are developing so quickly and mastering so many tasks during this stage, their feelings of self-efficacy can be advantageous (Seifert & Hoffnung, 1997). They are also developing the ability to control their impulses.

Play serves an extremely important function at this age, and it is through this medium that children learn how to be cooperative and take turns (Owens, 2002). However, they have difficulty understanding intentionality, so they are likely to misinterpret others' behavior and respond inappropriately (Vernon & Al-Mabuk, 1995). Because their emotional vocabularies are limited, they often express their feelings behaviorally. Toward the end of this stage of development, youngsters begin to acquire a better understanding of other people's emotions and can respond verbally or physically by, for example, apologizing or giving a hug when they think someone is sad.

Middle Childhood

During middle childhood, ages 6 to 10, physical growth is relatively stable, and children are able to master most motor skills (Bee, 2000;

McDevitt & Ormrod, 2002). By age 8, children enter the concrete operational stage, which has a positive impact on their problem-solving abilities. For these reasons, many consider middle childhood to be the best period in a person's life (Berger & Thompson, 1991).

As concrete operational thinkers, these children are able to think more logically, but they still do not reason abstractly or consider a wide range of alternatives, an inability that influences how they approach situations (Vernon, 1993). For example, if their best friend does not sit by them on the bus, they might assume that they did something to make the friend angry rather than consider other possibilities.

During this period of maturation, children's self-understanding improves (Owens, 2002), and they begin to develop a stronger internal locus of control (Vernon & Al-Mabuk, 1995). As they enter school and compare themselves to others, they become increasingly self-critical and may begin to feel inferior.

The ability to socialize effectively with peers is a critical developmental task during these years, as children confront the issues of acceptance, rejection, peer pressure, and conformity. Peer interactions may elicit joy, concern, and disappointment, but friendships serve important functions as well. As children develop perspective taking, they become more adept at interpreting social cues (Pruitt, 1998) and are better able to employ social judgment as a means to resolve interpersonal conflict (Cole & Cole, 1996). The ability to recognize and communicate feelings more effectively also contributes to their improved social problem solving skills.

Early Adolescence

Whereas middle childhood is generally thought of as the best period in a person's life, early adolescence (ages 11 to 14) is often considered the worst. It is during this period of development that young people feel increasingly vulnerable. Physical changes occur more rapidly during this time than at any other point in the life span, with the exception of infancy (Dusek, 1996). Because the rate of maturity varies tremendously across genders and individuals, self-consciousness and anxiety are prevalent. Males and females alike may become clumsy and uncoordinated because the size of their hands and feet may be disproportionate to their other body parts. Their rate of physical change affects their self-concept (McDevitt & Ormrod, 2002); it is a factor that is especially relevant for early adolescents, who want to be like everyone else to gain social acceptance and are anxious about appearing awkward or different (Owens, 2002). Additionally, physical and hormonal changes can cause a great deal of confusion and discomfort as sexual thoughts and feelings arise, and they are often accompanied by feelings of guilt, shame, and embarrassment (Vernon, 1999b).

Although the shift from concrete to formal operational thinking begins during early adolescence, this process is gradual and is not completed until at least age 15 (Kaplan, 2000). As adolescents move

into formal operational thinking, they begin to think more abstractly, develop the ability to hypothesize, reason more logically, and
predict consequences (Dusek, 1996; Kaplan, 2000). However, they
do not always apply these skills to themselves and often have difficulty linking events, feelings, and situations. Therefore, they may
fail to make the connection between flunking a test and not studying for it (Newman & Newman, 1991). Because considerable vari-
ability exists in the degree to which formal operational thinking is
attained and applied consistently during early adolescence, it is of
critical importance not to assume that these youngsters are capable
of more mature cognition (Cobb, 2001).

During this developmental period, early adolescents begin their
search for self-definition and integration and push for autonomy
(Cobb, 2001). However, because they are still immature and lack
life experiences to guide them (Weisfeld, 1999), they often feel vulnerable and may be somewhat more dependent on adults. This situation is confusing to them (Vernon, 1999b). Adolescents in this
age range tend to feel acutely self-conscious and assume that everyone is looking at them and that they are on display before what
Elkind (1988) termed the *imaginary audience*. As a result of this type
of thinking, adolescents fantasize about how others will react to
them and are overly sensitive about their performance and appearance. Needless to say, self-esteem usually decreases during this
period of development.

Another phenomenon that causes considerable concern during this
stage is what Elkind (1984) labeled the *personal fable,* which is the
belief held by many early adolescents that because they are unique,
special, and invulnerable, bad things may happen to others but not to
them. This type of thinking may explain in part why so many young
people engage in risk-taking behaviors such as unprotected sex
("Others can get pregnant or contract sexually transmitted diseases,
but it won't happen to me").

Peers play an increasingly important role in the lives of early
adolescents, and, although teens look to one another as a source of
support, they are also vulnerable to peer humiliation. Belonging
and rejection are major issues at this age, and desire for one and
fear of the other typically result in vulnerability to peer pressure.
Because they are still egocentric and have difficulty taking others'
viewpoints into account (Jaffe, 1998), young adolescents may be
limited in their ability to deal effectively with these problems.

Early adolescents ride an emotional roller coaster during this
developmental stage. Their emotional volatility is characterized by
moodiness, emotional outbursts, anger, anxiety, shame, depression,
and guilt. These negative emotions are typically overwhelming to
these adolescents and lead to feelings of anxiety about their vulnerability, an anxiety that is often masked by anger. This response in
turn keeps people at a distance and can result in increased conflict
with adults as well as peers.

Mid-Adolescence

Mid-adolescence (ages 15 to 18) is generally characterized by more stability than early adolescence, depending on when the onset of puberty occurs. Physical development is usually less rapid (McDevitt & Ormrod, 2002), resulting in a lesser degree of self-consciousness and fluctuation of emotions. Formal operational thinking continues to develop, and these new cognitive abilities allow adolescents to think and behave differently. Their thinking is more multidimensional (Owens, 2000), and they are better able to think abstractly, hypothesize, and consider future events and consequences. Additionally, they are less likely to conceptualize everything in either/or terms, the way younger adolescents typically do. However, inconsistencies in their thinking and behaving remain (Cobb, 2001). Although they may be able to see alternatives, older adolescents often lack the experience or self-understanding to make appropriate choices (Vernon, 1999b).

At this stage of development, adolescents are concerned about achieving independence and exploring various roles and responsibilities. Their interests may change, and they may engage in the process of self-questioning and experimenting as a way of establishing an identity (Vernon, 1999b). In addition, these older adolescents are generally more self-confident than they were in early adolescence.

Peer relationships continue to be very important and serve as vehicles to try out various roles and develop tolerance for individual differences. Depending on their degree of formal operational thinking, mid-adolescents approach peer relationships with more maturity than they possessed in earlier years and consequently may not be as dependent on friends for emotional support as they were in the past (Dusek, 1996). As intimate relationships develop, new challenges, such as dating and sexual experimentation, emerge (Newman & Newman, 1991).

The degree to which a formal operational thought process has been attained is especially important because it has a strong impact on adolescents' emotional state. For the most part, adolescents during this stage experience fewer mood fluctuations than younger adolescents. They also are not as overwhelmed by their feelings and are better able to deal with emotionally charged issues. They are not as impulsive or as likely to behave erratically in response to emotional upset. The way they manage their emotions still varies widely, however, and is dependent on their level of cognitive maturation (Vernon & Al-Mabuk, 1995).

IMPLICATIONS OF DEVELOPMENTAL STAGES

Practitioners working with children and adolescents need to tailor their assessment and intervention strategies, using games with younger children and concrete techniques with children of all ages to illustrate their points. They need to remain aware of the ways in which self-development, as well as emotional, social, physical, and cognitive development characteristics, influence how youngsters interpret their world. Interpretations of such factors carry important implications for accurate problem diagnosis and selection of appropriate interventions.

Perhaps the most important factor to keep in mind is that cognitive development significantly affects perceptions. For example, although children in middle childhood have acquired enhanced problem-solving skills, they are still limited by their concrete thought processes. Not being able to see all sides of an issue, taking things literally, and not being able to reason abstractly all have significant implications for how they process everyday occurrences. For these reasons, their perception of events is often distorted, and they frequently become upset because they have not judged problems accurately. This phenomenon also pertains to the 11- to 14-year-old age group and often extends into mid-adolescence, depending on the rate of cognitive maturity. For example, children in middle childhood often are quite eager to please the teacher because they want the teacher's approval. If the teacher fails to call on them or reprimands them, they may wrongly conclude that the teacher does not like them or that they can never do anything to please the teacher. If appropriate intervention does not occur, they may become discouraged or act out in negative ways to gain attention. Because they also lack the ability to generate problem-solving alternatives, their behavior may be misunderstood and result in conflict with parents or teachers, who assume they are able to recognize other possibilities. This type of behavior is exemplified by the 12-year-old who stayed for basketball practice and neglected to do her paper route. When her father asked her why she hadn't called home to ask her brother to deliver the papers, she said, "I honestly didn't think about it. The coach said we had to stay for practice or we would get kicked off the team, and that's all I thought about."

RELATIONSHIP BETWEEN REBT AND DEVELOPMENT

Because the stages of development, particularly cognitive development, play such a central role in how children and adolescents interpret their life experiences, therapeutic interventions must be developmentally sensitive if they are to be effective. REBT is uniquely suited for use with younger populations because it can be easily tailored for youngsters at any point in their development and employs a wide array of strategies that most appropriately address the problem. Furthermore, interventions aimed at correcting irrational thinking also help young clients gain cognitive perspective, which in turn enables them to deal more effectively with normal developmental problems as well as more situational factors.

The model shown on the next page illustrates the relationship between REBT and development. In the very center of the model (1) are the areas of development: self, emotional, social, physical, and cognitive. How clients respond to normal developmental problems

Relationship between REBT and Development

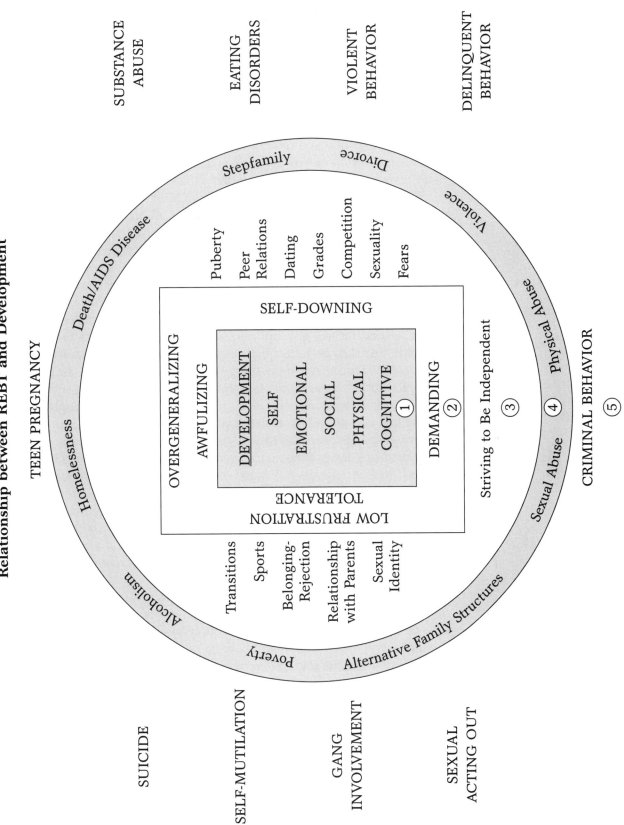

SUBSTANCE ABUSE

EATING DISORDERS

VIOLENT BEHAVIOR

DELINQUENT BEHAVIOR

TEEN PREGNANCY

SUICIDE

SELF-MUTILATION

GANG INVOLVEMENT

SEXUAL ACTING OUT

CRIMINAL BEHAVIOR

Stepfamily

Divorce

Death/AIDS Disease

Violence

Homelessness

Physical Abuse

Alcoholism

Sexual Abuse

Poverty

Alternative Family Structures

Puberty

Peer Relations

Dating

Grades

Competition

Sexuality

Fears

Transitions

Sports

Belonging-Rejection

Relationship with Parents

Sexual Identity

SELF-DOWNING

OVERGENERALIZING

AWFULIZING

LOW FRUSTRATION TOLERANCE

DEMANDING

DEVELOPMENT

SELF

EMOTIONAL

SOCIAL

PHYSICAL

COGNITIVE

Striving to Be Independent

① ② ③ ④ ⑤

11

such as peer relations, school performance, or transitions, which are depicted in the first circle (3), is influenced by their level of development. For example, a 6-year-old who is still quite egocentric and in the process of developing more prosocial skills, such as cooperating and compromising, will have more difficulty with peer relations than a 10-year-old who has more mature skills and is not as egocentric. Likewise, their level of development also affects how they respond to more serious situational problems such as abuse, parental divorce, or homelessness, shown in the outer circle (4). Because adolescents can think more logically and understand more complex issues, it would be easier for a 16-year-old, as opposed to an 8-year-old, to understand that it was not her fault that her father sexually abused her.

Not only does the level of development affect how children and adolescents respond to typical developmental problems—as well as to more serious situational problems that some youngsters experience—but their degree of irrational thinking also plays a major role. Listed in the inner square (2) are the core irrational beliefs: self-downing, low frustration tolerance, demanding, and awfulizing/overgeneralizing. A youngster who has low frustration tolerance will experience more difficulty with a normal developmental issue such as performance in sports because he will give up more easily, thinking, "This is too hard. I shouldn't have to do things that require this much effort." A fourth grader who engages in self-downing will make remarks such as "I'm so stupid; nobody is as dumb as I am" in response to missing several problems on a social studies test. This type of thinking can be problematic and is especially correlated with level of cognitive maturity. For example, self-conscious 13-year-olds whose abstract thinking skills are limited can easily overgeneralize and awfulize about having to give a speech in front of a class. Instead of realizing that others probably feel the same way, that everyone will not be staring at the barely noticeable pimple on their nose, and that they can tolerate this embarrassment for a short time, they may see only one option: skipping class to avoid the situation. They are not able to think of alternative ways to deal with the issue, nor do they usually anticipate the consequences of their actions.

To illustrate further, consider how young people respond to divorce, a situational factor that affects the lives of many children. Clients' level of emotional maturity, coupled with their ability to think rationally, will have a significant bearing on their level of distress. Eight-year-old Keisha told her counselor that she was very sad about her parents' divorce. But in her words, "It could be worse. My dad could move a long ways away, and I'd hardly ever get to see him then." Contrast this reaction by a logical thinker to that of a same-age classmate, who stated that he couldn't think of anything worse than his parents getting divorced because he knew he would never be happy again: Everything in his whole life would change, and if his parents remarried, he could never get along with a stepparent. In his case, his awfulizing and overgeneralizing resulted in depression and anxiety. His failure to realize that his situation, although very difficult, could definitely be worse had a negative impact on how he responded to this circumstance.

Having established that both their level of development and their irrational beliefs can influence how young people respond to typical developmental problems that they all experience in some form (as well as to more serious situational problems that far too many young people are subject to and have little control over), let's refer once again to the model on page 11. Around the outer edge of the last circle (5) are self-defeating behaviors such as self-mutilation, suicide, eating disorders, and substance abuse. Consider the fact that irrational thinking and the inability to put things in perspective make problems—be they typical or more serious—seem insurmountable. If adolescents in particular, but children as well, make inaccurate assumptions, lack persistence, engage in self-downing, fail to generate alternatives, and lack good coping mechanisms, they may resort to the behaviors listed around the outer circle as a way to escape or deal with their pain. The likelihood of this occurring seems stronger when they have both typical and situational factors to contend with. Of significant concern is that, once youngsters engage in these self-defeating behaviors, they often face other serious consequences that make it far more difficult, if not impossible, to remedy the problem. The following example illustrates this point:

> Jill, a high school junior, had been involved in a serious relationship with her boyfriend for over a year. Her parents did not approve of Matt because they perceived him as emotionally unstable and were quite certain that he was a heavy pot smoker. They did whatever they could to discourage their daughter from seeing him, and the arguments they had were frequent and intense. Jill felt trapped because on the one hand, she could see her parents' point, but on the other hand, she thought she loved Matt and could not consider the thought of breaking up with him; he had already threatened suicide when the topic had been raised. Jill also felt pressured to become sexually involved with Matt, which only added to her stress. In the midst of this, her grandmother became seriously ill. Because Jill felt much closer to her than she did to her mother, she became anxious and depressed. Her grades deteriorated, and that upset her parents. She dropped out of several activities and started drinking to forget about her worries. One night, after she had had too much to drink, she and her friends got picked up and charged with alcohol possession and intoxication. As a result, her infuriated parents grounded her for a month, during which time her grandmother died.

> After her grandmother's death, Jill became even more depressed. She felt that she had no support; she could

not spend time with her friends because she was still grounded. She worried incessantly about her boyfriend's faithfulness because of how upset he was about not being able to see her. As she sat alone in her room, waiting for Matt's phone calls, which seldom came, she felt worthless and rejected because she assumed he was out with another girl. All of this became too much for Jill, and she took an overdose of pills to "forget the pain." Fortunately for Jill, her mother found her and got her to the hospital before it was too late.

This case study underscores the potentially dangerous interaction of situational problems when coupled with irrational thinking and a lack of emotional and cognitive maturity. When Jill started counseling after her suicide attempt and discussed the events of the previous several months with her counselor, she described herself as feeling trapped and overwhelmed. She said she felt hopeless and thought that things would never get better. The fact that there were more effective ways to deal with this crisis than to attempt suicide had not occurred to her. She hadn't considered that she could eventually work through her grief over her grandmother's death and not feel so terrible, or that even if Matt rejected her and started dating someone else, she was not worthless and could get through it. It had not crossed her mind that her poor grades and her shaky relationship with her parents were problems that would eventually go away. And because, as a typical adolescent whose sense of time is in the "here and now," when she was weighted down with problems that seemed impossible to overcome, she reacted impulsively to stop the pain.

Understanding the characteristics of child and adolescent development and how irrational thinking and developmental levels affect so many aspects of young lives is critical in both assessment and treatment.

THE THERAPEUTIC RELATIONSHIP

Over the years, there has been considerable discussion among REBT practitioners regarding the nature of the therapeutic relationship. Ellis and Dryden (1997) recommended that therapists adopt an active-directive style with most clients, and they maintained that showing clients considerable warmth and caring may be detrimental because it can unintentionally reinforce their strong need for love and approval. Although both Dryden and Ellis strongly prefer the active-directive style, Dryden (1996, 1999) encouraged counselors to be flexible and modify their approach to fit the client. Dryden and Ellis (2001) emphasized that it is possible to vary the style and adhere to the theoretical principles at the same time. Walen, DiGiuseppe, and Dryden (1992) also encouraged REBT therapists to employ many different and equally effective therapeutic styles. In addition, they stressed that it is a misconception that being active and directive is incompatible with developing rapport.

Although there may be some difference of opinion concerning the nature of the relationship in the counseling of adults, REBT practitioners who work with younger clients would definitely agree that it is essential to establish a good relationship with children and adolescents if counseling is to be optimally effective. In fact, it may be a necessary precondition for change (Bernard & Joyce, 1984; Vernon, 1997, 1999a; Wilde, 1992). These professionals would argue that being forceful is not appropriate when working with most young clients and that a slower pace and a gentler approach are essential.

Because children and adolescents usually are referred for counseling by their parents or teachers, their degree of resistance or reluctance may range on a continuum from extremely resistant and unwilling—with overt hostility and refusal to cooperate—to acceptance and compliance. Whatever the case may be, it is important to acknowledge what the children perceive, perhaps saying, "I sense that you don't want to be here, and that's all right. But because someone else thinks you have a problem, maybe I can help you deal with that." In the case of the child who is self-referred or willing to be in counseling, the counselor can reinforce this fact by remarking, "I understand that counseling was your idea; I appreciate that because it will make it easier for us to work together and find ways to help you deal with what is bothering you."

It is also a good idea to ascertain what young clients' understanding of counseling is in order to address any misconceptions. Young children may think they are going to a medical doctor, who will give them a shot; many adolescents may assume they are going to a "shrink," who is going to psychoanalyze them or tell them what they have to do. Explaining as succinctly as possible that you are here to help them resolve a problem or a situation that is disturbing to them or to others is important. Reassuring them that they are not crazy and that having a problem does not mean they are bad or ill-intentioned people also helps to alleviate some anxiety. It is often useful to explain to them that if they had a sore throat or a broken leg, they would go to a medical doctor for help, and when they have a social, emotional, or behavioral problem, they can get help from a counselor.

Some younger clients like to read what others their age have said about being in counseling, so sharing a few anonymously written testimonials from former clients often works well. If the parent reports that a child is exceptionally anxious or resistant, writing a short letter explaining who you are and what counseling entails has proven to be an effective way to help ease the child into counseling. Obviously, if the counseling occurs within the school setting, some of these issues will not exist because clients may be familiar with the counselor or at least feel comfortable with the school environment. Regardless of where counseling takes place, many young clients are not sure what counseling is or why they need it. For these reasons, it is essential to address their preconceptions and reluctance in the very first counseling session. In doing so, it is important to deliver explanations in an age-appropriate and nonpathologizing manner. For instance, you can explain that counseling is a safe place to explore thoughts and feelings and solve problems. The counselor should normalize the experience of problems of daily living in order to provide a sense of universality. Clearly stating that all individuals, including adults, have problems may provide an immediate sense of relief.

Because children's sense of time is more immediate, it is also important to let them know that this type of counseling will help them address the problem quickly and that you will teach them skills they can use to change their thoughts, feelings, and behaviors so they can get better in a relatively short amount of time. Suggest to them that you might be asking them to participate in some "experiments" between sessions that can provide them with additional ways to resolve problems. Using the term *experiments* is often better than using the traditional REBT term *homework*, because children and adolescents often assign a negative connotation to the latter, which they associate with schoolwork.

Following are additional ways of establishing a good therapeutic relationship with younger clients.

Learn about their interests and hobbies, things they enjoy, and what they think they are especially good at. Also inquire about pets and family members. This information can be gathered in a variety of ways: by asking them to draw a picture or write a short story about one or more of these topics; by playing a game such as checkers and sharing something personal with each move; or by completing a name poem, in which they write each letter of their name down the side of the paper and then write (or draw) a word or phrase describing themselves that begins with each letter:

> **S**–Soccer player
>
> **A**–A and B student
>
> **L**–Loves to play Nintendo
>
> **L**–Loves to eat candy
>
> **Y**–Yellow is my favorite color

This information can then be used in several ways. For example, a young child shared during her first meeting with the counselor that she had a pet rabbit. In a subsequent counseling session, she expressed concern that her parents would think she was a bad girl because she accidentally wet the bed sometimes. Asking her if she thought her rabbit was a bad rabbit if he ever went to the bathroom outside his cage was a very concrete way to help this young girl see that her parents probably did not think she was a bad person if she wet the bed. Knowing about interests and hobbies also helped a counselor working with a 16-year-old who thought he was a total failure because he had flunked math. Aware that Adam loved working on cars, the counselor asked him if he would think the car was a total piece of junk if it had a flat tire. "Of course not; the tire just needs fixing," Adam replied. "Then think of yourself as the car with the flat tire. You are not a failure; you just need to study harder in math," explained the counselor. This analogy seemed to be an effective way of getting the point across.

Take a nonjudgmental stance. Young clients generally will not disclose much if they think you are judging them. Therefore, even though you may not agree with them, you must nonetheless accept them unconditionally. Watch your body language and nonverbal behaviors so you don't gasp when a 14-year-old shares details about her recent sexual experience. At a later time, you may help the client look at the risks inherent in early sexual activity, but conveying disapproval, either verbally or nonverbally, will sabotage the counseling relationship. Adolescents in particular are very sensitive about being judged. It can be helpful to explicitly state that "who you are is not what you do." For example, if they broke the law, they did something they should not have done, but that does not make them a bad person.

Be genuinely interested in their stories. It is too easy for adults to minimize children's problems, especially those of a typically developmental nature. To younger children, fighting with a best friend can be as upsetting as fighting with a spouse is to an adult; breaking up with a boyfriend can be as traumatic to an adolescent as a divorce is to a parent. It is important to remember that young clients may not have the ability to put their problems in perspective and therefore may overreact or act impulsively, responding in a way that can lead to significant negative consequences. For this reason, it is critical to listen carefully to their stories and see things from their perspective. Additionally, this nonjudgmental approach puts young clients in the position of being the expert on themselves, and you the expert in REBT, thereby creating a collaborative relationship. Doing so instills in them a sense of being respected and important. By being an active and interested listener, you will serve as a good role model and will be gathering important information that you will use later in problem resolution.

Whenever possible, normalize their issues and instill hope. Because of their developmental limitations, children and adolescents often do not understand why they think, feel, and act the way they do. Practitioners who understand what is typical for each age level often find themselves saying something like this: "You know, several other fourth graders I have seen have also been very worried about something bad happening to a parent, because at this age you are more aware of what can happen, but you sometimes don't understand all aspects of the situation. I think we can come up with some ideas about how to help you deal with this, and on this matter, you and I can share some things that have helped other kids your age." The only caution when using this approach is that you must be careful not to dismiss their problem with an offhand remark such as "Oh, that's nothing. All kids your age go through this."

Be honest with them about what you know about the issue. For example, you may know that Serita was picked up for shoplifting, but there is a good chance that she won't share that news with you because she might be ashamed or embarrassed about it. Rather than trying to tease it out of her or wait for her to bring it up, you can introduce the issue in the following way: "Serita, I want to be honest with you. Your father called and informed me that you have been charged with shoplifting. I assume that you have some feelings about what has happened as a result, and this might be a good place to help you deal with them."

Explain the nature and limits of confidentiality, and discuss with clients how you will be communicating with their parents and teachers. Do not promise to hold in confidence things you will need to share later; by doing so, you are likely to destroy the therapeutic relationship. Explain to them that adults in their lives may be concerned about them and may be contacting you. Whenever possible, ask young clients if there is anything they have shared with you that they do not want someone else to know. You may be surprised to learn that they put fewer limits on their sharing than you had imagined. In fact, they may appreciate your facilitating communication with adults on difficult issues. A 10-year-old recently asked me if I could help her mom understand that girls her age like boys. "It's just a girl thing; I'm not going to do anything yucky with them like hold hands or anything, but I want her to know that girls just talk about boys. That's just the way we are," said Natalia. Of course, all clients aren't going to have requests of this nature, but asking them what you can share and being honest with them if you cannot honor their wishes because of your duty to warn, for example, puts the issues out in the open. Consulting with them about these matters can strengthen your client-counselor relationship.

Be genuine; be human. Young clients will respond to you better if you come across as a "real person." When working with this population, you may find yourself on the floor playing a therapeutic game with an 8-year-old, or you might spend the first few minutes of a session looking through a 14-year-old's yearbook or listening to a tape of his or her latest favorite song. This helpful tip does not mean that you should shed your professional role and become a friend to the child or adolescent, but it does indicate that by being more real, you have a better chance of establishing a good relationship.

Don't act like a parent! Even well-meaning parents may nag, overcontrol, and offer unsolicited advice. Adolescents in particular resent this intrusion. Your relationship with young clients should be more collaborative. Establish goals mutually, help them look at the consequences of their behavior, and zip your lip so you can refrain from saying, "I told you so," or giving them advice about what they should and shouldn't do. Your clients will be more likely to change if they initiate the process because they see a reason for doing it, not because they are being coerced. If you act like a parent, they will most likely put up greater resistance.

Be a salesperson. Just because you exist, don't expect that clients are going to want your services. Young clients may not have participated in counseling before; consequently, they have no idea what to expect. Parents, too, may feel ashamed because their child has a problem or is a problem for them. Selling them on the idea of counseling can help in the rapport-building process. For example, you might say to 12-year-old Patrick that, because you have worked with other young adolescents who had trouble dealing with their anger, you think you can help him, too. You can point out that, if he expresses his anger differently, he will probably be able to get his parents and his teachers off his back; thus you will be teaching him a strategy that could benefit him. Be careful not to promise things you can't deliver, but keep in mind that many people think there are no advantages to counseling or that there is no need for them to get help for emotional problems. Selling them on the idea is often important. For clients who are particularly reluctant, contracting for a few sessions has proven to be a good way to initiate the process.

Be flexible and creative. Remember that it is not always easy for children and adolescents to pinpoint how they feel or describe what they are experiencing. If you are working with young clients who just will not talk, don't keep talking at them. Instead, shift gears. Play a game, read a story, engage in a role play, or invite them to write sentence completions.

Don't be afraid to self-disclose, but do so in a way that has therapeutic value. Young clients in particular are often curious about who you are. If you are playing a feelings game, share an appropriate experience related to that feeling. Or use yourself as an example: "I think I can understand why you are still so sad about your grandmother's death. I was also very close to my grandma, and it was a very sad time for me, too, when she died." Sharing in this way makes you human. Using common sense is important, however. Boasting to your adolescent clients about your teenage drinking escapades is obviously inappropriate. For one thing, it is very easy for them to misinterpret this message as permission to drink; for another, it is a violation of the boundary that must exist between client and therapist.

Have patience and adjust your expectations for the counseling process. Sometimes the harder you push, the less you gain; this can be especially true when counseling adolescents. Although at times it may seem as if you are getting nowhere, in reality you are engaging in problem assessment throughout the rapport-building process. Accurate problem conceptualization contributes to more effective intervention, which is the ultimate goal.

BUILDING RAPPORT

According to Walen et al. (1992), therapy actually begins with the first moment of contact with the client and develops as you establish a therapeutic alliance, initiate the assessment process, agree on the problem area, and establish treatment goals and strategies. They noted that it is important to delineate what clients can expect from therapy and what you expect from them; an understanding of these expectations can help ease clients' anxiety. This strategy imposes structure and ensures predictability, both of which are especially critical when working with young clients. The explanation needs to be simple: "I think we can work together to figure out ways to deal with what is bothering you. If you are open with me and will agree to try out the ideas we come up with, we should be able to make progress." Walen and her colleagues also emphasized that, although the goal of the therapeutic relationship is not friendship, demonstrating professional competence, credibility, respect, and commitment to helping the client are essential in building the therapeutic alliance.

Many REBT therapists believe that the best way to establish rapport is to engage in the therapeutic process—to begin working immediately on the client's problem (Walen et al., 1992). Although it is true that you can help clients believe in the process if they begin to feel better after the first session, it is important to remember that this quick approach may not work with younger clients, especially elementary-aged children. With this younger clientele, it is often necessary to ease into the process more gradually. The following activities have been helpful in breaking the ice with children and adolescents.

Strategies for Building Rapport with Children (Ages 5 to 10)

Because play is the language of a child, engaging younger clients in simple games or activities can be a good way to establish rapport. As you use these get-acquainted activities, it is important to interact with the client, ask extending questions to acquire more information, and be patient if the child chooses not to share. Although it may suffice to use only one of the activities during the first session, you may need to use more of them in subsequent sessions. Use your clinical judgment to determine how comfortable the child seems and to get a sense of how open he or she will be once you start working on the issues that prompted the call for counseling. Though the information gleaned from these activities may contribute to the assessment process, the actual intent is for the questions to be relatively nonthreatening and for you to build trust through mutual self-disclosure in a game format, which is a comfortable medium for young clients. Several examples of rapport-building activities for children follow.

Who Are You?

This is a simple activity that takes no more than 5 or 10 minutes. You begin the exchange by explaining to the client that this is a short activity designed to help the two of you become better acquainted. Indicate that you will take turns asking each other, "Who are you?" The person who is asked this question responds with something he or she is willing to disclose and in turn asks, "Who are you?" The other person responds and asks, "Who are you?" With younger children, it is often a good idea if the child asks the first question so that you can model a response. In this way, you can also establish some categories that you think will provide you with some good information about the client. This procedure can go back and forth for several rounds and can be repeated in subsequent sessions if needed. The following is a brief example of the activity:

Client: Who are you?

Counselor: I am a dog lover; I have three dogs. Who are you?

Client: I have a kitten named Fluffy. Who are you?

Counselor: I am someone who likes to read. Who are you?

Client: I'm someone who likes to roller blade. Who are you?

Button, Button

This activity works especially well with children who are 8 or younger and can be completed in 10 to 15 minutes. For this activity, you will need two buttons, one for the client and one for yourself, and some index cards with questions written on them. When it is your turn, you hide the button behind your back in one of your hands. The client tries to guess which hand the button is in, and if correct, draws an index card and asks you the question written on the card (be prepared to read for the child). If the child's guess is incorrect, it is her turn to hide the button and your turn to guess. The following are examples of questions that might be asked:

What is your favorite color?

What do you like to do most on Saturdays?

What is your favorite television show or video game?

If you ever feel scared, what do you do?

If you could make a wish, what would you wish for?

What is something you don't like to do?

What do you like or not like about your friends?

If you ever feel mad, what helps you get over your mad feelings?

Flip the Coin

This activity can be handled in several ways. The easiest method is for you and the client to pick either heads or tails, take turns flipping a coin, and share something personal when it turns up heads on your flip (if you picked heads). Past experience indicates that this activity is often not structured enough for young clients. If this proves to be the case, you can have questions written on index cards and pick one when it turns up heads on your flip. Questions on topics such as the following can be geared both to younger and to older child populations.

For younger children

A favorite toy or game

A favorite and least favorite food

A happy memory

Something that makes you laugh

Something that scares you or makes you cry

For older children

Something you do or do not like about school

A hobby or favorite activity

One of your best memories

Something you think you do well

Something you feel sad about

People, Places, and Things

For this activity, you will need to take a piece of tagboard and cut out a circle, dividing it into three segments labeled "People," "Places," and "Things." Using a tagboard arrow, make a spinner and fasten it to the center of the circle with a brass fastener so it will move. Explain the activity as follows:

Counselor: In order for us to get to know each other better, I'd like to have the two of us play this game for a few minutes. Are you willing?

Client: Sure!

Counselor: I'll start and spin. Oh, the spinner landed on "Places," so I'm going to share one of my favorite places with you. I love to go to my cabin, which is on a lake. Now it's your turn.

Client: *(Spins.)* Mine landed on "Things."

Counselor: What is one of your favorite things?

Client: I have lots of them, but I guess my favorite is my bike.

Counselor: Do you usually ride bikes alone or with someone else?

Client: Sometimes I go with my brother or my mom, but usually I go with my friend.

The game proceeds in this manner for a few minutes, with the counselor asking extended questions, when appropriate, to learn more about the client.

What's Your Bag?

For this activity, you will need two lunch-size paper bags, scissors, and several magazines. You and the client will each spend several minutes cutting out pictures of interests; hobbies; and favorite foods, clothes, cars, pets, colors, or places, for example. Next, each of you will place the pictures you selected in a separate bag, then take turns drawing them out of the bags and sharing them with each other.

It's Me!

This activity uses a game board and game cards. You may use the game board given in the Appendix or construct your own. Using three different colors of dot stickers, randomly place one colored dot on each space on the game board. Next apply twelve dot stickers, four of each color, to the same number of tagboard or index cards. On the other side of each card, write a question like the following:

What do you like best about being your age?

What do you like least about being your age?

What do you think you would like to do when you are grown up?

What is your easiest subject in school?

What is your hardest subject in school?

How do you feel when you make a mistake?

How do you feel if you don't do well on a test?

What kinds of things do you and your friends argue about?

If you have a fight with a friend, what do you do to work out the problem?

If someone calls you a name, how do you react?

If you are not getting along with a parent or a brother or a sister, what do you do?

What is something that really upsets you or scares you? What do you do to feel less upset or scared?

To play the game, place the index cards, which have the colored dot stickers affixed to them, in separate piles beside the board. Give the client a coin and a colored button or marker and take the same for yourself. Explain that the two of you will take turns flipping the coin, moving a marker along the dots (a flip to heads is a one-dot move, to tails is a two-dot move), drawing a card from the pile that corresponds with the color of the dot you land on, and responding to the question on the card.

Alphabet Soup

For this simple activity, you will need a set of alphabet letters that you can buy or make out of tagboard. Put the letters in a box or a hat. You and the client then take turns drawing a letter of the alphabet and sharing something that applies to you or your family. For example, 9-year-old Alejandro drew the letter *K* and stated that he loved to play kick ball.

Fish for Feelings

This is a good game to use with younger children because it not only helps them build a feeling vocabulary that facilitates self-disclosure during the counseling sessions, but it also gives you more insight into the troublesome feelings that may have prompted the need for counseling. For this simple game, you will need to make a set of tagboard fish labeled with feeling words such as *happy, scared, mad, sad, worried,* or *excited.* Each fish should have a hole in its nose.

You will also need a fishing pole (a short stick with a string attached to the end and a paper clip attached to the string). Place the fish on the floor. Take turns trying to snag a fish. Once you do, read the word on the fish and describe the situation in which you felt that way. By participating with the child, you can model self-disclosure, which makes it easier for the child to respond.

Strategies for Building Rapport with Adolescents (Ages 11 to 18)

Getting acquainted with adolescents may often be more difficult than it is with younger children. Although adolescents are better able to describe their problems, they also may be more defensive and reluctant to share them with you. It is important to keep in mind that adolescents are naturally self-conscious and vulnerable—and may feel even more so by merely entering a counselor's office and being asked to disclose things they may feel very confused or uncomfortable about. It is sometimes helpful for adolescents (as it is for children) to have something to fiddle with during the session. Clay, stress balls, Slinkys, or other manipulatives may help put them at ease.

It is essential that you be empathic with those in this age group and imagine how you would feel sharing personal thoughts and feelings with an adult who may be a total stranger. A good idea is to address this concern by first asking the referring parent or teacher how the adolescent feels about coming to therapy. If the adult concedes that the adolescent does not want to see you, don't take offense. Instead, simply proceed with caution. Acknowledge to the client that you can understand why he might not want to be there, but reassure him that you are there to help him. Sometimes it may be necessary to contract for at least three sessions; then, if the adolescent still has a strong aversion to coming, you can reevaluate the situation. If you are a good salesperson and can begin to connect with your client, he will likely be more amenable to counseling by the third session and grudgingly agree to more therapy. If you cannot sell him on the idea, perhaps it will be necessary to confer with his parents and discuss whether he may be more open to counseling sometime in the future. Like some adolescents, he may need to hit rock bottom before he agrees to seek help. The downside to this scenario is that, in the meantime, he may act impulsively and engage in self-defeating behaviors that could have long-lasting ramifications. Therefore, you need to do your best in the first few sessions to convince him to continue in counseling.

When working with this age group, it is imperative that you be patient. Many adolescents may test you with their silence, seeing how long you can wait them out. A classic line you are likely to hear is "I have to be here, but I don't have to talk." In response, you can acknowledge that, although that may be the case, it is also true that they probably won't have to come for as many sessions if they *do* start talking.

Another approach you can use is to permit them to remain silent. You can explain that, although you don't prefer this, you cannot force them to participate. You should casually suggest to them that it might be more beneficial to them in the long run if they did involve themselves in the process, because that could shorten the number of times they would have to come. By offering them the choice to remain silent, you will, in all likelihood, allow these adolescent clients to feel empowered and free to engage in counseling on their own terms.

Adolescents may also throw every obscenity in the book at you, anxious to see your reaction, be it verbal or nonverbal. Don't take the bait. Instead, let them finish their tirade and see what happens. In most cases, these clients will eventually back off. Even if you are offended by their language, the worst thing you can do is to react negatively, because that is exactly what they want. Once they see that they are not going to ruffle your feathers, you can request that they tone it down if you think your silence is condoning something offensive.

It is also important, when working with this age group, to maintain a sense of humor and perspective and not let them push your buttons. It may also be appropriate to use some humor with them, because they are better able, owing to their abstract thinking skills, to understand the intent. Without making fun of your clients, you can use exaggeration or humor to make a point or to help them see their situation in a different light. For example, a teenager was talking about how she threw fits to force her mother into giving in and letting her go to a dance. With a smile on her face, the counselor replied, "So, your 2-year-old temper tantrums worked rather well! Are there times when they don't, or when you feel rather foolish throwing a fit?"

Remember that adolescents will also try their best to engage you in a battle of wills, or they may test the degree to which you can be nonjudgmental by throwing out blatant statements or opinions. If you can refrain from overreacting, you can usually take the wind out of their sails, and they will ultimately be more amenable to counseling.

The following specific rapport-building ideas and activities may be useful with adolescent clients.

Sharing Information about Development

Most adolescents don't understand why they feel the way they do, so sharing information about typical adolescent development can be very useful. For example, noting that it is normal for teenagers to feel confused, overwhelmed, angry, or moody often brings relief and can facilitate their self-disclosure. Be accurate and specific about what you share. If you are discussing their emotions, explain in simple terms why teenagers tend to be moody: that their hormones are fluctuating and that this turbulence results in a chemical imbalance that is usually resolved once they are past puberty. Or help them understand that, because they are still in various stages of developing more complex thinking skills, it is common for them to misconstrue things or make assumptions, some of which can have negative effects on their ability to solve problems. Indicate that, for these reasons, it is important for them to consciously consider all sides of an issue.

Experience suggests that clients are often very interested in their own development and tend to ask lots of questions. *Developmental Assessment and Intervention with Children and Adolescents* (Vernon, 1993) is one good resource for information on this topic.

Games

Depending on your clients' developmental level, it is sometimes advantageous to play checkers or a card game, during which you engage in casual conversation that can help you get to know them better. Experience indicates that it is often better to induce casual conversation than to use a game that is more specifically geared to personal self-disclosure, because adolescents tend to resist activities of this nature. If you are initially low key, you can work into activities that are more self-revealing. For example, you can put feeling words or self-disclosing questions on checkerboard spaces and take turns responding as you and the client land on different spaces. Another game you can play is These Are a Few of My Favorite Things, in which you and the client write examples of favorite things (e.g., activities, hobbies, possessions, people, movies, music) on separate index cards. You then scatter the cards facedown on the table and take turns flipping over a card, elaborating on the significance of the favorite thing as each of you turns over the cards. (These activities are generally more appropriate for younger adolescents.)

Testimonials

Inviting teens to read about what their peers have experienced is another excellent way to help them see that they are not alone. Recently, a 17-year-old who had been referred by her school counselor was in my office. She alluded to being lonely but seemed reluctant to talk much about it. Remembering that a former client of mine who was also a high school senior had written about similar feelings, I invited her to read what this client had written:

> When I refer to feeling lonely, I mean that I feel alone. But being alone and feeling lonely are very different. I've felt lonely, on occasion, when I am alone, but it is not a severe feeling. I am perfectly happy being with my own thoughts. If I do feel this way, it is because I am remembering what it was like to have a real best friend who understood me well. Now I don't seem to have that. We've grown away from each other because our values have changed, I guess. But I really miss having that best friend, a kindred spirit.

> At one point in time I lost respect for my peers. They wanted to do things that I didn't. They didn't understand the restrictions I put on myself. All in all, I grew away from them, and I guess that just happens. I'm a senior in high school, and I probably won't see these people very much later in life. I miss the cohesive group that we had, but that is over.

> What I think creates the most problems now is not having a new group to fall into. In every class there are people that I should try to break down the barriers with so that I don't feel so alone. But that's hard. Slowly I am finding some people that enjoy "good, clean fun" again, and I'm beginning to develop some new friendships. But in reality, I think I will still feel this loneliness until I move away next year and have a chance to start over again. (Vernon, 1998c, p. 237)

When my client finished reading this, she immediately said that she felt exactly the same way and was relieved to know that she was not the only one who felt like this. She then proceeded to talk at length about what she was experiencing.

Artifacts

Other good ways to build trust include asking clients to bring favorite tapes or CDs, yearbooks, pictures, poems, artwork, or hobbies. Be genuine in showing interest in what they share with you, and don't suggest this activity unless you *can* be genuine. Not only can this interaction be a good way to break the ice with your clients, it may also be an excellent way to gain insight into their world.

Something You Can't Tell by Looking at Me

This simple strategy frequently yields some very useful information. Indicate to clients that we often make assumptions about others, but there are many things that others can't tell just by looking at us. Volunteer to share an example or two to model the process: "Just by looking at me, you don't know that I like to sleep late" or "Just by looking at me, you don't know that I don't like comedy movies." Invite clients to do the same, and then share back and forth for several minutes.

Inner-Outer Me

This activity can be especially effective with nonverbal adolescents who are reluctant to self-disclose. You will need an envelope, a pencil, and several strips of paper.

Explain that who we are on the outside can be very different from who we are on the inside, and that the purpose of this activity is for you to learn as much about your clients as they are willing to share. Invite them to write on the outside of the envelope words or phrases that describe how they appear to others. Then ask them to write on the strips of paper words or phrases they think describe themselves but that they do not readily share with others, and put these on the inside of the envelope. (Be sure to inform clients that they won't have to share these descriptions unless they choose to do so.)

One very angry adolescent wrote the following on the outside of her envelope: "Can be mean and snotty, smart, hateful, forceful, strong, loud." On the inside she wrote, "vulnerable, hurt, low self-esteem, and loner." Obviously, the discrepancy between the two lists generated good discussion and provided information for goal setting and therapeutic interventions.

Writing

Oftentimes it is less threatening for adolescents to write about what is bothering them than to share it verbally. Writing can take the form of a short paragraph; a letter to someone they feel is "causing" their problem; a poem; or a "Dear Abby" letter, in which they write to Abby about their problems.

❊ ❊ ❊

How long it takes to build rapport with a client is not something you can easily predict. With some clients, you just click; with others, you don't. Sometimes it takes a long time to develop a trusting relationship. It is unrealistic to expect that you will like every client or that every client will like you—and that certainly is not the goal of counseling, anyway. How you connect with children and adolescents, though, can have a major impact on how effectively goals can be accomplished. If you have good rapport with your young clients, they are generally less resistant or reluctant to come to counseling and more motivated to work on their problems.

ESTABLISHING GOALS

Most REBT therapists would agree that you should attempt to establish goals with your client within the first few sessions. With children and adolescents, this objective is sometimes more difficult to achieve or simply different than it is with adult clients—and for several reasons. First, it is not uncommon to hear young clients say they do not know why they are there, and that makes goal setting more complicated. Obviously, because of what their parents or teachers have shared with you, you have some idea why they are there; however, even though you may have an idea of a goal, the client might not see it that way. Second, goal setting may be an alien concept to many young clients. They may be somewhat familiar with the term if it is used in school, but it may not be a household word. Therefore, you may have to do some educating about what goals are and why it is important to set them. You may even find yourself using simpler language, especially with younger children. For example, you might say to 6-year-old Tyronne, "You and I talked today about how hard it is for you to go outside to play because you are afraid someone will come and take you away. Should we try to think of some things you can do to help you so you won't be so afraid to play outside?" Third, remember that children's sense of time is more immediate than adults' and that you will want to set more short-term goals so that they see that something is being accomplished. Finally, keep in mind that, whereas setting unrealistic goals is discouraging for adults, it is even more so for children, whose thinking is still very concrete. They tend to give up more quickly because they think they will never achieve the goal if they were unable to succeed the first time. This pessimism is exemplified by youngsters who are failing in school. If their goal is to pass all their classes, they find it very easy to conclude that they will never be able to accomplish this goal and thus decide not to try at all. A more reasonable goal for these youngsters would be to pass at least one class each semester.

The goal-setting process should involve a partnership that encourages success. This success occurs much more readily if a good working relationship has been established, as this short case example conversation with a 17-year-old illustrates.

Counselor: Marissa, in today's session we talked about your anger and frustration with your parents because they don't let you do things you think you should be able to do at your age. I'm wondering what you see as your goal for these counseling sessions.

Client: I don't know. Just for the arguing to stop, I guess. And I want them to start treating me like I'm 17 and give me more freedom.

Counselor: You identified two very clear goals: to stop the arguing and to convince your parents to give you more freedom. Both of these goals involve your parents to a large extent, but since you are the one who is here, let's first focus on you. What is *your* goal?

Client: I guess it'd be to get along better with them, and then maybe they'll let me do more.

Counselor: I think that makes sense. You are recognizing that you may have to change in order for them to change. Of course, we can't guarantee that they will behave differently, but we can focus on what you can do. So it sounds like your first goal is to decrease the arguing, correct?

Client: Yeah, I think that's the first step.

Counselor: With that goal in mind, is there something you think you could do to help move you closer to that goal?

Client: I think it would help if I stopped talking back to them. They hate that.

Counselor: That's a good specific example. Have you thought about how you might do that?

Client: I guess I just have to try and remember that it will only make things worse if I mouth off.

Counselor: I think you're right about that. I remember that one of my other clients taped a note on her bathroom mirror that said, "Zip your lip," as a reminder to herself to try and stop the mouthing off or arguing. Maybe that's something you could try.

Client: All right. I'll try it and see how things go.

Basic Principles of Rational Emotive Behavior Therapy

Rational emotive behavior therapy (REBT) was the first cognitive-behavioral therapy introduced into clinical practice (Ellis, 1957). It is practiced throughout the world both with adults and with children. In its nearly half a century of existence, it has been applied successfully to individual, group, marital, and family therapy (Ellis, 2001a), as well as to a wide array of problems such as fears and phobias, anger, depression, underachievement, lack of motivation, test anxiety, interpersonal relationship issues, low self-esteem, anxiety, impulsivity, cheating, aggression, and job performance (Bernard, 1991; Ellis & Tafrate, 1997; Wilde, 1992; Yankura, 1997). REBT is a well-established form of therapy that has been used in educational, industrial, and commercial settings and also in hospital and mental health facilities (Ellis & Dryden, 1997). Moreover, REBT is a multidimensional form of therapy that enables practitioners to use many kinds of cognitive, emotive, behavioral, and interpersonal techniques to facilitate the problem-solving process (Ellis, 2001a; Kwee & Ellis, 1997). One of the unique features that distinguishes it from many other forms of therapy is its emphasis on problem prevention (Ellis, 2000, 2001a; Vernon, 1997). REBT is designed as a self-help, educative therapy through which clients learn rational principles that will help them deal with present, as well as future, problems (Dryden & Ellis, 2001; Vernon, in press). Teaching people how to *get* better rather than simply *feel* better is a primary goal of REBT practitioners (Broder, 2001).

BASIC PRINCIPLES: THE ABC's OF REBT

REBT is based on the notion that how we think determines how we feel and behave. Practitioners can empower clients to deal with a wide array of problematic situations by helping them learn to identify and challenge the irrational thinking patterns that create their emotional disturbance (Dryden & Ellis, 2001). In developing this theory, Ellis relied on teachings from philosophers such as Epictetus, who stated that "men are disturbed not by things, but by the views which they take of them" (Walen et al., 1992, p. 3). Accordingly, Ellis (1996) noted that disturbance is largely a function of our perceptions and evaluations. He maintained that humans have a biological tendency to think dysfunctionally and irrationally and that virtually all people exhibit major irrationalities (DiGiuseppe, 1999; Ellis & Dryden, 1997). Despite having given up some irrational ideas, even intelligent humans often adopt new ones or fall back into self-defeating habits, according to Ellis. However, human beings have the ability to see how they disturb themselves and, consequently, how to change their thinking (Ellis, 2001b). With knowledge and practice, they can overcome their dysfunctional thinking and behave in less self-defeating ways.

Ellis developed the ABC conceptual model to illustrate the theoretical concepts and the process of change (Dryden, 1999; Dryden & Ellis, 2001; Ellis & MacLaren, 1998). In essence, the nature of emotional disturbance can be explained by recognizing that, as people attempt to fulfill their goals, they often encounter an activating event (A) that either blocks them from achieving their goal or helps them to achieve it. Activating events may be either positive or negative; they may be past, present, or future oriented; they may refer to real or perceived events; and they may be caused by a person's own thoughts or feelings. In general, an A can be anything that a person judges or evaluates that elicits emotional and behavioral reactions. However, most activating events that bring individuals to therapy are adverse or unfortunate current events that have created some emotional or behavioral difficulties. That being the case, most individuals enter therapy believing strongly that the activating events in their lives cause their emotional and behavioral reactions at C: A ➜ C

According to REBT theory, people have thoughts or beliefs (B) about the activating events that influence their emotional and behavioral consequences (C). Although we commonly think that the events "cause" our reactions, this is usually not the case, unless the events are very powerful, such as a war or an environmental disaster. There also are hormonal or biochemical factors that may contribute to or cause the C (Ellis & Dryden, 1997). In reality, although activating events (A) may contribute significantly to the consequence (C), beliefs (B) about the A actually cause the C and can be changed more readily than the activating event. Thus, instead of A ➜ C, REBT theory maintains that the beliefs (B) about A ➜ C. According to this theory, the A, the B, and the C are closely related and do not usually exist independent of one another; when you *think* negatively about an event or an experience, you usually *feel* bad and *act* dysfunctionally (Ellis, 1996). This basic tenet of REBT theory may be difficult for individuals to grasp initially, but it will ultimately empower them because it gives them a method to gain self-control when faced with adverse events.

Take the case of an adolescent who interviewed for a job and was not offered the position (A): The fact that she didn't get the job did not *cause* her to feel angry; rather, her belief that she should have gotten it and that it was unfair that they offered it to someone else (B) triggered her anger. On the other hand, one of her classmates who also interviewed for the same job and didn't get it was only disappointed. Although the classmate thought she had good qualifications and had hoped she would be selected, she recognized that employers have the right to hire the person who best meets their qualifications. A third classmate was overjoyed when she was not selected because she did not want a job and could now spend more time with her friends. As this example illustrates, the same event resulted in three different emotional consequences (C) because of differences in thinking (B).

Irrational Beliefs

The beliefs that people hold may be rational and eventually lead to self-enhancing or self-helping behaviors, or they may be irrational and subsequently result in self-defeating behaviors. Irrational beliefs emanate from absolutistic evaluations, which ultimately sabotage a person's goals. The core irrational belief is a *must,* and it has several derivatives:

1. I absolutely must, at practically all times, be successful at important performances and relationships—or else I, as a person, am inadequate and worthless!

2. Other people absolutely must always treat me considerately, kindly, fairly, or lovingly—or else they are no damned good and deserve no joy in their existence.

3. Conditions under which I live absolutely must be comfortable, pleasurable, and rewarding—or else it's awful, I can't stand it, and the goddamned world is no good! (Ellis, 1996, p. 13)

These three basic irrational beliefs share four key elements: demands, awfulizing, low frustration tolerance, and global rating of self or others. Irrational beliefs result in negative emotions (C) such as anxiety, depression, anger, resentment, self-pity, worthlessness, and rage. Withdrawal, avoidance, fighting, violence, procrastination, and addiction are typical behavioral manifestations. These irrational beliefs result in maladaptive behaviors and emotional upset, therefore interfering with a person's happiness.

In contrast, rational beliefs emanate from realistic preferences that typically result in moderate negative emotions and constructive behavior patterns when activating events (A) fall short of desired outcomes (Dryden, 1999). Therefore, a rationally thinking student who studied hard for a test and got a grade lower than the A she was expecting would not feel elated about receiving the lower grade; that would be illogical. It would be understandable for her to feel disappointment, a moderate emotion that is often an outcome of rational thinking. Had she been thinking irrationally, she might have labeled herself a stupid person for getting an average grade and felt devastated, which would have been an overreaction to a disappointing outcome.

Ellis and Dryden (1997) distinguished between healthy negative emotions, which are related to rational beliefs, and unhealthy negative emotions, which are related to irrational beliefs. For example, clients who think rationally but still have negative feelings would feel concern versus anxiety, sadness versus depression, regret versus guilt, disappointment versus shame, and annoyance versus anger.

To illustrate further, rationally thinking parents prefer to have their children perform well in school. But if they don't perform well, it doesn't mean that their children are complete failures and will never succeed in academic tasks or that the parents are doing a poor job of parenting. In contrast, irrationally thinking parents would magnify this problem by assuming that their children's poor academic performance was an indication of their failure as parents, that their children were deliberately performing horribly to spite them, and that their children will always be losers. The parents who think rationally would probably feel disappointed but not devastated, whereas the parents who think irrationally would most likely feel angry or depressed—reactions that would have a negative effect on the parent-child relationship.

Rational beliefs are logical and can be validly inferred from earlier premises. For instance, a young client says he wants to get an A in math and that studying for tests and doing the homework will help him achieve his goal. His rational conclusion is that he very much wants to get an A, and this conclusion is logical. Irrational beliefs, on the other hand, are illogical and are not validly inferred. In this example, the fact that the client wants to get an A and believes that studying for tests and doing homework will help him get the A does not validate the conclusion that he absolutely must get the A and that the teacher cannot give him anything except an A.

Disputation

Once these irrational beliefs and their emotional and behavioral consequences have been identified, the next step in the paradigm is to dispute the irrational beliefs (D). This step is accomplished by challenging or poking holes in the belief system, which can be achieved in a variety of ways: through modeling, Socratic questioning, persuasion, humor, vigorous disputing, role reversal, rational emotive imagery, and homework assignments (DiGiuseppe, 1999; Ellis & Blau, 1998; Ellis & MacLaren, 1998). In the disputing process, a wide variety of cognitive, emotive, and behavioral techniques are employed. Asking how the belief is helpful, how consistent it is with reality, and how logical it is can prove useful (Ellis & Dryden, 1997). Using the previous example of the parents who were angry and resentful that their children did not perform well in school, an REBT therapist would challenge their assumption that the children were doing poorly to spite them by asking for the evidence that this is true. The therapist might also have them make a list showing how their children's failure to perform well makes them bad parents. Asking them for examples of more horrible events could help them put this situation in perspective by showing them that this problem does not mean the end of the world for them and their children. If the parents are particularly resistant about giving up their irrational beliefs, the therapist could switch roles, playing the part of the irrational parent who is awfulizing about his or her children's performance and having the client assume the role of the therapist who is challenging the irrational beliefs. A homework assignment for the parents could involve writing a paragraph explaining how their children's failure doesn't mean they are failures as parents.

Rational Beliefs/Moderation of Feelings and Behaviors

Because disputation is the heart and soul of this therapeutic process, it may take many attempts and several different forms of disputing before clients are ready to surrender their irrational beliefs and adopt a more rational perspective. It is important that practitioners remember that rational thinking does not imply that clients will feel wonderful about a negative event. Rather, as they give up their absolutistic thinking and their consequent demand for perfection and comfort, they will reduce the intensity of their negative behaviors and emotions, which is the goal of the therapeutic process. In doing so, they will be able to adopt a more realistic outlook, one that is based on rational beliefs. Ellis and Blau (1998) described this as the E—effective new philosophy or effective rational beliefs. As clients begin to apply these rational beliefs to the problems of everyday living, they consequently experience less intense negative feelings and behaviors (F), and this application results in a happier existence.

SPECIFIC APPLICATIONS TO CHILDREN AND ADOLESCENTS

Although the basic theoretical principles of REBT remain in effect in work with younger clients, there are considerable differences in the way the theory is applied to them and to adults. As noted in chapter 1, it is extremely important to establish a good therapeutic relationship with the younger clients. It is also imperative that therapists working with youth be flexible and creative, taking into account the developmental considerations discussed in that chapter.

Furthermore, whereas Ellis and Dryden (1997) advocated the importance of helping clients change through the philosophic restructuring of irrational beliefs, this task may be more difficult or not always possible with younger clients because of their lower cognitive developmental level. In some cases, it may be impossible. For example, adults can arrive at the rational conclusion that it is sad, but not the end of the world, if their parents decide to divorce; they realize how futile it is to think that such a thing should never happen.

However, because children are naturally more dependent on their parents for support and nurturance, it may take longer for them to understand that they can learn to adjust to a change so potentially devastating as a divorce, that they cannot control what their parents decide to do, and that life goes on. Ellis and Dryden also noted that, in some instances, clients may also make direct changes in the situation at A (the activating event). Although this is not the preferred way of practicing REBT, it is sometimes necessary in the case of children and adolescents. For example, because of young people's concrete thinking, it can be difficult to dispute an 8-year-old's belief that a best friend should always be fair and loyal and never associate with other classmates. A practical solution to this problem might be to help the child expand his circle of friends and not rely on one best friend.

Although REBT practitioners are encouraged to use a wide variety of cognitive, emotive, and behavioral techniques when working with clients (Ellis, 2001a; Dryden, 1999), practitioners working with children and adolescents must be even more flexible in order to connect in meaningful ways with this younger clientele and to employ the ABC process effectively. Because younger clients are generally less skilled at expressing themselves verbally or may not be able to understand concepts as readily as adults, the practitioners' freedom to be creative and flexible allows them to target the problem more specifically and make the therapeutic process more interesting and engaging for both client and counselor. The remainder of this chapter will describe specific adaptations and effective strategies to employ with children and adolescents, beginning with the assessment process.

Problem Assessment

Accurate problem assessment is important not only in identifying the client's irrational beliefs and disturbing emotions, but also in determining if this is a practical problem (e.g., not knowing how to make friends or how to study for a test) or an emotional problem (e.g., feeling anxious about interacting with peers or panicking when taking a test). Furthermore, it is imperative that the counselor assess whether the problem is representative of the child's age group and whether the child's emotions and behaviors are normal expressions, or if the child is overreacting with an atypical response. Because children and adolescents are dealing with normal developmental problems in addition to more serious issues requiring various degrees of intervention, professionals must examine the frequency, intensity, and duration of the symptoms to determine the exact nature of the problem. Furthermore, it is also critical that counselors identify who owns the problem: Is it the child's problem, or the parent's or teacher's problem about the child, that is the main issue? Counselors should keep in mind that parents and teachers sometimes refer a child who is exhibiting relatively normal behavior because they either don't understand child and adolescent development or are experiencing conflicts with the young client.

Once it has been established that a problem exists, and once the ownership has been determined, the problem analysis phase occurs, resulting in a determination of the client's dysfunctional cognitions, emotions, and behaviors. From an REBT perspective, assessment is ongoing, and there is no clear distinction between assessment and intervention because, in every session, the therapist is constantly analyzing cognitions, emotions, and behaviors as they relate to the problem (Vernon, 1997). Therefore, within the same session, there may be an assessment of one aspect of a given issue and an intervention for another. In addition, it is not uncommon during an intervention for new information to surface that provides more assessment data.

There are several distinguishing features of REBT assessment for children and adolescents: (a) the relationship between the practitioner and the young client, (b) parental involvement in the assessment process, (c) the developmental level of the client, (d) the assessment of problematic emotions and behaviors, and (e) the assessment of irrational beliefs and cognitive distortions. In addition, because younger clients often are not very verbal or skilled at expressing themselves, assessment with this population may be more challenging than it is with adults. Consequently, the counselor must be prepared to use a variety of approaches in order to identify irrational beliefs and accurately define the problem.

The Relationship between Practitioner and Client

As mentioned earlier, the relationship between the practitioner and the young client is an important aspect of the entire counseling process, including assessment. Utilizing the rapport-building strategies described in chapter 1 may need to be the counselor's first step if the client is anxious or reluctant to share. Although not specifically related to the ABC assessment process, these activities usually generate some useful information.

Parental Involvement

When working with younger children, it is often very helpful to bring parents into the first session to explain the reason for the referral and to assist with the initial assessment. This approach is also beneficial because younger children may be more willing to go into an office with their parents if counseling is taking place outside the school setting. Even if the parents are present, however, it is preferable first to ask the children to explain why they are coming to counseling. If the child gives a typical "I don't know," then the counselor should ask the parents (or parent) for input. Once the counselor has a clear picture of the issue from the parents' perspective and has discussed how he or she anticipates involving them in the counseling process, the counselor can usually excuse the parents and begin the relationship-building process with the child.

For several reasons, it is usually advisable for practitioners to see adolescent clients alone during the initial visit so they can get the clients' perspective on the problem: First, in order to effectively join with them, it is important to hear their version before anyone else's. Second, adolescents are generally more private than adults and don't want to share with their parents. Third, what parents share about their children may put adolescent clients on the defensive, thus causing them to be even less likely to open up with the counselor. In the case of adolescents, parental involvement in the assessment process often occurs with the initial phone call, when clients are referred. This contact allows the practitioner to hear parental perceptions and concerns, but at the same time honors adolescents by validating their perspectives without a parent being present.

When conducting problem assessment with parents, it is helpful to the practitioner to undertake a specific analysis that includes identifying (a) the problem from the parents' perspective; (b) individuals other than the parents who are involved (e.g., how it is affecting other family members); (c) the duration of the problem; (d) any specific precipitating circumstances or transitions; (e) instances in which the problem is manifested; and (f) strategies that the clients, parents, and other key individuals have employed in previous efforts to address the problem.

Developmental Level

With regard to the specific assessment strategies that are employed, accurate assessment must take into account not only the developmental level of each client, but also how the client's problem is conceptualized:

> Is this a typical problem for a child this age?

> Are his or her reactions typical for someone at this developmental level?

In addition, it is important for therapists to remember that children and young adolescents may have a myopic view of the problem because, as concrete thinkers, they may not be able to see all perspectives. Although it is always important that they hear what these youngsters say and to accept their version of reality, practitioners must, at the same time, keep in mind that the youngsters' reality may be distorted. For example, it is not uncommon to hear adolescents claim that their parents *never* listen to them and that they are *always* unfair. In some cases this may be true, but very often these statements are overgeneralizations that result from adolescents' concrete categorizations and their inability to recognize exceptions or see all sides of the issue.

Because children and young adolescents may not be able to verbalize specifically how they are thinking, feeling, and behaving, it is often necessary to employ a variety of developmentally appropriate assessment strategies, such as the following.

Chapter 2 • Basic Principles of Rational Emotive Behavior Therapy

Sentence Stems

Sentence stems can be adapted for all age levels and can be completed either orally or in writing. Because the goal of using an assessment of this nature is to stimulate discussion that gives counselors more information about their clients, it is not necessary to use more than 8 to 10 sentences. If, on the basis of initial intake information, counselors have a general idea of the problem, they can develop sentences that elicit more specificity about the particular issue. If counselors are still unclear about the problem, they can use more general sentences. For example, if the counselor knows that the presenting problem of the client is school phobia, the following sentence stems can generate more information about the child's school experience:

When I have to go to school, I feel . . .

When I have to go to school, I think . . .

When I have to go to school, I try to . . .

The worst parts of the school day for me are . . .

The best parts of the school day for me are . . .

Last year school was . . .

My teachers are . . .

When I think about going to school, I . . .

If I could change something about school, it would be . . .

If the counselor doesn't have a sense of the problem, the following sentence stems can elicit information in several areas:

My friends are . . .

At home I feel . . .

My parents are . . .

School is . . .

What I do best is . . .

What I'm not good at is . . .

What I like best about my life right now is . . .

What I'd like to change most about my life right now is . . .

The following examples of sentence stems are designed specifically to assess rational or irrational thinking:

When I make a mistake, I feel . . .

I should . . .

I really need . . .

I just can't forgive myself when . . .

To be a good person, one must . . .

When others reject me, I feel . . .

Other people should . . .

I can't stand it when . . .

It would be awful if . . .

Writing Activities

Through various types of writing activities, it is possible to generate important assessment data. Diaries; logs; journals; and self-composed songs, poems, and stories are excellent sources of information. Examples of writing assignments that can be used to assess a variety of factors include journal entries that highlight key feelings and triggering events; written analyses of songs the clients think describe their circumstances; and original stories or poems that describe how they are thinking, feeling, and behaving.

Self-Monitoring Activities

Involving young clients in monitoring themselves often yields helpful information; the major drawback is that this approach is highly subjective, and results vary according to the clients' investment in the process and their level of honesty. Nevertheless, it is worth a try. Examples include behavior frequency graphs, on which clients plot a line to illustrate how often they experienced targeted behaviors during the week; worry boxes, in which clients write things they worry about on slips of paper and keep them in a box that they bring to share at the next therapy session; a troubling-times tin, for which they write examples of troubles and put them in a tin can to share during counseling; and a feelings chart, on which, for a week or two, they identify the intensity of specific feelings such as anger, depression, or anxiety on a scale of 1 (low) to 5 (high) for each hour of the day.

Assessment of Problematic Emotions and Behaviors

The first step in assessing problematic emotions and behaviors is to determine how accurately the clients are able to identify feelings and behaviors. It may be necessary, especially with younger children, to build a feeling/behaving vocabulary by using the following techniques:

Feeling Flash Cards

Put feeling words on flash cards, and have clients define or act out the words described on the cards.

Feeling Chart
(Featuring Pictures of Feelings and Feeling Words)

Invite young clients to select feelings from a chart that includes words or pictures that describe how they currently feel or how they felt during the time between sessions.

Behavior Chart
(Featuring Pictures of Behaviors)

Ask clients to select pictures from a chart that depict their behaviors during the past several days.

For an accurate assessment, it is important to see how adolescents as well as children define the feelings or behaviors they describe. One client's conception of anger, for example, may be another's description of irritation. A good clarifying question to ask is "When you say, 'irritated,' what exactly do you mean?" Suggest that clients be more specific by describing how they look, sound, or act when they are angry. What they were thinking or how others would know they were angry can give you a clearer idea of how they are defining terms. Role-playing how they act when they feel a certain way or drawing a picture of the feeling or behavior is also a good way for less verbal clients to express themselves. Having younger children use puppets to convey feelings and behaviors is also very effective.

With older clients, having them keep a feeling/behaving journal is a good way to determine how they are defining terms. To initiate this activity, invite clients to take a few minutes each day to describe how they felt and behaved in response to incidents at home, at school, or with friends. (If they are willing to share what they have written, their descriptions will give you insight.)

Feeling and behaving charts are also excellent assessment tools. These charts can be easily made by writing the days of the week across the top of a sheet of paper and the hours of the day and evening down the side. Instruct clients to keep a record throughout the week by indicating on a scale of 1 to 5 how they were feeling or behaving (1 being very depressed, angry, or whatever feeling you are attempting to assess, and 5 being feeling very good; or, for behaving, a 1 could be having lots of behavior problems, and a 5 could be having very few or behaving well). Invite them to bring this to the counseling session the following week. Using the data, ask more specific questions about what the feeling or behavior was like for them, how they feel about the ratings, and so forth. Note how many times a week they experienced certain feelings and help them draw connections between the feelings, behaviors, and any activating events to identify patterns.

You must also assess the frequency, intensity, and duration of these feelings and behaviors. A good way to measure intensity is to use subjective units of distress scales (SUDS) after the emotions and behaviors have been identified (Ellis & MacLaren, 1998). For example, if a client says she was mad at her teacher, ask her to pinpoint her degree of anger on a scale of 1 to 10, with 1 meaning hardly mad at all (just irritated), and 10 meaning furious.

A visual method that can be used is a "thermometer of emotions," in which the client actually moves the scale from cold to hot emotions (using a tagboard thermometer into which a red strip of paper can be inserted and moved up or down) according to the strength of the feeling. This thermometer gives you and the client a specific indication of the intensity of the emotion. The frequency of the emotion can be assessed as well by using the following scaling question: "On a scale of 1 (not at all) to 10 (many times a day), how many tantrums did you have this week as a result of your anger?"

The methods described here can also be used to gather data on frequency and intensity. You can assess duration by asking clients how long the targeted feeling or behavior lasted—minutes, hours, days?

Practical versus emotional problems. Differentiating between practical and emotional problems is also a distinctive aspect of REBT assessment (DiGiuseppe, 1999; Vernon, 1999a). Practical problems are realistic difficulties, whereas emotional problems are uncomfortable feelings about the practical problems that are generated by irrational beliefs. For example, if an adolescent is angry and ashamed because she lacks organizational skills that interfere with her ability to complete her schoolwork, then she might be irrationally thinking that she shouldn't have this problem and that she is stupid and incompetent. The emotional problem frequently prevents clients from doing what they need to do at the practical level, so it is critical to deal with the emotional problem generated by the irrational beliefs first, or attempts at problem resolution will, at best, be temporary. A good example of this scenario are parents who try to coerce their AD/HD children into taking their medication. Because parents, teachers, and many professionals don't deal with the emotional problems—the shame, guilt, or feelings about being different—the behavior management strategies that they frequently employ are generally effective only in the short term. Practitioners can expect far better results if they first address the underlying emotional issues before they attack the practical problem.

Secondary problems. Another distinctive feature of REBT is that it assesses for secondary emotional problems, such as being depressed about being depressed or being anxious about being anxious. It is also very common for adolescents to feel ashamed or embarrassed that they are depressed. Thus it is generally recommended that the secondary emotional problems be dealt with first, with certain questions, such as the following, having to be posed:

What does it say about you if you are depressed?

Where's the proof that others who aren't depressed are better than you are?

How will it help you get over your depression if you also have to deal with your depression about being depressed?

Helping clients dispute their irrational beliefs about their emotional disturbance is a critical step—indeed the first step—in dealing with the primary problem of anger, anxiety, or depression (Ellis & Dryden, 1997).

Appropriate versus inappropriate negative reactions. It is also essential to differentiate between appropriate and inappropriate negative emotional reactions (Ellis & Dryden, 1997). Concern, irritation, and disappointment are reasonable emotions that result from rational thinking, whereas anger, rage, and devastation emanate from irrational beliefs. Counselors should keep in mind that, because young clients do not always accurately label their feelings, they may express irritation but, in reality, may be quite angry. For accurate assessment, it is important to probe further and uncover the beliefs, as the following example involving a sixth grader shows.

Counselor: So how did you feel when you found out your parents were getting divorced?

Client: Oh, I guess I was irritated.

Counselor: Irritated? In what ways?

Client: Well, it'll be a hassle to go back and forth between houses, and it won't be as much fun when I have to go to my dad's, since my pool and trampoline are at my mom's.

Counselor: So there are things you will miss by not being at one house all the time, and that can be irritating and certainly disappointing. I'm wondering if there are other things you're irritated about regarding this situation, or if you have any other feelings about it.

Client: Not really.

Counselor: Well, can you share with me how you reacted when you first found out about this?

Client: I just shut myself in my room and stayed there for a long time.

Counselor: And when you were in your room, what were you thinking about?

Client: How I hate my parents for doing this, and I think they shouldn't have ever gotten married in the first place if they can't stay together now.

Counselor: So it sounds like you might have been more than just irritated—sounds like you were pretty mad.

Client: Yeah, I was.

One goal of treatment is to move the client away from the extreme emotional reactions that accompany irrational beliefs. Therefore, practitioners must assess the emotion accurately and not necessarily take what the client says at face value without probing further.

Accurate emotional assessment also must include looking at all possible emotional reactions. I clearly recall a case in which an adolescent was extremely upset because she hadn't been selected for an honor band. My immediate assumption was that she was upset with herself for being rejected and felt inadequate, but I was wrong. She was angry at the system and the band instructor, who deemed her unacceptable. A more specific question (e.g., "What do you mean by upset?") might have gotten her to specify her anger. Then I would have asked her whom she was angry with: herself or others?

Assessing the behavioral consequences of different emotional reactions should not be ignored. Asking clients who reported feeling angry to describe what they did when they were angry gives insight into the intensity of the emotional reaction and the accompanying thought process. If the clients say they punched the wall, then obviously they were intensely angry. If they merely pouted, then they may have been more irritated than angry. These differentiations should be pointed out to clients. It is also important to assess whether their reaction is a common response to similar events, how much control they perceived that they had over their behavioral reaction, and how they felt about the way they behaved. Finally, practitioners should inquire about their clients' understanding of the consequences of their behavioral reactions.

Assessment of Irrational Beliefs and Cognitive Distortions

Although the major objective of the REBT assessment process is to identify irrational beliefs, practitioners should keep in mind that not all beliefs are irrational. A major clue to the existence of irrational beliefs is the intensity or duration of the feeling or behavior. If, for example, a client reported that he felt sad when his dog died, and he cried himself to sleep for several nights, the practitioner should not assume that there is anything irrational about the client's behavior because it is normal to feel sad and cry when a pet dies. However, if he is still crying and can't sleep months after the event, the duration of the symptom is an indication that he is irrationally thinking that his dog's death is the worst thing that could ever happen, that he can never be happy without his dog, and that he can't stand this discomfort. It would also be normal for an adolescent to be upset when his girlfriend breaks up with him. But if he is suicidal and thinks he can't go on living because the two of them are no longer together, he is thinking irrationally—that this is the end of the world, that he will never fall in love again, and that he can't stand the pain.

As described earlier in this chapter, irrational beliefs are distorted thoughts that result in self-defeating behaviors and intense negative emotions. Ellis (1996) identified demanding, low frustration tolerance or discomfort anxiety, and global ratings of self and others as core irrational beliefs. Waters (1982) expanded on Ellis's core beliefs, identifying the following irrational beliefs for children:

It's awful if others don't like me.

I'm bad if I make a mistake.

Everything should go my way; I should always get what I want.

Things should come easily to me.

The world should be fair, and bad people must be punished.

I shouldn't show my feelings.

Adults should be perfect.

There's only one right answer.

I must win.

I shouldn't have to wait for anything. (p. 572)

Waters (1981) enumerated the following irrational beliefs for adolescents:

It would be awful if peers didn't like me; it would be awful to be a social loser.

I shouldn't make mistakes, especially social mistakes.

It's my parents' fault I'm so miserable.

I can't help it—that's just the way I am, and I guess I'll always be this way.

The world should be fair and just.

It's awful when things don't go my way.

It's better to avoid challenges than to risk failure.

I must conform to my peers.

I can't stand to be criticized.

Others should always be responsible. (p. 6)

It is sometimes difficult to explain the concept of irrational beliefs to young clients, so practitioners may want to use terms such as *junk thoughts, unproductive thoughts, muddy thoughts,* or *insensible thoughts.*

In assessing cognitions, therapists should pay attention to their young clients' ability to distinguish between facts and assumptions. It is characteristic for children and adolescents to make assumptions without checking the facts. They might assume that their best friend doesn't like them because the friend sat with someone else at lunch, or they might assume that their parents will not let them go to a movie because their parents said no the last time they asked. These assumptions result in disturbing emotions that can also affect behavior, as illustrated in the following example:

Nate was irate because his girlfriend hadn't called him the night before, as promised. He told the therapist that he knew she hadn't called because she was out with another guy and that this must mean she didn't like him anymore. He informed the therapist that he had waited over an hour for her to call, and when she didn't, he went out and picked up two female friends and rode around with them the rest of the night.

When his therapist asked him if there was any proof that his girlfriend was out with someone else or whether there were previous indications that she didn't like him, he admitted that there was no basis for his assumptions—and that he hadn't considered the possibility that maybe she hadn't called because of some other, extenuating circumstance. As it turned out, she had been grounded from using the phone, but when she heard from friends that Nate had been out with other girls, she became angry with him, and a major fight ensued.

Had Nate not jumped to conclusions and allowed his assumptions to rule his emotions and behaviors, the scenario would have been significantly different. This is why, as clients describe their problem, it is important to initially accept their perception of the circumstance but then help them to distinguish between facts and assumptions as you work through the ABC process. Teaching young clients this distinction is also an excellent prevention technique because, if they are able to differentiate between facts and assumptions, in the future they will have a clearer perspective of the problem. This fresh perspective can help alleviate some of their emotional upset and impulsive behavior. The following activities may be helpful.

Fact, Fact, Fact

Activities such as Fact, Fact, Fact (adapted from Vernon, 1980, p. 96) are effective in helping younger children distinguish between facts and assumptions. Such activities also help children to understand that they have failed to take into account all perspectives of the situation. To play Fact, Fact, Fact, you will need an 8½ × 11–inch sheet of paper designed as a tic-tac-toe board.

Indicate to the client that you will be reading some statements, and that both of you need to think about whether what you are reading are facts (i.e., true statements that can be proven) or assumptions (i.e., statements that the client supposes are true but have yet to be verified). You and the client alternate turns and place an *F* for *fact* or an *A* for *assumption* on the board. Designate the client as 1 and yourself as 2, so when you put the letters on the board, you can also put a number beside each of them to indicate each player's response. As in tic-tac-toe, the first person to get three numbers in a row is the "expert" on facts and assumptions:

> *Some examples of facts:* Broccoli is a vegetable; milk comes from cows and goats; lakes are smaller than oceans; pigs can't fly; Iowa is a state located in the United States.

> *Some examples of assumptions:* All third graders are smarter than all second graders; winter is the best season of the year; cats are better pets than dogs; all presidents like their job; parents never have to do things they do not want to do.

Tunnel Vision

Another activity that is effective in helping younger children to distinguish between facts and assumptions is Tunnel Vision (adapted from Vernon, 1998a, pp. 237–239). To play Tunnel Vision, you will need a kaleidoscope (either a real one or a toy).

Introduce the activity by sharing the kaleidoscope with the client and asking him to look through it. Ask the following: "Do you see just one thing or a variety of changing patterns as you turn the dial?" Then discuss what it is like to be in a tunnel (e.g., It is usually dark, and you can't see around you; you just see what is straight ahead). Contrast the experience of being in a tunnel to that of looking through a kaleidoscope and seeing a variety of things in multiple patterns. Introduce the term *tunnel vision,* explaining how people sometimes act as if they are in a tunnel and don't see all aspects of a situation. These people may assume something is true, but they don't bother to check its veracity or consider other possibilities. Discuss how having tunnel vision could possibly create problems at home, at school, or with friends.

Emphasize the difference between having tunnel vision and considering a variety of perspectives, as would be the case with *kaleidoscope vision.* Next, designate one chair as the "tunnel" chair. Ask the child to sit in that chair. As you read several of the following situations, he is to state an *assumption* about each one. Then have him switch to the "kaleidoscope" chair and state at least two different possible points of view. The following are examples of tunnel vision situations:

> Tom was supposed to be home at 5:30, but he didn't get home until 6:00.
>
> Shiron got a bad grade on his science test.
>
> Daphne had $5 on her dresser, but when she got ready for bed, she noticed that the money wasn't there. Her sister had been in her room to borrow a sweatshirt earlier in the day.
>
> Donita didn't sit by her friend on the bus.
>
> Aaron didn't go to ball practice last night.

After the client has responded to these situations, discuss how the concepts of tunnel vision and kaleidoscope vision apply to his life.

The following strategies are effective in helping children and adolescents identify irrational beliefs.

Sentence Stems

Have the client complete these sentences: When that happened, you were thinking _____. When you felt so angry, you were thinking _____.

Inference as a Hunch

Ask the client something like "Some kids your age might think nobody liked them if they didn't get invited to a birthday party. What do you think about not being invited?"

Labeling

Although this technique should be used sparingly because it is better for the client to supply her own thoughts, it is effective with the younger client who has trouble expressing herself. The practitioner can ask, "Are you thinking . . . ?" and then complete the sentence with a thought that would result in a dysfunctional emotion or behavior. Some examples: "Are you thinking it is awful that your mother was 10 minutes late to pick you up?" "Are you thinking that you are bad or different because you have to take medicine to help you control your behavior?" If the client agrees that she was thinking along these lines, the practitioner can probe for other irrational beliefs related to the specific activating event (Bernard & Joyce, 1984).

Visuals

Use a visual, such as a head with thought bubbles surrounding it. After the client describes the activating event and feelings, point to the head and ask what he was thinking. Write the thoughts in the bubbles and ask probing questions to generate additional thoughts. Oftentimes these thoughts are automatic thoughts that aren't irrational, so you will need to ask additional questions about self-downing, demanding, and low frustration tolerance.

Rational or Irrational? Game

This game helps adolescents learn to distinguish between rational and irrational beliefs. Before you start, you will need a set of rational beliefs and a set of irrational beliefs, with each set written on separate index cards.

Rational Cards

I hope I get invited to the party.

If I miss one or two math problems, it isn't the end of the world.

It would be nice if I won the contest.

I really hope my friends call me to go skating.

If I don't get a good grade, I am still a worthwhile person.

Irrational Cards

I can't stand it if I don't get invited to the party.

I can't imagine anything worse than missing one or two math problems.

If I don't win the contest, I will be very upset and depressed for a long time.

I'll be devastated if my friends don't call me to go skating.

If I don't get a good grade, I might as well stop trying—it will just prove how stupid and worthless I am.

Chapter 2 • Basic Principles of Rational Emotive Behavior Therapy

To play, shuffle the cards and put them facedown, five in one row and five in another. Ask the client to turn over a card, state whether it is rational or irrational and why, and then turn over another card to try to find the first overturned card's rational or irrational counterpart. If he gets a match, those cards can be taken off the board. If there is no match, they both get turned over. Proceed until all cards have been matched.

Think-Aloud Technique

Assign the client a task in the counseling session that is similar to one she is having trouble with, such as completing math homework. As she is working, ask her to verbalize what she is feeling and thinking (Genest & Turk, 1981).

Expansion/Contraction Technique

As the client describes in his own words his thoughts or feelings about a problematic situation, the practitioner asks questions such as "When you said that you thought it was awful, what was it about that event that you thought was so awful?" or "I'd like you to describe for me the first thing that comes into your mind when you think about . . . " The purpose is to ask questions that help the client expand on his thoughts (Bernard, 1981).

Inference Chaining

Because younger children are not as adept at verbal expression as adolescents, the prompts "and . . ." and "because . . ." are useful in that they can encourage the children to continue verbalizing. For example, if the child says she was angry when the teacher didn't call on her, the practitioner's use of "because . . ." can help her complete the thought.

Distinguishing between Inferences and Evaluations

Owing to their developmental level, children and adolescents often make inferences, which are automatic thoughts or interpretations, rather than evaluations that relate to the core irrational beliefs. For example, a young adolescent might state that his girlfriend doesn't like him; in actuality, that is an inference. The evaluation is that there must be something wrong with him (self-downing). In assessing irrational beliefs, it is important to distinguish between inferences and evaluations and attempt to get to the evaluations. The therapist can accomplish this task by asking a series of questions such as "Suppose he doesn't like you—what does that say about you? Are you what he says you are? And suppose you are. Does that mean you are no good?" Using the analogy of peeling away the layers of an onion is a concrete way for practitioners to help young clients understand that the therapist is going to be asking them certain questions to get to the basis of what they are thinking. Although it is preferable to identify young clients' core beliefs—if one is to practice the most elegant form of REBT—it is important that therapists be sensitive to each client's developmental level in the disputation of these core beliefs. It would be difficult, for example, for a first grader who was abandoned by his mother to understand that he is still lovable, even though his mother deserted him.

Assessing Cognitions

In assessing cognitions, counselors should also assess for automatic errors in thinking. The following such errors are quite common among younger populations (Beck, Rush, Shaw, & Emery, 1979):

> *Overgeneralization*—drawing a general conclusion that is based on one or more isolated incidents and applying it across the board. Example: "I didn't get an A on this test, so I will never get an A in this class."

> *Personalization*—relating external events personally when there is no basis for the connection. Example: "The bus driver didn't wait for me; therefore, she doesn't like me."

> *Magnification or minimization*—evaluating the significance of an event inappropriately. Example: "So what if I got picked up for possession? It's no big deal."

> *Selective abstraction*—focusing on a detail out of context or ignoring significant details of the situation. Example: "My mother didn't wash my jeans, but she washed my sister's, which proves that she cares more about my sister than she does about me. It shouldn't matter that my sister followed the rule and had hers in the laundry hamper and I didn't. Mom should have done mine anyway."

> *Arbitrary inference*—drawing a specific conclusion in the absence of evidence to support the conclusion or in the presence of evidence to the contrary. Example: "Since I only studied an hour for my test, I'll flunk it, even though I only studied an hour last time and got a B."

Once the irrational beliefs and the disturbing emotions and behaviors have been assessed, the treatment phase of the process can begin.

The ABC Process

As noted earlier in this chapter, a distinct advantage of REBT is that its ABC model provides a framework that helps to structure the counseling process. This framework is especially helpful in counseling children and adolescents, because, as a rule, it is more difficult to keep them (as opposed to adults) focused and willing to work through the steps necessary to bring about change. In employing this model, practitioners have a mental map to guide them as they assess the problem and subsequently design interventions that help clients think rationally and behave sensibly.

The A—Activating Event

In conceptualizing the problem, REBT therapists can usually expect children and adolescents first to describe the A, or the activating event. This would be what the children experienced, what happened. Occasionally, they may first discuss their feelings, in which case their therapists would encourage them to discuss their emotions and accompanying behaviors and then identify the activating event.

Unlike less directive therapists, REBT practitioners do *not* encourage children to elaborate extensively on the event because such detail is often unnecessary and time consuming. Practitioners need to judge how much to allow clients to elaborate on the activating event. Certainly, a traumatic event merits more time than a friendship dispute, and it is always important to allow some time for young clients to tell their stories because they may not have adults in their lives who are there to listen to them. Unfortunately, many practitioners mistakenly believe that, because of the method's active-directive nature, listening isn't essential in the practice of effective REBT. In reality, listening is extremely important, as is the ability to ask well-directed questions that elicit information about clients' emotional and behavioral reactions and irrational beliefs. This strategy is especially important when working with resistant youngsters and those with backgrounds that differ markedly from the therapists'. In general, it is often during the initial session that more elaboration occurs; but once therapists have established rapport and have acquired an overview of the problem, it is important to begin actively working on the problem.

The C—Emotional and Behavioral Consequences

Although the core of the REBT problem-solving process is the identification and disputation of irrational beliefs, it is reached only after the emotional and behavioral reactions are assessed. Therefore, after the activating event has been described, the next step is to ask clients to discuss how they felt and how they acted relative to the particular event. The intensity of their feelings and behaviors is important in determining whether they are holding irrational beliefs, plus their specific emotions help target the core belief. For example, if clients report feeling depressed and worthless, they are most likely engaging in self-downing, whereas if they are angry and resentful, they are probably engaging in demanding, "shoulding," and other-downing. So, not only do feelings and behaviors facilitate the assessment process, they also make up an integral part of the therapeutic process. Especially with younger children, it is important that therapists listen to their feelings.

Strategies for Children

It is often difficult for children to describe their feelings, so it may be necessary for them to brainstorm a list of feeling words and select which ones apply to them relative to their current situation. Drawing a picture, acting out how they feel, demonstrating with puppets, or pointing to feeling faces on a chart of feelings are also effective strategies.

In addition, Feel Wheel (Vernon, 1989a, pp. 25–26) and other games, such as Fabulous Feelings and Not-So-Fabulous Feelings (Vernon, 1998a, pp. 27–34), are also good ways to facilitate identification and expression of feelings.

Feel Wheel

Feel Wheel involves cutting a large circle out of tagboard and dividing it into 13 pie shapes, with each slice assigned a feeling word: *excited, grouchy, sad, happy, mad, angry, nervous, frustrated, upset, lonely, worried, scared, furious.* Make an arrow out of tagboard and attach it to the center of the circle with a brass fastener so it will spin. Invite the client to spin the spinner. When the arrow lands on a feeling, have the client first explain what the feeling means, and then have her give an example of a time when she felt like that.

Fabulous Feelings and Not-So-Fabulous Feelings

Fabulous Feelings and Not-So-Fabulous Feelings are games that help younger children identify positive and negative feelings. For these games, you will use the bottom half of two 1-quart milk cartons, one labeled Fabulous Feelings, and the other labeled Not-So-Fabulous Feelings. In addition, you will need two sets of cards: one set consisting of Fabulous Feelings words and the other set consisting of Not-So-Fabulous Feelings words. The Fabulous Feelings cards should have written on them the following feeling words: *proud, happy, excited, calm, cheerful, wonderful.* The Not-So-Fabulous Feelings cards should have written on them the following feeling words*: mad, scared, jealous, worried, furious, sad.* (Each word—the fabulous and the not-so-fabulous— should be written on two separate cards.) You will also need the Fabulous Feelings Scenarios and the Not-So-Fabulous Feelings Scenarios.

Fabulous Feelings Scenarios

You haven't seen your grandparents in a long time, and they are coming this weekend.

Your birthday is next week, and your parents have hinted that you will be getting a special present.

You just got your math paper back, and you got all the problems right.

You have wanted a kitten for a long time. Today your mom is going to take you to the Humane Society to pick one out.

Your cousins are coming over to play.

Your new baby sister is coming home from the hospital tomorrow.

Not-So-Fabulous Feelings Scenarios

You are outside for recess, and one of your friends makes fun of the way you run.

You are at the market with your mother. She buys your sister some candy and won't buy any for you.

You are taking swimming lessons because you don't know how to swim.

You got your reading worksheet back. You didn't get very many right.

Your brother takes your roller blades without asking if he can use them.

Your dad is in jail for selling drugs.

To play this game, mix up the scenarios and read them to the client, who then selects either a Fabulous Feelings card or a Not-So-Fabulous Feelings card and puts it in the corresponding milk carton. Once he has done so, discuss the meaning of the word on the card. Proceed with the activity, continuing to discuss the meanings of the words on the cards the client chooses to help increase his feeling vocabulary.

Continuum of Emotions

Because younger children are active and like to move around, Continuum of Emotions is an activity that works well. Place a strip of masking tape on the floor and designate two opposite degrees of an emotion that relates to something they are experiencing. For example, if they are angry, you could label one end "Slightly Irritated" and the other end "Furious." After discussing their particular situation, identify the extreme emotions at either end of the continuum and then elicit from them other emotions that would fit across the continuum (e.g., very angry, somewhat angry, pretty ticked off). Then ask the clients to stand on the line at the spot that most accurately describes how they feel about the problem they are experiencing.

Strategies for Adolescents

With adolescents, it may be necessary to share a chart of feeling words and ask them to select the term that describes them. You can also share excerpts from a motion picture that portrays emotions in a circumstance similar to theirs. Examples may include scenes from the movie *Dead Poets Society* that depict the relationship between a teenage male and his controlling father or scenes from the film *Pump Up the Volume* that highlight the anger and confusion commonly experienced by adolescents.

Reading about Other Teens' Feelings

Teens also seem better able to self-disclose and express their feelings if they have read about other teens' feelings. By reading about how others their age feel, they realize they are not alone, and they are relieved to discover that. Consider sharing the following poem, written by a 17-year-old (Vernon, 1998c, p. 48).

Anger Is . . .

Anger is inside you.
It burns you, like the gates of hell.
It controls you, fills you up.

Anger is red.
It is hot, like the sun.
It is powerful, like money.

Anger takes hold.
It grabs your arms and your legs.
It breaks you down.

Anger is a bright flash.
It is the emotional battle you're trying to win.
You against anger, who's keeping score?

Two stories written by adolescent clients are also helpful to share:
The Emotional Roller Coaster (Vernon, 1998c, pp. 43–44) and Like a
Yo-Yo (Vernon, 1998b, p. 187).

The Emotional Roller Coaster

I am 15. For the past several months I have been having lots of mood swings. I can wake up in the morning
feeling excited about going to school to see my friends.
But before I even get out the door I might be in a bad
mood. Maybe it's something as little as not getting my
hair to look right or not liking what I have to wear. But
most of the time I just feel down for no apparent reason; there doesn't seem to be anything major that
makes me feel the way I do. Oh, sometimes I may get
in a fight with a friend, or I might get mad at my mom
if she won't let me do something I want to do, but usually the moods just happen with no warning. Once I
get to school I may snap out of it, but if I don't, I don't
even want to talk to anybody.

The bad part of it is that when I feel down, I get
scared. Sometimes it seems like the bad feelings will
never go away, and I feel like giving up. When I'm
down I tend to think of other things that make me feel
more down, and then it just gets worse. It confuses me
that I can feel that bad, and then those moods can shift
and I can feel real up and happy. That's how I'd like to
feel more of the time. Then I can laugh, do crazy
things with my friends, and just feel good.

Sometimes when I'm down I get argumentative. I'll
yell at my mom or go off on my friends for no good
reason. Then later I feel guilty because I acted like
that. The last time I was with my dad I blew up at him

in the restaurant. People started looking at me and I felt pretty embarrassed. It's not like I really planned to act that way; I just didn't feel like I had any control. The one thing that helps me get out of the bad moods is to force myself to get out and do something. It takes a lot of effort, but if I do it, I usually feel better. I know that when I mope around I think about things that don't help my moods, so I try to stay "up" by getting involved in something other than myself. That isn't a guarantee that I'll stay "up," but at least it helps for a while. Doing things with my friends helps, too. We can have fun just hanging out.

I don't mean it to sound like I have a terrible life or am depressed all the time. It's not like that. I think I'm a pretty normal teenager. But sometimes no matter how hard I try it just isn't quite enough, and the moods take over. I know a lot of my friends feel like this, too. I guess we just have to ride the "roller coaster" and try not to let things get to us. I keep trying to remind myself that this won't last forever, and that helps.

Like a Yo-Yo

I am 14 years old and in eighth grade. Since the end of last year I have been feeling strange. Sometimes I am really happy, and I can joke around and laugh with my friends. Then I change, and I can't figure out why. I might get real angry or just depressed. Sometimes it doesn't even have anything to do with what's going on. Like yesterday. I was walking down the hall with one of my friends, and all of a sudden I just went off on him. He hadn't even said anything, but I just got mad. When I'm like that I yell at my friends for no reason, and then they get mad at me. It happens with my parents, too. Sometimes I just want to be left alone, but they keep asking me what's wrong, and I just blow up. Afterwards I feel really guilty that I treated them like that, and I don't even understand why.

Today I was walking home with a bunch of kids. We were just goofing off and having fun. I felt so good. Then later I was hanging out in my room and I just started to get depressed. Nothing had happened; my feelings just changed. I hate it, and I don't understand why this happens.

I know some of my friends feel like this, too, because some days they just go off on me for no reason. But if I'm in a bad mood, I get ticked off at them, and then we get into big fights, so that creates more problems.

It's like none of us knows what to do to stop this from happening.

I just wish I could feel the same way for longer than a few hours or a day. Sometimes I wake up and I know it's going to be a good day, but then it can change. Other days I wake up and I'm already in a super-bad mood, and then things just get worse for a while. I wish I knew what to do about it.

Concrete Analogies

It is also useful to come up with concrete analogies to help children and adolescents describe their feelings more accurately, such as the following:

Is your anger more like water boiling slowly on a stove and then eventually spilling over, or is it like a rocket ship that just takes off suddenly?

Is your anxiety so intense that you feel like it's a wave washing over you, or is it just a little ripple?

✳ ✳ ✳

It is generally easier for children and adolescents to identify behaviors than to identify emotions, but it still may be necessary with young clients to have them draw, pantomime, or act out with puppets how they behaved when they felt a certain way. Establishing the connection between feelings and behaviors is very important, and this connection is something that children and adolescents may not think about. A couple of questions that counselors might ask them are "So when you were so angry, how did you behave? Were there consequences of those actions, and if so, how did you feel about those?" Throughout the ABC process, the practitioner should strive to help clients understand how their behaviors help them or hinder them, how to assess the consequences of their behaviors, and how to control their behaviors.

The B—Beliefs

Once the disturbing emotions and behaviors have been identified and discussed, the practitioner helps clients to identify their beliefs and see the connection between thinking, feeling, and behaving. If, during the assessment process, it is determined that the feelings and behaviors are moderate and appropriate and the beliefs are rational, it is important for the therapist to talk to the client in a reassuring manner, saying something like this:

It is normal to feel sad about your best friend moving away. You said that you will miss her and that it might be hard to adjust to her being gone, and that is understandable. Had you been thinking that you can't stand this and can't imagine living in this town without your best friend, you would probably be depressed and more upset. But because you have told yourself that you can get along without her but at the same time wish she didn't have to move, you are able to cope with this situation even if you don't like it.

The D—Disputing Irrational Beliefs

If, on the contrary, it is determined during the assessment process that the beliefs are irrational, the therapist must now dispute them. With children and adolescents, practitioners need to be more creative in their disputation techniques than they are with adult clients and not rely solely on verbal challenging. Some suggestions follow:

Just Pretend

Have your client pretend she is her best friend: What would she say to a friend who was insisting that she always had to be perfect or was sobbing because it was so awful to be grounded for a day?

Exaggeration

Used with some degree of caution, exaggeration can be effective in showing young clients how irrational their beliefs are. Before using this technique, be certain that your client is old enough to understand the concept of exaggeration. For a teenager whining about curfew, you could say something like this: "Maybe your parents should be locked up in jail because their crime of making you come in at 10 o'clock on a school night is so severe."

Reverse Role Play

In reverse role play, you play the part of the irrational student who, in this case, insists that it is the end of the world if she gets a failing grade. The client, meanwhile, attempts to help you dispute your irrational beliefs about this.

Humor

Humor, which is a strategy that can be somewhat similar to exaggeration, must also be used appropriately and cautiously so that it doesn't seem as if you are making fun of your young client. You might say to him, for example, "You, who have never made a mistake in your life, made one—and you are still alive to tell about it?"

Empty Chair Technique

This technique, which involves movement, is a very graphic way to help children understand the disputational process. Use two chairs. Designate one chair as the irrational chair and the other as the rational chair. First, have the client sit in the irrational chair and verbalize the thoughts she has about a problematic situation. Then have her shift to the rational chair and attempt to dispute her irrational beliefs. The following transcript is from a 6-year-old who learned this process after it was modeled by the therapist for a different problem:

Irrational chair: My mom never pays any attention to me. The only one she cares about is my baby sister.

Rational chair: Just because my mom is paying attention to the baby doesn't mean she doesn't love me. My sister can't do anything for herself, so she has to help her.

Irrational chair: I know she loves me, but it's not fair that she only reads one book to me before bed and rocks my sister for a lot longer.

Rational chair: That's just the way it is. You can throw a fit about it or just read another book to yourself.

Survey Technique

The survey technique, which involves a homework assignment, works well for a client who stubbornly hangs on to his irrational thoughts. Suppose he insists that his parents are the worst in the world, *never* letting him go anywhere or do anything and *always* making him do all the work in the family. To help challenge his overgeneralizations, work with him in the session to develop a survey he can use to ask his classmates about their parents. For example, he could ask his friends if their parents let them do anything they want, never have any rules for them, never make them do any chores, and give them as much money as they want. Just by generating the questions, the client usually sees how he is exaggerating his situation and, consequently, is better able to put it in perspective.

Paradoxical Technique

Suggest that the client set a time limit to be deliberately irrational. During this 10- to 15-minute period, she should think of all the awful things she can't stand, make lists of her mistakes, or create poems or songs about her irrational beliefs and behaviors. Once the time period is up, she should tell herself that she can't be irrational the rest of the day and will make every attempt to think rationally and act sensibly. During the next session, as she shares the results of her experiment, ask her to identify what changes she had to make in her thinking to be rational.

Erase the Irrational

Activities such as this one (Vernon, 1989a, pp. 217–218) teach children and adolescents how to replace irrational thoughts with rational ones. After explaining the concept of rational versus irrational beliefs and discussing the idea of erasing something, give the client the following

Chapter 2 • Basic Principles of Rational Emotive Behavior Therapy

list of irrational beliefs and ask him to "erase" the following irrational beliefs and write rational replacements:

I should be perfect in everything I do.

My friends should always do exactly what I want them to do.

If I make a mistake, I'm dumb.

Everyone should like me. I can't stand it if everyone doesn't.

I'm the only one around the house who ever does any work.

The way I'm working on my project is the best way, and others should do it my way.

I shouldn't have to go out of my way to make friends. People should come to me.

It's not my fault that I'm unhappy all the time.

Other kids shouldn't just stand there during a game—they should put in as much effort as I do.

My friends should always listen to what I have to say.

Challenging Irrational Beliefs

This activity (Vernon, 1989b, pp. 49–51) helps adolescents learn to challenge their irrational beliefs. Once your client has learned the process, she can substitute her own irrational beliefs and challenge them. Although the original version of this activity was intended for use in a classroom or small group, it can be adapted for use with you and a client. You will need to use the following list of scenarios:

You have a chance to win the game for your team, and you miss the shot.

You don't get all A's on your report card.

Your best friend moves away.

You've got the flu and have to miss the only school party of the year.

Cheerleading tryouts are tonight, and you're nervous.

A teacher blames you for something you didn't do.

You have tests in four subjects tomorrow.

Someone you have a crush on ignores you.

Your parents are getting a divorce.

A group of kids has been giving you a hard time about your clothes being ugly.

Take turns reading the items aloud. When it is your turn, identify two irrational beliefs that could be associated with the particular situation; the client then identifies a challenge for each irrational belief. For example, for the situation of the best friend moving away, the irrational beliefs might be that you can't stand it and you will never find another best friend again. One challenge could be that you can stand it even if you think you can't. Another could ask for the evidence that you will never find another best friend ever again. After the client understands the process of identifying and challenging irrational beliefs, have her identify personal examples she can work on.

Change the Channel

Use the metaphor of changing the channel on the TV to help remind your client that if he is "tuned in" to an irrational channel, he can switch to a more rational channel by disputing his irrational beliefs.

Bibliotherapy

Bibliotherapy is another excellent way to help children and adolescents understand the concept of rational and irrational beliefs and the disputational process. Waters's (1979) *Color Us Rational* stories are excellent for younger children. After reading one of the stories, involve your client in writing a story with a rational ending that relates directly to a situation in her own life. Recently, a 9-year-old client wrote that, although he was sad that his parents had gotten a divorce, he realized that it could be worse—one of his parents could have died: "I don't like what they did, but I know they both love me. I can choose to be mad and sad, or just accept it and try to be happy." *Instant Replay* (Bedford, 1974) is also a good story to use. The concept of instant replay helps children think about their behavior and identify ways to replay the scenario and react more rationally. After children understand this concept, they can act out instant-replay scenarios with puppets or draw instant-replay cartoon scenarios.

Traditional Disputing Strategies

More traditional disputing strategies involve asking the client to show the evidence that something is true, challenging his assertion that he is not able to tolerate something by asking him if it is unbearable (which most clients respond to by saying it is bearable—they just don't like it), or asking him to show you the rule or law that says that something "shouldn't" happen. Another good challenge is to ask him how his rigid thinking helps him. If he actually makes a list of all the ways his irrational thoughts are and are not working for him, he will have a visual reminder that these thoughts aren't very functional.

Keep in mind that, when working with children and adolescents, you will usually not be as forceful in disputing as you would be with adults; it may take more effort and a combination of strategies before children and adolescents truly understand how to identify and dispute irrational beliefs. Since younger clients may never have heard of the terms *rational* and *irrational*, substituting terms such as *sensible, flexible,* and *helpful,* or *insensible, rigid,* and *unhelpful* is often necessary.

The E—Effective New Philosophy

If the REBT process has been effective, clients should feel less disturbed and behave more sensibly because they will be thinking more rationally. Especially with younger clients, it is important to reinforce what they have learned so they can continue to handle the present situation, as well as future incidents, more effectively. To that end, the following strategies have worked well.

Tape Recordings

Because most young people are technology junkies, tape-record the session with your client so she can hear herself working through the ABC process and can thus listen to how she learned to challenge her irrational beliefs.

Concrete Images

Teach your client concrete images he can use to help him dispute irrational beliefs. I recall working with an adolescent male who claimed he just could not stop thinking about what his girlfriend was doing when he wasn't with her. He admitted that he allowed his imagination to run wild, picturing her with other guys and having sex. When he had those thoughts, he would get depressed, thinking that she was rejecting him because he wasn't good enough, and that if they broke up, he would never find anyone he loved as much as he loved her. Despite my efforts at disputing, he was struggling to develop a rational perspective. Finally, it struck me that, because he was a visual learner, it might help him to imagine that his head was a giant "bug zapper." If he could visualize it as such, then—just as bugs would be eliminated when they hit the zapper—his irrational beliefs would be eliminated if he turned on his zapper each time he started to think irrationally. This concrete example was just what this client needed, as is so often the case with children and adolescents. They may find it helpful to visualize a stop sign in front of them when they start to make assumptions, engage in self-downing, or act impulsively. The stop sign can be a signal to stop and reevaluate. Other examples that have proven useful include visualizing a superhero zooming in and snatching them away from situations when they are tempted to act out; imagining that there is a radio inside their head that switches to another channel when irrational thoughts are predominant; seeing a billboard with the words "Think sensibly, act smart"; or picturing a rearview mirror as a reminder not to dwell on past negative thoughts, feelings, and behaviors.

Rational Verses

Involve your young client in writing rational verses such as the following:

> *Jack and Jill went up the hill to fetch a pail of water.*
> *Jack fell down and broke his knee.*
> *Jill said, "This is bad, but not a catastrophe."*

Rational Limericks

Teach your client to write rational limericks, in which the first, second, and fifth lines rhyme with each other, while the third and fourth lines also rhyme:

There once was a boy named Moe,
Who wanted to go to a show.
But when he got there,
He could not find a chair;
So sad but not mad, home he did go.

Rational Songs

Teach your adolescent client to compose rational songs to familiar childhood tunes, or suggest to her that, for songs she frequently listens to, she rewrite them from a more rational perspective. A fourth grader who was upsetting herself about her best friend's lack of attention made up the following lyrics (to be sung to the tune of "All I Want for Christmas Is My Two Front Teeth"):

All I want for Christmas is my best friend back,
My best friend back, oh, my best friend back.
But, gee, if I never get my best friend back,
Then I will have to make some new ones.

Analyzing TV Shows or Movies

Suggest that your client analyze TV shows or movies for examples of self-downing, demanding, overgeneralizing and awfulizing, or low frustration tolerance and rewrite the episodes to reflect a more rational perspective.

Rational Bumper Stickers, Posters, or Banners

Invite your client to create rational bumper stickers, posters, or banners as a way of remembering rational concepts. A fifth grader who was having problems concentrating on schoolwork because he was anxious about his performance drew a two-part poster of himself surrounded by balloons with slogans such as "You can't do it" or "If you miss one, you're a total loser" or "Nothing is more awful than doing a bad job on this test" on one side of the poster. On the other side he drew a picture of himself popping these balloons. He said the poster was a reminder that he could get rid of his negative thoughts.

Rational Advice Column

Suggest to the client that she write a rational advice column, in which she takes examples of problems she has been dealing with and writes suggestions about how to think more rationally and behave more sensibly.

The F—Effective New Feelings

One of the goals of REBT is to reduce the intensity of negative emotions, an objective that is particularly important for young clients, who easily become overwhelmed by their emotions and often don't know how to deal with them. The result of working through the ABC model is that clients can adopt an effective new philosophy that will consequently result in more moderate feelings. This is not to say that clients who have experienced a negative event that they were depressed about will feel elated, but that they can feel less depressed, sad, or regretful. These moderate feelings facilitate problem solving and prevent the client from staying stuck.

Homework

Homework, which helps clients change more quickly and profoundly, is an essential component of REBT (Ellis, 1991; Ellis & MacLaren, 1998; Walen et al., 1992). The premise is that, through persistence and practice, clients can continue to work on getting better—independent of the counseling sessions. This form of self-help is empowering for children and adolescents and is often a good way for young clients to share what they are working on with parents and teachers. Various types of cognitive, emotive, and behavioral homework can be used: conducting short surveys or experiments, creating rational coping statements, making lists of advantages and disadvantages of maintaining unproductive behaviors, practicing self-talk in front of a mirror, or using bibliotherapy. Homework is usually assigned at the end of the counseling session, and when possible, it is a good idea to involve clients in the design of the task. The following example illustrates how the counselor involved Antonio in developing his homework task:

> For several sessions, 10-year-old Antonio had been working on his low frustration tolerance, noting that it negatively affected his ability to complete tasks. In his next session, the counselor had him read the ever-popular children's story *Little Engine That Could* (Piper, 1986) to introduce the idea of positive self-talk. In this story, a little engine's goal was to get over the hill, but because he was smaller than all the other engines, he had to work harder to achieve his goal. As the story goes, the little engine kept saying to himself, "I think I can, I think I can," as he chugged up the hill, and "I thought I could, I thought I could," as he raced down. After reading the story, the counselor and Antonio discussed how the little engine used positive, instead of negative, self-talk and how he had to work hard and be persistent in achieving his goal. The counselor asked Antonio what he thought he could do during the week to practice these ideas at school, and he came up with

the idea of making an "I think I can" can to set on his desk to remind him of the message in the story. Together they came up with the idea that he could paste a list of the advantages of persistence on the can and look at that list several times a day as a reminder. The counselor suggested that, each time he persisted and completed something, he write it on a sheet of paper and put it in the can, reviewing the contents every few days to help him remember what he had accomplished.

In introducing homework to younger clients, it may be preferable to use the term *experiment* to avoid the negative connotation of *homework*. It is also important not to react negatively if they don't complete the homework, which is often the case with this age group. However, if the assignments are engaging and creative, there is a greater likelihood that they will complete the task.

Evaluation

Evaluation can be accomplished as a monitoring process that occurs at various points during counseling or as an overall evaluation at the end (Bernard & Joyce, 1984). If it occurs periodically, you can modify treatment as needed. Several forms of evaluation can be used: subjective client reports such as journals, feeling charts, sentence stems, and behavior graphs; objective measures such as depression inventories, anger checklists, feeling thermometers, and ABC self-help sheets; or input from parents and teachers. Parents and teachers, for example, can be asked to keep logs of behavior or evidence of feelings such as anger, anxiety, or depression. It may also be helpful for parents to complete standardized evaluation forms. Especially when working with younger children, evaluation from parents and teachers as well as the child is optimal, because, depending on the nature of the problem, younger children may tell you what you want to hear. If behavior at school is a problem, for example, they may be unwilling to admit that they haven't made much progress and therefore report that everything is fine, in which case teacher input is essential. This reluctance can also be the case with adolescents, particularly if they were not self-referred. If they don't want to be in counseling, their feeling charts or behavior logs may show dramatic improvement because they want to terminate counseling, not because there has been drastic change in their behavior. One way to get parental input without making adolescents feel defensive is to have clients write a note to their parents indicating specific improvements they've made and explaining why they think they can terminate. My experience with these young clients has been that they are more honest about their own self-evaluation if they know that their parents may differ in their opinion of progress.

Regardless of which method is used, evaluation as an ongoing part of the therapeutic process results in data that can be used to reevaluate and revise goals and is a viable way to assess progress, both from the client's and the counselor's standpoint. In addition, frequent evaluation provides for accountability for all stakeholders. If, during this evaluation process, it appears that the client is making good progress, sessions can be scheduled less frequently, thus giving the client the opportunity to work on the problems and utilize homework assignments.

Evaluation conducted at or near the end of the counseling process compares the current functioning to criteria related to the goal. For example, if the goal was to decrease anxiety about spending the night away from home, evaluation in the form of self-report or parental input will indicate whether the goal has been achieved. This type of overall evaluation is important in determining what has been accomplished and whether termination is appropriate. If the client has made good progress, but you sense she is not quite ready to terminate, you can suggest decreasing the frequency of sessions but still doing some periodic checkups to see how well she is maintaining her progress. In my experience, many young clients seem to like this approach because they can continue to have the support and structure if they need it. Usually after one checkup, they are ready to terminate completely.

As part of the overall evaluation process at the end of therapy, it is particularly helpful to young clients to invite them to list both the changes they have made and what they need to continue doing to maintain those changes. Brainstorming together can often result in creative strategies that help keep them on target, as the following example illustrates:

> Kelsey, who had been in counseling to work on anger management, made a list of her "before and after" behaviors. She was proud of the progress she had made in decreasing the frequency of her temper tantrums. When she had first come to counseling, she had been asked to rate herself on a frequency scale to show how many times she had temper tantrums each day. Her self-report, along with input from her parents and teachers, indicated that she averaged at least five tantrums a day. At termination, she only occasionally had one. To maintain her progress, Kelsey decided to make a videotape of what she looked and sounded like when she used to have tantrums. She would then play this video whenever she had more than one tantrum a week to remind herself how foolish she looked when she threw herself on the floor, and how ridiculous she sounded when she demanded to have her way over trivial things.

Evaluation, coupled with strategies intended to maintain progress and self-evaluation, is an inherent part of the counseling process. Informal evaluative measures can be used with more formal procedures, as needed, to provide comprehensive treatment.

CHAPTER 3

Interventions for Internalizing Problems

The challenges faced by youth today are greater than in any previous generation (McWhirter, McWhirter, McWhirter, & McWhirter, 1998), making access to high-quality mental health services more critical than ever. McWhirter and colleagues noted that "numerous social, demographic, and economic factors have weakened the ability of families to provide healthy and developmentally appropriate environments for their children" (p. 260). Social changes, coupled with technological advances, have resulted in children's and adolescents' exposure to new influences and experiences that are often overwhelming and inappropriate for their age level.

As a society, we are seeing the ramifications of these changes. The pregnancy rate for U.S. teens is almost double the rate in other industrialized countries (Coley & Chase-Lansdale, 1998). Depression, once considered to be an unusual condition typically reported by women (Seligman, 1995), is now recognized as a prevalent problem for all people of all ages (Cicchetti & Toth, 1998). According to Seligman, depression, "has become the common cold of mental illness and it takes its first victims in junior high school—if not before" (p. 37). Today 3 to 6 million children suffer from clinical depression (Lockhart & Keys, 1998) and are at high risk for suicide, which is the second leading cause of death among youth ages 15 to 24 (King, Price, Telljohann, & Wahl, 2000). School counselors now find themselves serving increasing numbers of students who have serious mental health problems, including depression and anxiety (Lockhart & Keys, 1998).

As noted in chapter 1, children and adolescents often lack the support and skills necessary to cope effectively with situational and developmental problems and consequently feel anxious, depressed, or guilty. They may have very low self-concepts or engage in irrational risk taking or violence as a way to cope with their confusion, anger, or frustration. It is imperative for practitioners to identify effective interventions to help young people deal with life's challenges in self-enhancing ways.

The purpose of this chapter is to identify cognitive, emotive, and behavioral interventions to be used in individual counseling for common internalizing disorders of childhood and adolescence: self-downing, anxiety, perfectionism, guilt, and depression. Interventions both for children (ages 6 to 10) and for adolescents (ages 11 to 18) will be described, including a case study to illustrate concepts. Many of the interventions are very brief and are intended to be incorporated into the counseling session to reinforce concepts or help with disputing. Others are more detailed and will constitute most of the session.

Self-Downing

REBT theory posits that all human beings are fallible and will make mistakes, and it also emphasizes that self-worth is *not* contingent on one's performance. It promotes the concept of unconditional self-acceptance, which does not involve global self-rating or evaluation (Ellis & Dryden, 1997) but does allow for rating different aspects of self. Therefore, although it is possible to evaluate and focus on negative aspects and do something to improve them, global rating of self as good or bad is anti-REBT, as is the notion of considering oneself a total failure on the basis of a few negative characteristics. The concept of unconditional self-acceptance (USA) implies that all individuals are multifaceted and have strengths as well as weaknesses, that human beings are complex and are constantly in the process of change, and that it is impossible to render a single legitimate global rating of any person. The concept of USA is in sharp contrast to the notion of self-esteem, which does imply a single rating. For this reason, REBT practitioners use the term *self-acceptance* rather than *self-esteem*.

When clients do not understand or practice the concept of self-acceptance, they engage in *self-downing*: "I'm no good because I didn't pass that test" or "Because I didn't get asked to the party, it must mean no one likes me and I'm a loser." It is particularly easy for children and many adolescents to experience self-downing because, as concrete thinkers, they see things in either/or terms. This view makes it more difficult for them to separate their self-worth from their performance or to understand the difference between global self-rating and the rating of individual aspects of self. Because their self-downing can easily result in depression, anxiety, and guilt, it is critical to start addressing this problem at an early age.

Concepts related to self-acceptance/self-downing include the following:

Who you are isn't what you do (your behavior does not define who you are as a person).

There is no such thing as an "all good" or an "all bad" person; everyone has strengths and weaknesses.

You are worthwhile just because you exist.

Making mistakes is natural, and each of us can learn from them.

The following interventions can be adapted as needed, depending on the specific age or developmental level of the child or adolescent.

If Who You Are Is What You Do

RATIONALE This intervention is designed to teach children that who they are isn't what they do—that their self-worth isn't based on their performance.

MATERIALS
▷ A sheet of construction paper

▷ Scissors

▷ A pencil

PROCEDURE
1. When a child is putting herself down because she isn't good at something, teach her this song, which is sung to the tune of "Yankee-Doodle":

If Who You Are . . .

If who you are is what you do, then when you don't, you aren't,
But just remember this, my friend, that you are great regardless.
Yes, you are a super kid, even when you goof it up,
So remember, don't be glum and don't you cry or hate yourself.

2. After teaching her the song, discuss its meaning and how it applies to her situation.

3. Have her cut a musical note out of the construction paper.

4. Have her write a few words or phrases that she thinks will help her remember the words of the song and how she is a good kid regardless of how she performs.

I Can, I Can't

RATIONALE   This is a simple intervention to help children accept themselves as individuals with both strengths and weaknesses.

MATERIALS
- ▷ An empty vegetable can labeled "I Can" and another labeled "I Can't"
- ▷ 10 to 12 strips of paper
- ▷ A pencil

PROCEDURE

1. When the client discusses how dumb he feels or how he can't do anything right, engage him in some experiments that prove what he can and can't do. Examples might include jumping up and down on one foot for several seconds, singing a song, lifting something heavy, writing his name with the hand opposite the one he usually writes with, or reciting the alphabet backwards. Be sure to include tasks you know he can do, as well as some he can't.

2. After he has completed the assignment, have him list on individual slips of paper the activities he was able to do and put them in the can labeled "I Can." Then have him do the same for the can labeled "I Can't."

3. Process the activity by discussing the fact that all people have things they can and can't do, and that just because this particular client can't do something, it doesn't mean he is no good; it only means he can't do certain things.

This Package Is Valuable

RATIONALE When children are dealing with self-acceptance issues, they frequently have difficulty understanding their own value or worth because they equate it with their performance. Consequently, if they don't perform well, they get down on themselves. This intervention is a concrete way of helping them learn that they are valuable or worthwhile regardless of their accomplishments.

MATERIALS ▷ A small box with a lid that has the word *valuable* written in several places on the outside

▷ A picture of the client you are working with (or her name, if a picture is unavailable) on the inside

PROCEDURE 1. Begin by asking the client to examine the box and guess what might be in it, discussing the meaning of the word *valuable*—that it means something is worth a lot.

2. Encourage her to think about something she may have gotten in a box that she considered valuable, and discuss why she considered it valuable. For example, was it valuable because it was special or unique?

3. Have her open the box to see what is inside. After she sees her picture or her name, ask her to share her reaction to what was in the package and how she considers this package to be valuable.

4. Point out to the client that she is valuable or worthwhile just as she is; she doesn't need to find talents or accomplishments in the box to prove her worth.

Burst or Bounce Back?

RATIONALE This intervention is a very concrete, visual way of helping younger clients understand that they are not like balloons—they will not pop and disappear as though they were worthless, just because they make a mistake or fail at something.

MATERIALS
▷ A balloon

▷ A safety pin

▷ A Nerf (or rubber) ball

PROCEDURE
1. When the client comes to a counseling session upset about his mistakes or failures, ask him to blow up a balloon and pretend he is the balloon.

2. Give him a safety pin and ask him to recount his most upsetting mistake or failure. As he discusses this, instruct him to pop the balloon and note what happens to his "self" (there is nothing left).

3. Give him a Nerf ball and ask him to recall the same mistake or failure, but to use the pin on the Nerf ball. Discuss what happens when he sticks the pin in the Nerf ball; the ball doesn't disappear—the pin just makes a tiny hole in it.

4. Explain that, when he makes mistakes or fails at a task, it doesn't mean that he is no good and will disappear like the balloon because he is worthless; it just means that there is a minor problem to work on, as illustrated by the pricking of the Nerf ball.

IAWAC

RATIONALE This intervention is a concrete way of helping teenage clients understand that they don't have to take every criticism or comment personally and put themselves down as a result. Adapted from Dr. Sidney Simon's activity *The IALAC Story,* as described in Howe and Howe (1975), it helps build emotional muscle and resiliency.

MATERIALS ▷ An 8½ × 11–inch sheet of paper with the letters *IAWAC* written across it (punch a hole at the top corners of the page and attach a piece of string so you can wear it around your neck like a necklace for purposes of demonstration)

▷ A copy of the IAWAC story (p. 76)

PROCEDURE 1. When working with a client who is upset because she has been teased, rejected, put down, or overly self-critical, incorporate some of her examples into the IAWAC story to illustrate how she can use rational self-talk to combat her self-downing.

2. Before telling the story, put on the necklace and explain to the client that the letters stand for "I Am Worthwhile and Capable." Explain that the story you are about to tell shows what happens when people allow others to control their thoughts, feelings, and actions and what they can do to counteract the negative effects.

3. Read the story to the client.

IAWAC

Ann *[the client]* forgot to set her alarm for school, so her dad yelled at her to get up. "Can't you ever be responsible and set your alarm? Fifteen-year-olds shouldn't have to be reminded to do these things," he said. So Ann rolled out of bed, feeling stupid. *[Tear off a piece of the IAWAC sign.]* She showered quickly and threw on her clothes, grabbing a toaster pastry on her way out the door. "Don't forget you have a piano lesson after school," her mother shouted at her. "I can't go—I have play rehearsal," Ann said. "Well, you should know better than to schedule two things in one day. Don't you ever think ahead? How stupid can you be?" *[Tear off another piece of the sign.]*

So Ann walked to the bus in a worse mood than ever, only to find that the friend she usually sat with was sitting with someone else. They totally ignored her; she felt like a nobody. *[Tear off more of the sign.]*

Ann got to school and went to her first-hour class, algebra. They were doing a drill on the board. Ann missed all her problems, and that totally embarrassed her. *[Tear off more of the sign.]*

After her first class, the rest of the morning went all right, but things started to deteriorate again at lunch. The group she usually sat with left her out of the conversation, and she felt invisible. *[Tear off more of the sign.]* Then, as she walked out of the lunchroom, she tripped on someone's shoe, and a bunch of boys started chanting, "Clum-sy! Clum-sy!" *[Tear off more of the sign.]*

By this time, Ann was feeling terrible and couldn't concentrate during English class. When the teacher called on her, Ann just gave her a blank look, and the teacher snapped at her, saying, "Get your head in the game, or you'll fail this class." *[Tear off more of the sign.]*

Ann couldn't wait for the day to end, and she was feeling so bad that she skipped play practice and went home. Her mother was furious, ranting and raving about how Ann had better get her act together. *[Tear off the rest of the sign.]*

4. After reading the story and tearing off pieces of the sign, as instructed, discuss what factors contributed to the elimination of Ann's sense of being worthwhile and capable.

5. Introduce the idea of *rational self-talk* as a way of preventing that from happening again.

> For example, when Ann's father put her down for being irresponsible, Ann could have said to herself, "I should have remembered to set my alarm, but that doesn't mean I'm always irresponsible or that I'm stupid or worthless because I didn't."
>
> Or, when she felt rejected by her friends or left out of the conversation, Ann could have said to herself, "Just because they aren't paying attention to me doesn't necessarily mean they don't like me or that I'm unlikable."
>
> Or, when her teacher chastised her for not concentrating, she could have said to herself, "I do need to concentrate, and I don't want to fail this class—but I'm not a failure if I don't do well."

6. Review with the client how she can use rational self-talk as a means to prevent her self-worth "sign" from disappearing. Give her a copy of the story, and encourage her to make a sign and work through her own example and to use the IAWAC intervention to remind herself that she is worthwhile and capable.

IAWAC

Ann forgot to set her alarm for school, so her dad yelled at her to get up. "Can't you ever be responsible and set your alarm? Fifteen-year-olds shouldn't have to be reminded to do these things," he said. So Ann rolled out of bed, feeling stupid. She showered quickly and threw on her clothes, grabbing a toaster pastry on her way out the door. "Don't forget you have a piano lesson after school," her mother shouted at her. "I can't go—I have play rehearsal," Ann said. "Well, you should know better than to schedule two things in one day. Don't you ever think ahead? How stupid can you be?"

So Ann walked to the bus in a worse mood than ever, only to find that the friend she usually sat with was sitting with someone else. They totally ignored her; she felt like a nobody. Ann got to school and went to her first-hour class, algebra. They were doing a drill on the board. Ann missed all her problems, and that totally embarrassed her.

After her first class, the rest of the morning went all right, but things started to deteriorate again at lunch. The group she usually sat with left her out of the conversation, and she felt invisible. Then, as she walked out of the lunchroom, she tripped on someone's shoe, and a bunch of boys started chanting, "Clum-sy! Clum-sy!"

By this time, Ann was feeling terrible and couldn't concentrate during English class. When the teacher called on her, Ann just gave her a blank look, and the teacher snapped at her, saying, "Get your head in the game or you'll fail this class."

Ann couldn't wait for the day to end, and she was feeling so bad that she skipped play practice and went home. Her mother was furious, ranting and raving about how Ann had better get her act together.

Don't Soak It Up

RATIONALE This simple intervention helps adolescents remember that they don't have to be like sponges, soaking up criticism and put-downs that lead to self-downing.

MATERIALS ▷ A sponge

▷ A sheet of paper

▷ A pencil

PROCEDURE 1. When the adolescent describes how terrible he feels because others have criticized his looks or actions, give him a sponge.

2. Explain to him that when others say things about him that feel like put-downs, he needs to examine the content of the message and not just "soak it up." For example, if someone says he is ugly or stupid, he needs to look at the evidence, asking himself if he is really ugly or really stupid—and if he isn't, then he doesn't have to "soak it up."

3. Acknowledge that, although he doesn't like to hear others say these things, he doesn't have to allow himself to be put down.

4. Explain that, even if he does stupid things or people say he looks ugly, it still doesn't mean he is a bad person. By telling him this, you will inoculate him against extreme self-downing and depression.

5. After discussing the concept of not soaking it up, invite the client to jot down three recent examples of times he absorbed criticism or put-downs. Have him identify things he could say to himself to help him avoid "soaking it up" and engaging in self-downing in the future.

USA

RATIONALE Unconditional self-acceptance (USA) means accepting yourself as you are, avoiding global self-rating, and rating only individual traits and behaviors. The following intervention helps adolescents understand the concept of unconditional self-acceptance.

MATERIALS ▷ A paper bag labeled "USA" that contains five strips of paper, each with one of the following terms written on it: *school performance; peer relationships; sports, music, or drama; jobs or chores; son or daughter*

▷ A pencil

PROCEDURE 1. When the client discusses her failures in the counseling session, hand her the paper bag labeled "USA."

2. Discuss the concept *unconditional self-acceptance,* which means accepting yourself as a worthwhile person and not rating yourself as either "all good" or "all bad."

3. Invite the client to open the bag and take out the index cards.

4. Ask her to rate herself on a 1 (low) to 5 (high) scale in each of these areas, encouraging her to think about her performance in these areas over time, as opposed to thinking about how she performed in one or two isolated incidents.

5. Invite her to share her ratings, explaining how her ratings might be lower in some areas than in others. Emphasize that all of these dimensions contribute to who she is, and explain that it is in her best interests to accept herself unconditionally as a complex person who may perform better in some areas than in others—but that she is neither "all good" nor "all bad."

A Good CD, One Bad Song

RATIONALE   To help adolescents deal with their tendency to rate themselves as no good when they make mistakes, try this intervention.

MATERIALS   ▷ A CD player

▷ Several CDs that are very popular with this age group

PROCEDURE   1. When the client says he is no good because he made a mistake, share the CDs with him and ask him to select the one that he is most familiar with.

2. Invite him to play his favorite song, and then ask him how many cuts on the CD are among his favorites.

3. Ask him if there are any songs that he doesn't like, and invite him to play one.

4. When he is finished playing this song, ask him if he would rate the entire CD as horrible just because there are a few songs on it that he doesn't like. Draw the following analogy between CDs and human beings: Even if there are parts of a person that aren't as good as the rest, we wouldn't rate the whole person as terrible and no good.

Anxiety

As Wilde (1996) noted, anxiety is not caused by events, but rather by our perceptions of events. For children and adolescents, this idea is often complicated by their limited cognitive skills, which may interfere with their ability to perceive events correctly, and they may naturally tend to extrapolate ideas from one context and then apply them inappropriately to another situation that may be totally different (Vernon, 1997). Ellis (1998) noted that there are many types and degrees of anxiety. He distinguished between healthy and unhealthy anxiety, describing healthy anxiety as concern or vigilance that helps people cope with difficult or dangerous situations. Healthy anxiety is almost always based on a realistic fear, such as worrying about crossing the street at a very busy intersection where there is no traffic light and there is a realistic chance of being hit by a car. In contrast, unhealthy anxiety is an "emotional response to perceived dangers that seem real but are mainly imaginary because so little probability of occurrence exists" (Wilde, 1996, p. 94). The fears associated with unhealthy anxiety are exaggerated, unrealistic, or irrational, such as being terrified about riding on a roller coaster for fear it could crash. Although it is *possible* that this could happen, the *probability* is very slight; it rarely happens. According to Ellis (1998), unhealthy anxiety frequently makes you restrict your activities when there is no need to do so, or it makes you lose control of yourself because the physical and psychosomatic symptoms of panic, phobia, trembling, or shaking interfere with your ability to cope adequately.

When children are anxious, they assume something bad might happen in the future, and they irrationally believe that if this were to occur, it would be so bad that they wouldn't be able to stand it. Thus they not only minimize their ability to cope with very bad things, they also catastrophize, assuming that their worst fears will become reality. They may hear about something bad happening to someone else and assume this could happen to them. Their overgeneralizations or exaggerations increase their anxiety. They may become so anxious that they can't think about anything else and therefore often beg for a guarantee that their fears won't materialize. Even though the best way to deal with anxiety is to face the feared situation, anxious parents may inadvertently reinforce their children's anxiety by protecting them from this exposure.

It is important to understand that younger children become anxious because they may lack the cognitive skills to put things in the proper perspective. The case I vividly recall is the one in which a father of a third grader called me because he had found his young son's will. The father asked me if John had appeared anxious or depressed in our recent counseling sessions to discuss his parents' separation. Although I hadn't noted any anxiety or depression on John's part, I was concerned about what his father was reporting and scheduled an appointment with John for the next day.

When John and I met, I explained that his dad had found the will and was very worried. I questioned John about being very sad or anxious and worried about something, and he said the reason he had made the will was that, in his social studies class, they had been talking about how some kids his age had been trapped in a cave and had died. He was afraid that would happen to him, so he wanted to be sure his brother got his baseball glove and baseball cards and his friends could have his favorite toys.

This example clearly illustrates how children can cause their own anxiety because they don't have the ability to put the situation in its proper context. Adults need to be cognizant of this tendency and attempt to alleviate children's anxiety before it occurs by carefully explaining the difference between probability and possibility.

Often when young clients feel anxious, they experience secondary emotions. For instance, they feel anxious about being anxious or put themselves down for being anxious and then feel depressed. Irrational beliefs resulting in anxiety are related to personal inadequacy, awfulizing, "I-can't-stand-it-itis," and other forms of all-or-nothing thinking or overgeneralizing, including the following (Ellis, 1998):

Something bad might happen; it must not happen.

I can't stand being anxious.

I should not feel anxious.

I am a rotten person because I can't cope with my anxiety better.

If something bad happens, it would be awful and terrible, and I couldn't stand it.

The following interventions can be adapted for use with children and adolescents who are experiencing anxiety.

Anxious Albert

RATIONALE This story can be used with younger clients to help them learn how to cope with anxiety.

MATERIALS Anxious Albert story (pp. 83–84)

PROCEDURE
1. When working with a client who expresses feelings of anxiety, share this story about Albert, who is having his own problems dealing with anxiety.

2. Discuss with the client the types of strategies that Albert used to cope with his anxiety. If you wish, give her a copy of the story to keep.

3. Explain to her the difference between the *possibility* that something bad could occur and the *probability* of something terrible happening.

4. As a homework assignment, invite the client to draw a picture of something she is currently experiencing anxiety about. Have her include drawings or words and phrases depicting what she can do to cope with her anxiety.

Anxious Albert

For weeks, Albert's Boy Scout troop had been selling candy bars and fruit to raise money for a trip to the amusement park. All the boys had really worked hard, and they hoped they would find out at tonight's meeting that they had achieved their goal. All day in school, everyone was talking about what rides they wanted to go on and which ones were the scariest. As soon as they got to the meeting, the scoutmaster announced that they had enough money, and so he had scheduled the trip for next Saturday. As the boys started jumping up and down and chattering about how they wanted to ride the new, really scary roller coaster, nobody noticed that Albert had left the room. As he quietly hurried away to the bathroom with a feeling of queasiness in his stomach, Albert could hear two of the boys talking about how they had heard that the Log Roller was even scarier than the new roller coaster and how they couldn't wait to try them both out to see which was more terrifying. Albert felt sick. He couldn't admit to his friends that he didn't want to go on those rides because he was scared, but he was. He had heard about roller coasters crashing, and he knew that would happen to him. He didn't want to die, and he was certain that if the roller coaster crashed, that's what would happen.

Albert stayed in the bathroom as long as he could. When he finally went back to the meeting, they were working on a project, and the discussion about the trip was over, at least for the time being. But when Albert went home that night, he couldn't stop thinking about the trip and what he would do. He was so anxious, his stomach was tied in knots, and he couldn't get to sleep. Finally, he did, but he had a bad dream about being on a roller coaster that crashed. He woke up shaking.

The next day, he dreaded going to school because he knew everybody would be so excited about Saturday's trip. Albert knew he had to figure out some excuse not to go; he knew he couldn't stand riding on the scary rides, but he didn't want his friends to think he was a chicken if he didn't. The more he thought about it, the more anxious he became.

That night at supper, his parents informed him that they had volunteered to drive on Saturday, and Albert felt even worse. He had figured that he could just pretend to be sick and not go on the trip, but since his parents were driving, he knew he would have to go.

All through dinner, Albert was really quiet, and finally his dad asked him what was on his mind. "Nothing," Albert said. "Come on, Albert, I know something is bothering you," his dad replied. Finally, Albert admitted that he was really anxious about riding on the scary rides because he knew they would crash and he could be killed. Instead of laughing, as Albert thought he would, his dad said, "Well, we just have to figure out a way to help you with this. I remember when things like that used to make me anxious, and I did a little scientific experiment. I stood by the roller coaster for half an hour and watched the people as they rode. You know what I saw? Almost everyone was laughing and having a great time, and during that whole time, the roller coaster didn't crash. But I still wasn't convinced, so I asked the man who was operating it how long he had been doing it and if it had ever crashed. He told me that he had been doing it for several years and there had never been one accident. So then I told myself that, even though roller coasters sometimes do crash, it wasn't very likely that it would, and probably if I took my chances, nothing bad would happen. So then I tried it, and everything was fine—I even rode it again and again because it was so much fun."

(Continued from p. 83)

After Albert's dad told him what he had done in a similar situation, Albert considered the possibility of trying that out for himself. As his dad had said, bad things could always happen: The car could even crash on the way to Adventureland, but if the drivers were careful, the chances of that happening weren't as great—and people rode in cars every day. So Albert started to think that, although it was true that a roller coaster could crash, it was pretty unlikely that it would, and he had to decide if he wanted to take his chances and have fun, or if he just wanted to stay anxious about it. By the time Saturday arrived, Albert was ready to ride the roller coaster. Although he was a little anxious, he kept telling himself to relax and not think about the worst that could happen. And once he did that, he actually had fun!

Adios, Anxiety

RATIONALE   When working with young clients who are anxious, playing the game described in this intervention can be a concrete way of helping them say adios (goodbye) to their anxiety. The game is played like hopscotch.

MATERIALS   ▷ A plastic, flannel-backed tablecloth with a hopscotch board drawn on it in marker (see sample on p. 86)

▷ A sheet of paper

▷ A pencil

PROCEDURE   1. As the client discusses being anxious about such things as taking a test, riding on an airplane, staying all night at a friend's house for the first time, or doing something he has never done before, indicate that you will be his secretary.

2. Tell him that your job is to write down all the thoughts he has concerning whatever it is he is anxious about. For example, if he is afraid to swim in a pool, have him tell you his specific fears. (Common fears that people have of swimming include the fear that they will drown, that they won't have fun, that others will splash them or try to hold their head under water, that they will get water in their ears and nose and be unable to stand that discomfort, and so forth.)

3. Invite the client to stand on the first square of the hopscotch board, and then tell him you will read off something that he is anxious about. If he can identify something that he can tell himself so he is less anxious, then he can hop to the next set of squares.

4. Read the next item and encourage him to think of something he could tell himself so he is less anxious and can jump to the next set of squares.

5. Continue in this manner until the client reaches the top of the board, at which time he can shout, "Adios, anxiety!"

6. Discuss with him the concept of *rational self-talk* as a way of coping with anxiety, emphasizing that when we are anxious, we usually assume the worst, and when we use rational self-talk, we look

at things more realistically. For instance, a couple of examples of rational self-talk that could be used to counter the fear "I might drown" are "Because there are so many lifeguards around, they would probably *see* me and save me if I started to go under" and "Even if I get water in my ears and nose, I can stand it."

7. Encourage the client to think of other examples of rational self-talk he could use to cope with things he is anxious about.

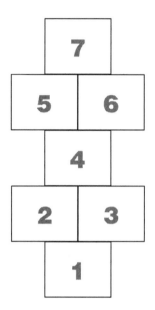

Feel Your Fears

RATIONALE   Younger clients (ages 6 to 8) readily engage in make-believe. This intervention, which uses puppets, helps them to identify the thoughts that create anxiety and to learn how to deal with them in a "let's pretend" format. Because children readily verbalize when they are playing with puppets, this intervention is an effective way to help them identify their anxious thoughts.

MATERIALS   ▷ 2 puppets

PROCEDURE   1.   When your client begins to describe something she is anxious about, invite her to use a puppet to act out her feelings.

2.   After she has acted this out for a while, ask her to take a different puppet and pretend that this puppet isn't anxious or worried about this same event. (What would this puppet be saying and doing?)

3.   After the two versions have been presented, discuss what the differences were between the two puppets—their thoughts, feelings, and actions.

4.   Point out that it is not the event that makes us anxious, but rather what we tell ourselves about it. Explain this phenomenon, referring frequently to the two puppets as a way of making this distinction concrete for the client.

Fraidy-Cat Frieda

RATIONALE This intervention helps children learn how to respond to common childhood fears.

MATERIALS
▷ A pair of dice

▷ 2 coins of different value (one for you and one for the client)

▷ Game board (from the Appendix or one of your own design)

▷ Scary Situation Cards (p. 89)

PROCEDURE
1. To play the game, take turns rolling the dice with the client, each player moving the coin the designated number of spaces and drawing a card.

2. After the person who rolls the dice and draws a card reads the example on the card, discuss whether it is something either you or your client is or has been afraid of, or whether it is something that neither of you is or has been afraid of. (The counselor should base his or her examples on childhood experiences. For the purposes of this intervention, however, we will assume that the client is rolling the dice.)

   If the client is not afraid of the example, ask him to think of how he would help a friend who fears it.

   If he used to be afraid but no longer is, have him explain how he overcame his fear of it.

   If he is still afraid, brainstorm what he believes he can think or do to overcome the fear.

3. Continue rolling the dice and moving along the board. At the end of the game, have the client make a list of three things he learned that he can apply to his fears.

Scary Situation Cards

Loud thunder and lightning	Ghosts or bogeymen
Staying all night with a friend for the first time	The dark
Riding in an airplane	Getting lost in a shopping mall
Tornadoes or hurricanes	Being picked on by a bully
Going to a new school	Taking a test
Getting scolded by the teacher	Diving off the high dive

A Is for Anxious,
B Is for Behaving

RATIONALE   When clients present with anxiety, talking about the problem is the first step toward alleviating the anxiety, but generally, action is necessary as well. The intervention described here is designed to help clients get to that next step of taking action.

MATERIALS   ▷ Index cards

▷ A pencil

PROCEDURE   1. Clients often describe feeling anxious about interpersonal relationships or performance. For example, your client could be a 16-year-old female who is anxious about going to a dance because she is worried that she might be clumsy and trip, or she might say the wrong thing or look stupid.

2. As the client describes her anxiety, ask her to write down every single anxious thought, one per index card.

3. Ask her to think about what she could say to herself to counteract each anxious thought.

> In the case of this 16-year-old who is anxious about dancing, she may find it useful to say: "I might not trip, but even if I did, I wouldn't trip during the entire dance. Maybe my partner will trip, too."

> Or she may find it useful to say, "If I say the wrong thing, I can stand it; everybody probably won't laugh or call me dumb."

4. Have the client write these responses on the back of the corresponding index cards.

5. After you have the client complete these rational coping statements, ask her to put the statements into practice by doing what it is she is anxious about. As she does so, have her keep the index cards in her pocket so she can review them before the event as a way of helping her cope with the anxiety-provoking situation.

A-A—Anti-Anxiety

RATIONALE Adolescents are easily overwhelmed by their anxiety and need simple strategies to help them cope. This intervention has worked well with teenage clients.

MATERIALS ▷ A tape recorder

▷ 2 chairs

Note: Before conducting this activity, be sure to tell your client that you are going to tape-record the session.

PROCEDURE 1. When the adolescent client describes what he is anxious about, help elicit his specific anxiety-provoking thoughts. Some of these thoughts might include the following:

"I know I'll never pass the Spanish test, and that will be awful."

"I know Jana's going to break up with me, and I don't know how I'll stand it."

"I know I'll get a miserably low score on the ACT and never get accepted into college."

2. Discuss with the client how it is not the event itself that is creating his anxiety (e.g., one of his friends could experience the same event and react differently); rather, it is what we tell ourselves about the event that largely determines our feelings.

3. Invite the client to sit in a chair and verbalize the anxious thoughts he has relative to a specific situation.

4. Have him switch chairs and pretend he is a friend who is experiencing the same situation but who is not as anxious about it. Ask him to verbalize his friend's thoughts—those thoughts that wouldn't create as much anxiety. Tape-record this conversation as well.

5. Play back the two taped dialogues and discuss the differences between them and how the client can change his degree of anxiety by changing his thoughts.

Anxiety Attackers

RATIONALE   This intervention can be used as a way of helping adolescent clients recognize how catastrophizing contributes to their anxiety.

MATERIALS   ▷ A sheet of paper

▷ A pencil

PROCEDURE   1. When the client describes her anxiety, suggest that she pretend to be a sensationalist news writer who exaggerates everything about this anxiety-provoking event.

2. Ask her to write a short article about how anxious she is, how awful that is, the terrible things that will probably happen, or how weak she is because she can't cope with the anxiety.

3. After she has written several paragraphs, ask her to underline anything that is similar to what she has thought about on those occasions when she has been anxious.

4. Talk about her writing and discuss how catastrophizing does or does not contribute to her own anxiety in actual situations. Identify ways to attack the catastrophizing by having her ask herself a series of questions such as the following:

   "What is the worst that could possibly happen, and what is the likelihood of that actually happening?"

   "Suppose the worst did happen; then what? Would I *really* not be able to stand it, or do I just *think* I couldn't?"

   "Have terrible things happened in similar situations before, and if so, was I able to stand it?"

   "What good does it do always to assume the worst?"

   "Does anxiety stop bad things from happening?"

5. Discuss with your client how this type of self-talk is a good way for her to defend herself against anxiety.

Let It Go

RATIONALE Oftentimes it is helpful for adolescents to have a visual reminder that they can let go of things they are anxious about.

MATERIALS ▷ Several balloons

▷ Several strips of paper

▷ A pencil

PROCEDURE 1. When the client discusses things he is anxious about, have him write them on separate strips of paper.

2. After working with him to dispute the irrational beliefs associated with these issues, ask him to rank the strips from the most to the least anxiety provoking.

3. Suggest that he select one strip that he ranked less anxiety provoking and agree to "let it go" by putting that strip in the balloon, blowing up the balloon, and literally letting it go into the air. Invite him to do the same with other anxieties he is ready to let go of as a result of disputing his irrational beliefs.

4. As a homework assignment, suggest that he set a goal to practice disputing and to let go of another anxiety every few days until his list is exhausted.

Perfectionism

Perfectionism is related to anxiety and self-downing. Behavioral manifestations of perfectionism include high achievement, compulsiveness, obsessiveness, and procrastination. In addition, perfectionists may overdo things for fear of leaving something out or failing to distinguish between what is really important and what isn't. They also have trouble prioritizing, go to great lengths to avoid making mistakes, have trouble acknowledging mistakes, and often become defensive if someone points out a mistake (Barrish, 2000).

Perfectionistic children often experience heightened anxiety before a test or a performance; they also experience guilt, depression, and self-downing if they fail to achieve their high standards. According to Ellis and Dryden (1997, p. 16), perfectionism is related to a basic must: "I realize that I did fairly well, but I *absolutely should* have done perfectly well on a task like this and am therefore really an incompetent person!"

As Barrish (2000) noted, irrational beliefs associated with perfectionism include the following:

> What I do must be perfect. I must not be incorrect or make mistakes.
>
> If I try hard enough, I can avoid making mistakes.
>
> I can't stand it when what I do isn't perfect or when my work isn't as good as someone else's.
>
> I must not let anyone see me make a mistake.
>
> I can't stand mistakes that others make, particularly if they affect my life.
>
> My entire worth depends on how I perform.
>
> No one will like me if I'm not perfect, or they will criticize or reject me—and that would be awful!
>
> If I make a mistake, I am incompetent—a failure.

The following interventions can be adapted for use with perfectionistic children and adolescents.

Perfect, Please

RATIONALE This story illustrates some of the problems associated with perfectionism and can be used with young clients to stimulate discussion about their own need for perfectionism.

MATERIALS Perfect, Please story (p. 96)

PROCEDURE 1. Share the Perfect, Please story with your client.

2. Discuss with your client what the word *perfect* means and how it affected Paula and Pedro. Adapt the concepts of perfectionism to her own personal experiences and identify some of the negative, self-defeating aspects of having to be perfect all the time.

3. If you wish, give a copy of the story to your client to keep.

Perfect, Please

Paula and Pedro sat at the edge of the playground. They really wanted to play, but the wind was not blowing quite perfectly—and Paula certainly didn't want her hair to get windblown. Besides, Pedro thought there was a little too much dew on the grass. As they sat on the sidewalk, several of their friends came over and invited them to play. Paula and Pedro were torn: Kick ball looked like fun, but they didn't want their hair to get mussed or their feet to get the slightest bit wet. Then a teacher approached them and asked them if they would like to play on the new playground equipment. It did look neat, but they decided not to because the kids who were waiting to use the slide weren't lined up perfectly, and Paula and Pedro absolutely could not stand it when the lines were less than perfect.

After a while, Paula and Pedro were getting a little bored, so Pedro suggested that they walk around the edge of the playground. Paula stood up, ready to go, but then told Pedro that they shouldn't go because she only liked to take walks when it was perfectly quiet and still outside, and she knew she wouldn't enjoy walking around the playground with so many kids yelling and laughing. So instead, Paula suggested that they play tic-tac-toe in the dirt pile behind them. Pedro didn't like that idea because he didn't want to get his perfectly white shirt dirty. So they continued to sit and look at their classmates, who were all having fun.

I'm Not Perfect

RATIONALE   When young clients experience anxiety or self-downing as a result of trying to be perfect, engage them in this activity to help them see that they don't have to perform perfectly in order to accept themselves.

MATERIALS   ▷   3 pencils (one with an eraser but no lead, one without an eraser, and one very short pencil with lots of teeth marks on it)

PROCEDURE   1.   When your client is dealing with problems related to perfectionism, show him the three pencils and ask him to pick the perfect one.

2.   After he has made his selection, discuss his choice and ask him if any of the pencils is really perfect, considering that one has no lead, one has no eraser, and the other is very short and all marked up. (Be sure to emphasize that, regardless of their condition, all of the pencils can perform some function.)

3.   Stimulate discussion about how people are like pencils: Some perform better than others, but they all function to some extent.

4.   Discuss with the client those occasions on which he has performed perfectly and those on which he hasn't.

5.   To help the client remember that he doesn't have to perform perfectly in order to accept himself, teach him the following rational rhyme:

> *Pencils aren't perfect, and neither am I,*
> *But I do my best and try, try, try.*
> *If I perform perfectly or even if I do not,*
> *I'm still a great kid whom others like a lot!*

P Is for Perfect

RATIONALE   This simple game helps young clients learn that it is natural to make mistakes.

MATERIALS
- ▷ A penny
- ▷ Game board (from the Appendix or one of your own design)
- ▷ 3 different colors of dot stickers
- ▷ *P* Is for Perfect Sentence Stem Cards (p. 99)

Note: Randomly place one colored dot sticker on each space on the game board. Next apply a colored dot sticker to the back of each P Is for Perfect Sentence Stem Card. Use an equal number of each color (e.g., four yellow, four blue, four red cards). If you construct your own game board, you could arrange the dot stickers in the shape of a P.

PROCEDURE
1. Begin the game by having your client toss the penny in the air. If it lands on heads, she moves the coin ahead one dot; if it lands on tails, she moves it ahead two dots.

2. When she moves her penny to a colored dot, have her pick a card that has a dot of the same color on it and then ask her to complete the statement on the card.

3. Engage her in a discussion of the concepts related to perfectionism and her propensity for making mistakes.

4. After some discussion, have her toss the penny again and move ahead one or two dots, as determined by the coin toss, once again selecting a card that corresponds to the color of the dot.

5. Discuss the concepts related to perfectionism and continue to proceed like this throughout the game.

P Is for Perfect Sentence Stem Cards

A time when I did something perfectly
and how I felt was . . .

If I try my best and it's not perfect, I . . .

A time when I made a mistake
and how I felt was . . .

I don't think I have to be perfect,
because . . .

A time when I did something almost
perfectly and how I felt was . . .

Someone I think expects me
to be perfect is . . .

A time when I made lots of mistakes
and how I felt was . . .

I can remember that whether I perform
perfectly or not has nothing to do with my
being a good kid, because . . .

Something I think to myself or tell myself
when I make a mistake is . . .

I don't have to get down on myself
if I don't do everything perfectly,
because . . .

I'm even OK when my performance
is not perfect because . . .

When I put pressure on myself
to perform perfectly, I feel . . .

Can't Be Perfect

RATIONALE To help children understand that it is impossible always to do everything perfectly, engage them in this brief experiment.

MATERIALS ▷ 3 tennis balls

PROCEDURE
1. When the client brings up perfectionism issues, ask him first to try juggling two tennis balls, then a third.

2. As the client attempts to juggle the balls, talk about how difficult a task it is for him.

3. Volunteer to juggle the balls yourself so the client can see how difficult a time you are having as well.

4. When the experiment is completed, debrief the activity by discussing with him how, except for professional jugglers, most people can't perform this act perfectly—at least at first. Draw an analogy between your client's juggling and his life: What does he expect himself to do perfectly? Is this expectation realistic, and what does it say about him if what he is doing isn't perfect?

Putting *Perfect* in Perspective

RATIONALE   As they grow older and feel the need to be more competitive in school and extracurricular activities, it is common for adolescents to expect perfection from themselves as well as from others. This expectation often results in anxiety, guilt, frustration, self-downing, and anger, all of which are unhealthy emotions. When adolescent clients present issues related to perfectionism, the following intervention can be helpful.

MATERIALS   ▷ A sheet of paper

▷ A pencil

PROCEDURE   1. As the client discusses her need to be perfect, draw a line across a sheet of paper, labeling one end "Perfect" and the other end "Imperfect." Discuss with the client that there are many points along the "Perfect–Imperfect" continuum.

2. Have your client rate a recent performance by placing a mark at a point somewhere on the continuum to signify how she felt she performed.

3. Ask her to identify how she feels about this rating and elicit her beliefs about her performance that contribute to her feelings.

   If she was closer to the "Imperfect" end of the spectrum, for example, and felt angry and upset, she could have been thinking that she *should* have done better or performed perfectly.

   If she felt depressed, however, she might have been thinking that her less-than-perfect performance detracted from her worth as a person (i.e., "I am worthless or incapable because I did not perform perfectly").

4. Help the client challenge her irrational thinking by asking her if she thinks it is *always* realistic to expect perfect performance and what it says about her when she does not perform perfectly.

Emphasize to her that there are many degrees of success and that perfection is a rare, most unlikely outcome. (In other words, she could be close to perfect in most things most of the time or at other points along the continuum, but it would be unrealistic to expect herself to be at the "Perfect" end of the continuum in everything she does.)

The Price of Perfection

RATIONALE   Along with the demand for perfection comes the emotional price people pay for it. By assessing and highlighting this negative characteristic of perfectionism, you can enable adolescents to look more realistically at what they should be expecting of themselves.

MATERIALS   ▷ A sheet of paper

▷ A pencil

PROCEDURE   1. When the client presents irrational beliefs and negative feelings related to perfectionistic issues, ask him first to list, in one column, all of the advantages of striving for perfection.

2. Ask him to think about the "price" he pays for having to be perfect and then to list, in a second column, the physical, emotional, and behavioral consequences he experiences when he tells himself that he *has* to be perfect.

3. Discuss the two lists and ask the client to think about the following:

What does it say about you if you aren't perfect?

Is the price you pay (high anxiety, headaches, stomachaches, etc.) worth it?

What do you think you could do to put less pressure on yourself to be perfect?

A Preference for Perfect

RATIONALE   It can be helpful for young people to differentiate between the *demand* for perfection and the *preference* for perfection. Certainly, it is reasonable to want to do well and be as close to perfect as possible, but when this desire for perfection escalates into a demand, adolescents may assume they have to perform perfectly at all times to fend off failure or mediocrity.

MATERIALS   ▷ 2 plastic cups

▷ Several strips of paper

▷ A pencil

PROCEDURE   1. To help the client who is having problems related to perfection, take two plastic cups and label one "Need to Be Perfect" and the other "Prefer to Be Perfect."

2. Hand her several strips of paper, have her write on them her "reasons" for needing to be perfect, and put them in the "Need to Be Perfect" cup.

3. As your client proceeds with this activity, help her to look realistically at the logic behind the statements she is making.

> If she says, for example, that she needs to be perfect because her parents demand it, ask her if this is a fact or an assumption.

> If she says she needs to be perfect, maintaining that if she isn't, her team might lose a game, challenge her thinking about how awful that really would be and whether her team's performance rests solely on her shoulders.

4. Discuss her thoughts, feelings, and behaviors associated with *needing* to be perfect: what it says about her when she doesn't perform perfectly and what others might think about these imperfections, for instance.

5. Introduce the client to the concept of *preferring* to be perfect: striving to do her best but not having it be the end of the world when she doesn't do everything to perfection.

6. Engage your client in *rational emotive imagery,* a mental exercise in which she takes deep breaths to get relaxed and then closes her eyes and imagines she is in a situation in which she thinks she has to perform perfectly.

7. Have the client think about this situation in vivid detail: that she has to get all the answers right, that she has to have every letter on her paper written perfectly, or that she has to spend countless hours getting every single homework assignment done to perfection.

8. Ask her to signal you when she is in touch with the significant stress or anxiety she feels when she thinks she has to be perfect.

9. When your client indicates that she feels her emotional distress, ask her to repeat the same exercise, but this time change the *demand* to be perfect to a *preference:* something she would like to do without putting so much pressure on herself to have every single thing perfect.

10. When she indicates that she has calmed herself down, discuss how she felt as she achieved this emotional change (i.e., "What did you tell yourself that enabled you to change your feelings?").

11. If the client was successful in changing her demands to preferences, then she can move her strips of paper to the "Prefer to Be Perfect" cup.

12. Encourage her to practice rational emotive imagery daily to help her counteract the demand for perfection.

Less-Than-Perfect Circles

RATIONALE   Perfectionistic adolescents not only equate self-worth with performance, they also think that if they make one mistake or don't do well in one area, then they are complete failures. This intervention addresses these issues.

MATERIALS   ▷ A sheet of paper

▷ A pencil

PROCEDURE   1. As your client describes his lack of worth or his feeling that he is a complete failure if he performs poorly in some areas, hand him a sheet of paper and ask him to draw a large perfect circle and then a smaller perfect circle inside the larger circle.

2. Ask him to divide the inner circle into four sections and to label them as follows: "R" (for relationships), "SP" (for school performance), "EP" (for extracurricular performance), and "JP" (for job performance).

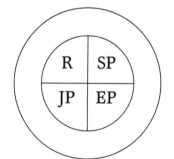

3. Ask the client to identify three recent past "performances" in each of the four areas, list them on the corresponding inner circle, and rate each on a scale of 1 (poor) to 5 (excellent), according to his perception of how well he did. For example, in the area of extracurricular performance, he may have missed three notes on a song (2), moved up from third to second chair in the orchestra (4), and played a solo and received a standing ovation (5).

4. After your client has completed this activity, review and discuss his ratings, noting his range of numbers and emphasizing that it would be very difficult to be perfect (scoring all 5s) in *all* areas.

5. Help him see his areas of strength and weakness and challenge his belief that he is worthless or a complete failure if he does less well in some areas than in others. One way to help your client remember this concept is to invite him to write, on the outside of the circle, "I accept myself as less than perfect, with many different strengths and weaknesses."

Guilt

Guilt is related to self-downing and occurs when individuals consider themselves very bad or wicked for something they did. They are upset not only with their behavior but also with themselves; they believe that they must not act badly, and that if they do, they are rotten people. Children and adolescents who aren't able to separate themselves from their performance are especially susceptible to guilt.

Furthermore, egocentric youths who see themselves as the center of the universe often take on the responsibility for others' choices and feel guilty when negative consequences occur. Because of their developmental limitations, it is often difficult for them to distinguish between guilt and regret. Regret is a normal reaction that stems from the realization of having done something wrong, while accepting the fact that all fallible human beings will occasionally make mistakes and bad choices. Guilt, on the other hand, is associated with the irrational notion that people who act badly are bad people.

When guilt occurs, clients have to believe they have done something wrong, either by omission or commission (Walen et al., 1992), and condemn themselves for doing this wrong thing. In reality, they may have done something wrong, either with respect to their own value system or against the law. In this case, clients had better acknowledge and take responsibility for what they did. The REBT therapist does not dispute this reality. Instead, the self-denigration component is targeted, with the goal being for clients to accept their fallibility without self-condemnation in order to help them refrain from repeating the same guilt-inducing mistakes in the future.

Irrational beliefs associated with guilt include the following:

> I did something wrong; therefore I am a horrible, rotten person.

> I must not act badly; and when I do, I'm awful.

The following interventions can be adapted to help children and adolescents deal with guilt.

Goodbye to Guilt

RATIONALE   This story can be used with younger clients who have difficulty forgiving themselves for behaving badly. Because these youngsters may not be familiar with the word *guilty,* the word is not directly referred to in this story but can be introduced and defined after reading the story in order to help build a feeling vocabulary.

MATERIALS   Goodbye to Guilt story (p. 110)

PROCEDURE   1. Share the Goodbye to Guilt story with the client.

2. Discuss with your client the concept of feeling bad about something without putting yourself down. Invite her to relate this story to a personal situation in which she was feeling bad about something she did and was blaming herself and thinking she was a bad person for doing it.

3. Give the client a copy of the story if you wish.

Goodbye to Guilt

George and Georgianna were playing in their tree house when Gabriella came walking across the lawn. George saw her first and whispered to Georgianna, "Let's lie down and pretend that we're not up here. . . . I don't want to play with her because I don't like her." Georgianna agreed, and together they crouched down along the side of the tree house so Gabriella couldn't see them from the ground. But when she got to the base of the tree house, she called out to them and asked if they would let the ladder down so she could come up and play. Even when she didn't get a response, she just stood there and stared up at them. Finally, Georgianna was frustrated because Gabriella wouldn't go away. Georgianna didn't want to have to stay hidden forever, so she quietly reached over and shook a tree branch loaded with apples. Just as she had hoped, several apples tumbled down, some even landing close to Gabriella. But still she didn't budge from her spot at the base of the tree. So then George picked an apple and threw it down, aiming it at Gabriella's feet. However, his aim was bad, and the apple landed hard on her head. Off Gabriella ran, crying. George and Georgianna looked at each other, and George said, "I am as rotten as that apple for hitting Gabriella. I'll never be able to look at her again."

Suddenly, it didn't seem as much fun to be in the tree house, so George and Georgianna climbed down. When they reached the porch, their dad asked if they knew why Gabriella was crying when she left the yard. The two children looked at each other, and then Georgianna told him what had happened. George told his dad that he felt just as rotten as the apple he threw, and his dad asked why. "Well, I shouldn't have thrown that apple at her. I just wanted to scare her away or hit her foot—I didn't mean to really hurt her," George said. "And it's my fault because I started it by shaking the tree," said Georgianna. "Well, it's true that you shouldn't have done what you did, because you did hurt her. But that doesn't make you rotten or bad kids. . . . It just means that you did something wrong, and hopefully you learned a lesson," said Dad. George nodded and said, "Yes, I won't try to scare someone away or try to hurt them again." Georgianna nodded her head in agreement. "Well, that's good. How do you feel now that we've talked about this?" asked their dad. Both children said they still felt bad about what they did, and their dad acknowledged that it wasn't something they should feel good about. When Georgianna suggested that they apologize to Gabriella, George agreed that was a good idea. As they were preparing to leave, their dad reminded them that they had done a bad thing, but they weren't bad kids.

Don't Beat Yourself Up

RATIONALE We want children to recognize when they have done something inappropriate, and feeling sorry about what they have done is a healthy response. However, some children "beat themselves up" over inappropriate actions, often keeping those feelings inside. To help them distinguish between healthy and unhealthy responses, try this strategy.

MATERIALS ▷ A stick or a plastic bat

▷ A pillow

PROCEDURE 1. When your client is beating himself up because he has done something he feels very guilty about, get out a stick (or a plastic bat) and a pillow.

2. Ask him to imagine that he is the pillow.

3. Give him the stick or bat and instruct him to verbalize the horrible, terrible thing he has done and then beat himself up (by beating on the pillow).

4. As the client beats the pillow, you can contribute by exaggerating the awful, terrible things he has done. For example: "This is the worst thing anybody could do" or "No one in the world will ever forget these terrible things."

5. Discuss with the client the difference between feeling sorry about what he has done and beating himself up over it, emphasizing that it is easy to exaggerate the "awfulness" of something when in fact it might not have been that bad.

6. Have your client list the things he feels guilty about and then identify whether he thinks any of these things merit his beating himself up over them. By doing this, your client may be better able to decide that these are things he can just feel sorry about and try not to do in the future.

G Is for Guilt

RATIONALE
: This story helps children learn to distinguish between (a) something they deliberately did that they may feel guilty about and (b) something that someone else did that they as children assume blame for and consequently feel guilty about. Because youngsters are still concrete thinkers, it is not uncommon for them to assume guilt for something they did not do and, as a result, put themselves down.

MATERIALS
: *G* Is for Guilt story (p. 113)

PROCEDURE
: 1. Share the *G* Is for Guilt story with the client.

  2. Engage the client in a discussion of the concepts presented in the story and how they apply to the client's own situation.

  3. Give the client a copy of the story to keep if you wish.

G Is for Guilt

Tamara's parents argued every night, and Tamara usually went to sleep with the pillow wrapped around her head in hopes that she wouldn't have to listen to them yell at each other. Their fighting was so frequent that Tamara never knew what caused it, but she tried extra-hard to be good so they wouldn't fight about her. One night Tamara just couldn't get to sleep because her parents were so loud, and the next day in school she fell asleep. Tamara was ashamed to tell her teacher the truth when he asked her why she was so tired, so she just said she didn't know. Nevertheless, the teacher sent a note home with her to give to her parents.

Tamara was afraid to give the note to them, so she just left it in her lunch box. However, when she was cleaning out the empty wrappers, the note fell on the floor and her mother read it. "How could you fall asleep in class?" her mother yelled. "If you start getting bad grades, you're going to be in trouble. You'd better figure out a way to stay awake or I'll tell your father."

Worried, Tamara snuck off to her room and wondered how she could prevent this incident from happening again. Later that night she heard her mother yell at her father: "It's all your fault! . . . Now Tamara is falling asleep at school because you yell at me all night!"

"Don't blame me!" her father yelled back. "It's not my fault!" Tamara kept thinking that if she hadn't gotten in trouble at school, her parents wouldn't have fought about her that night; and when she heard her dad say that it wasn't his fault that they yelled at each other, she assumed that it must be hers. She felt guilty and was upset with herself for being so stupid.

The next day at school, the same thing happened again. This time when the teacher awakened Tamara, he walked her down to the counselor's office. When the counselor started talking to Tamara about the problem, Tamara was close to tears. She finally admitted that she couldn't help falling asleep because she had been up so late at night listening to her parents argue. She told the counselor that it was all her fault that they argued, even though she tried to be good.

The counselor helped Tamara see that, even though she had fallen asleep in school, her parents did not have to yell at each other about it. She explained to Tamara that this was not something she needed to feel guilty about. This was her parents' problem, not hers, and probably no matter how hard she tried to be good, her parents would find something to argue about. She asked Tamara to give her an example of something she had done in the past that she had felt guilty about, and Tamara recalled that she had felt that way when she called her friend a name, because it was something she shouldn't have done. The counselor told her that, although it was helpful for her to feel bad about calling her friend a name—as it would prevent her from doing so in the future—it was unhelpful for her to feel responsible for falling asleep in class and upsetting her parents. In the first example, she meant to call the friend a name when she knew it wasn't right; in the second situation, she hadn't intended to fall asleep, but did so because her parents' fighting had kept her awake. It wasn't something she had intended to do. After explaining her situation, Tamara felt less guilty and realized that she could do her best to be good, but if her parents fought, it was not her fault, and she didn't need to feel guilty.

Guilty but Sorry

RATIONALE   When children do something they shouldn't have done, their parents sometimes tell them how bad they are for doing that; consequently, this admonishment makes the children feel bad or guilty. It is important to help children understand that it is normal to regret (feel sorry about) what they did and to change their behavior, but it is also important to teach them that they are not bad kids because of what they did.

MATERIALS   ▷ An 8½ × 11–inch sheet of construction paper with two holes punched in the top—one hole on each side—to which you attach a string to make a necklace. On the sign, write, "Guilty but Sorry."

▷ A sheet of paper

▷ A pencil

PROCEDURE   1. To illustrate the point of this intervention, instruct your client to wear the sign.

2. Discuss the concept of feeling guilty or sorry when she does something wrong that might be hurtful to others.

3. Share some specific examples, such as calling someone a name, cheating on a test, lying to parents or teachers, or taking something from the store without paying for it.

4. Give the client a sheet of paper and ask her to write several examples from her own personal experience. Then indicate to her that you will read these examples, and that, as you read them, she should begin tearing off pieces of the sign in the following manner:

   If she doesn't feel guilty or sorry about whatever example you are reading, she should tear off a big piece of the sign.

   If she feels somewhat guilty or sorry about it, she should tear off a medium-size piece.

   If she feels guilty and very sorry about it, she should tear off a tiny piece.

Chapter 3 • Interventions for Internalizing Problems

5. After all the examples have been read, examine what is left of the sign and point out to the client that if she did things that she feels guilty and very sorry about, there should still be a lot of her sign remaining. Explain to her that, if a lot of the sign remains, then she can rest assured that she isn't a bad kid, but a kid who made bad choices.

6. Explain that, if she actually did things that were wrong and hurtful and didn't feel guily or sorry, there wouldn't be much left of the sign. Point out that, if indeed little of the sign remains, the child still shouldn't think of herself as a bad kid. However, make sure she is aware that she not only made bad choices, but that she also needs to think about what she has done, realize that it is appropriate to feel guilty and sorry about her actions, and consequently change her behavior.

Give Up Guilt

RATIONALE This intervention works well with adolescents who hold onto their guilt by helping them see that it is unproductive to do so.

MATERIALS ▷ 2 sheets of paper

▷ A pencil

PROCEDURE 1. When your client describes how guilty he feels for something he has or hasn't done, ask him to divide one sheet of paper in half by drawing a line down the middle.

2. On one half of the paper, have him list the advantages of hanging onto the guilt. On the other half, have him list the disadvantages.

3. Review both lists and dispute those irrational beliefs that are associated with guilt by asking questions such as these:

> "Just because you did something you regret doing, does that make you a totally rotten person who should condemn himself forever?"

> "In hindsight, you probably could have acted differently, but what can you do about that now, and how long do you need to punish yourself?"

4. After helping your client with several disputations, ask him to write a letter to himself about how he will give up his guilt. Emphasize that, although it is appropriate for him to regret what he did, excessive guilt over a long period of time is not a productive emotion.

I'll Take *Some* Blame

RATIONALE   Some adolescent clients seem to put the responsibilities of the world on their shoulders, automatically assuming blame and feeling guilty about things they aren't responsible for. The strategy described here can help them address inappropriate self-blame.

MATERIALS   ▷   A big sponge

▷   2 buckets (one labeled "Things I Did"; the other labeled "Things Others Did")

▷   A sheet of paper

▷   A pencil

PROCEDURE   1.   When your client discusses those things she feels guilty about, ask her to make a list of them.

2.   Hand her a dry sponge and ask her to imagine she is soaking up the guilt about one of the items on her list.

3.   Have her pretend to wring the sponge into one of the two buckets:

4.   Into the bucket labeled "Things I Did" she should wring out the things *she* feels guilty about because she did something she didn't think was right.

5.   Into the bucket labeled "Things Others Did" she should wring out those things other people did that *she* somehow assumes she also should feel guilty about.

6.   As she wrings the sponge into one of the buckets, have her discuss the issue in more depth. Help her distinguish between things she can assume some responsibility for and regret and things she doesn't need to feel guilty about because they are other people's issues.

Guilt or Regret?

RATIONALE   Although we hope that clients will regret things they shouldn't have done, it is important to teach them to differentiate between regret, which is a healthy emotion, and guilt, which is an unhealthy emotion.

MATERIALS   ▷ A sheet of paper

▷ A pencil

▷ A long strip of masking tape

▷ A marker

PROCEDURE   1. When your client describes issues related to excessive guilt and self-downing, ask him to make a list of things he feels very guilty about.

2. Discuss what it is about his acts of omission or commission that he feels guilty about.

3. Place the strip of masking tape on the floor; using the marker, label one end "Guilt" and the other "Regret."

4. After explaining the difference between these two terms, ask the client to take each item on his list and move to a place on the line that identifies the degree of guilt or regret he feels.

5. Tell him that feelings of regret for wrongdoings are normal, but that excessive guilt that involves berating yourself forever isn't healthy because all people make mistakes, and self-condemnation does not prevent future mistakes.

6. It may be important to stress that something that is illegal and deliberately instigated to cause excessive harm and damage is wrong, and, although the perpetrators don't have to condemn themselves for it, intentional harmful behavior is to be taken seriously and not simply regretted.

Guilty as Charged

RATIONALE   Adolescents can accept responsibility for things they wish they hadn't done, but they don't have to hang onto the guilt or self-condemnation forever. The strategy outlined here helps them learn to let go by using rational emotive imagery.

MATERIALS   ▷ A sheet of paper

▷ A pencil

PROCEDURE   1. As your client discusses things she feels guilty about, have her make a list of these things and invite her to participate in a rational emotive imagery exercise.

2. Instruct her to close her eyes, take several deep breaths, and relax.

3. Ask her to recall the incident she feels most guilty about and to get in touch with her guilt by thinking of the terrible thing she did, how it affected so many people, how others look down on her as a result, and so forth.

4. After she has gotten in touch with this guilt, instruct her to work on changing the feeling from guilt to regret. (What will she have to tell herself in order to do this?)

5. Indicate that she should signal you by opening her eyes when she feels regret as opposed to guilt.

6. Invite her to explain how she was able to change the feeling— what she was telling herself that enabled her to experience regret instead of guilt.

7. Repeat this procedure for other items on her list, emphasizing how she can use this strategy in the future as a way to help her let go of guilt and self-condemnation.

Depression

Depression is related to a belief about one's personal inadequacy, how awful and hopeless things are, and how terrible it is not to have what one "needs" (Walen et al., 1992). Although depression includes an affective component that involves feelings of low self-worth, it is also a clinical syndrome that includes emotions, thoughts, and behaviors. The emotional component is characterized by despair, guilt, sadness, and irritability. Behaviorally, depressed clients may be tired and lethargic, inactive, socially withdrawn, and unable to derive enjoyment from things that normally give them pleasure. Furthermore, changes in appetite, weight, and sleep patterns may occur. Depressed clients suffer from distorted cognitions that relate to worthlessness and self-deprecation. They also tend to think dichotomously; overgeneralize; and engage in selective abstraction, viewing only the negative aspects of their behavior (Bernard & Joyce, 1984).

Seligman (1995), in noting that depression is at epidemic proportions among children and adolescents, cited irrational thinking as a major contributor to this problem. He identified the following three cognitive errors associated with depression: permanence, pervasiveness, and personalizing. Seligman explained that children and adolescents who are most at risk for depression believe that the causes of bad events that happen to them are *permanent,* as opposed to temporary. Therefore, they are more likely to think about their failures, rejections, or challenges as *always* this way, or *never* getting better. Depressed children also incorrectly assume that the cause of something negative is generalizable across all situations, or *pervasive,* as opposed to situationally specific. For example, if two students are in a contest and work hard, but neither is selected as the winner, the pervasive thinker would consider himself a total loser who never does anything right. The nonpervasive thinker, on the other hand, would recognize that, although she did not win the contest, it does not mean that she never does anything right. The former view represents a global negative thought pattern that contributes to depression. *Personalizing* refers to the concept that when bad things happen, we blame either ourselves or others. Children and adolescents who continually blame themselves for everything feel depressed, guilty, and ashamed. In contrast, children who realistically evaluate each situation do not consistently internalize blame and are not as readily prone to depression.

Irrational beliefs that contribute to depression relate to a negative, pessimistic view of self and the future and include notions of hopelessness, helplessness, and worthlessness (Wilde, 1996):

I'm no good and will never amount to anything.

No matter what I do, I will never succeed.

Nobody could love me, because I am worthless.

I can't do anything right.

I deserve the rotten treatment I get.

What's the point of going on? I'll never get over this.

I can't change the horrible things that have happened to me, so I'm doomed forever.

There's no way out.

Life sucks now and always will.

The following interventions have proven helpful in working with depressed children and adolescents.

So Sad

RATIONALE   Although depression is expected among adolescents and adults, increasing numbers of younger children are also subject to depression. This is especially true in families in which one or both parents are depressed and there is a strong family history of depression. This intervention helps youngsters deal with extreme sadness and depression.

MATERIALS   So Sad story (p. 123)

PROCEDURE   1. Share the So Sad story with the client.

2. Discuss the concepts in the story and how the client can apply these ideas to his own life to help him deal with depressed feelings.

3. If you wish, give the client a copy of the story to keep.

So Sad

Sid was so sad. Everything in his life seemed awful. His mom and dad were getting a divorce, his grandma was very sick, and his best friend had just moved away. Sid felt as if the whole world was falling apart. Even though he didn't feel like getting out of bed, his mom made him go to school, but he flunked two tests because he couldn't concentrate. At home he just moped around and yelled at his little sister for messing with his stuff. It didn't seem that things could get much worse.

Days went by, and Sid's mother just kept dragging him out of bed and shoving him out the door. At school he stopped going out for recess, and his grades went from bad to worse. At night he cried himself to sleep. Finally, one day his next-best friend, Francisco, yelled at him for moping and ignoring everybody: "You think you have it so bad? Sure, your parents are getting a divorce—but they're both still alive, and you get to see your dad every week, don't you? Just think about Sal: His dad got killed in a car crash, so he can't ever see him. Sure, it's tough that your best friend moved, but don't you have other friends? You've got me, but you won't if you keep ignoring me and crying about how much you miss Simon. Get a grip! Things are bad now, but they're not as awful as they could be." On that note, Francisco ran off to play with his other friends.

At first, Sid was mad at Francisco for yelling at him, but then he started to think about what Francisco had said. It was true that he still got to see his dad every week, and his dad was still alive. And he knew that even though his grandma was very sick, she was strong and could probably get better. And although he missed Simon a lot, he did have other friends. The more Sid thought about it, the more he realized that things weren't totally awful; because he couldn't make his parents get back together, his best friend move back to town, or his grandma get better, the only thing he could do was to concentrate on how to make himself less sad. But what could he do?

Sid thought and thought. Soon he realized that it had been a long time since he had watched cartoons, and they always made him laugh. He also remembered that it had been a while since he had listened to music, and music usually cheered him up. Then he thought about visiting the old man next door who usually had a surprise for him or a joke to tell. Finally, he thought it might help just to get his mind off all his troubles and run around and play.

So Sid proceeded to try his strategies, and little by little he felt better. It did help him to remember that things could be worse and that, even though he felt sad now, he wouldn't stay this way forever unless he just continued to mope and feel sorry for himself and keep dwelling on how awful his life was. So even though nothing in Sid's life changed, once he put his problems in perspective and started doing something about his sad feelings, he didn't feel so depressed.

Sick of Being Sad

RATIONALE When clients are sad or depressed for long periods of time, it is easy for them to become discouraged. Helping children identify things that help them feel less sad is empowering and can be a way of encouraging them to work harder to change their negative feelings.

MATERIALS
▷ 2 puppets

▷ A pencil

▷ Sick of Being Sad song (p. 125)

PROCEDURE
1. To introduce this intervention to younger children, teach them the Sick of Being Sad song.

2. After teaching the song, invite the client to designate one puppet as the Sick of Being Sad person and the other puppet as the one who suggests ways to get over being sad.

3. The Sick of Being Sad puppet starts by singing the first verse of the song, and the other puppet responds (not necessarily mimicking the tune of the song) with ideas it thinks would help get rid of the sad feelings: calling a friend to play, reading a favorite story, or writing about the sad feelings in a journal, for example.

4. If you wish, give the client a copy of the song. (It would be a good idea for you to write suggestions on the song sheet so you can give them to the client as reminders.)

Sick of Being Sad
(Sung to the tune of "The Farmer in the Dell")

I'm sick of being sad,

It really makes me mad.

But what do you think that I can do

To keep from being so blue?

You could find something fun to do,

And if you don't have a clue,

Try make-believe or some other fun,

But don't sit in your room and be glum.

Down the Drain

RATIONALE   This is a concrete intervention that helps children remember a strategy for getting rid of sad and depressed feelings.

MATERIALS
- A glass of water
- Blue food coloring
- A sink or a bowl
- A sheet of paper
- A pencil
- A copy of the Down the Drain Faces (p. 128)

PROCEDURE

1. When your young client talks about feeling really sad or depressed, have her write down the things she is sad about.

2. After your client has created a list of things she is sad about, have her select the one thing that bothers her the most and write it on the line below one of the sad faces on the Down the Drain Faces page.

3. Help elicit thoughts the client has about that situation or perception. For example, if the situation is that she has gotten a bad grade on a test, her thoughts might include the following:

   "I'm dumb."

   "Others will laugh at me."

   "I'll never understand this subject."

4. Once she has identified her thoughts, help her learn to dispute them. For example, you might ask her the following questions:

   "Where is the evidence that you are dumb just because you got a bad grade on one test?"

   "How do you know others will laugh at you, and can you stand it if they do?"

   "Who says you will never understand this subject?"

5. After helping her with the first example, have her select the second most bothersome thing on her list and write it on the line below one of the other sad faces. Then help her dispute these irrational beliefs.

6. Repeat Steps 4 and 5 as you again help her to dispute her irrational beliefs.

7. Have her place a drop of blue (sad) food coloring in the glass of water after each irrational belief is successfully disputed.

8. Invite her to pour the blue (sad) water down the drain to help her remember that she can get rid of her depressed feelings by identifying and disputing her irrational thoughts.

9. Continue the activity until the items on her list have been exhausted.

Down the Drain Faces

What Works When with Children and Adolescents © 2002 by Ann Vernon. Champaign, IL: Research Press (800) 519–2707

Silly Songs

RATIONALE Music is a good medium for children, and the rhymes and rhythms help them remember important concepts. Engaging them in music making can help them cope with sad or depressed feelings.

MATERIALS
▷ A sheet of paper

▷ A pencil

▷ Optional: bongos, maracas, or other musical instruments

PROCEDURE
1. Take familiar childhood tunes and help your client write his own lyrics that empower him to deal with the concepts of depression and sadness.

2. After he has composed his songs, engage him in a discussion of the concepts and how he can use these ideas to help himself deal with sad feelings. The following songs are examples.

Song 1

(Sung to the tune of "Three Blind Mice")

Three sad kids,
Three sad kids,
See how they cry,
See how they cry.
They all got tired of crying so much,
They ran around and made faces and such,
You've never seen these kids laughing so much,
The three happy kids, the three happy kids.

Song 2

(Sung to the tune of "This Old Man, He Played One")

This sad kid, he sat and cried,
All he wanted was to hide;
With a knickknack patty-whack,
Give this boy some hope;
Now this kid knows how to cope.

This sad kid, he no longer cried,
He went to play and did not hide;
With a knickknack patty-whack,
Sensible thinking was the key;
Now this boy can sing with glee.

When You Need a Helping Hand

RATIONALE   This concrete strategy helps adolescents remember that they can control their thoughts that contribute to their depression and sadness.

MATERIALS   ▷ A sheet of drawing paper

▷ A pencil

PROCEDURE   1. Invite your client to identify specific situations that she is depressed about.

2. Explain to her that it is not the event that depresses her, but rather what she tells herself about it.

3. Help her identify her thoughts that contribute to her depression. For example, if she broke up with a significant other, she might be thinking that this is the end of the world and she will never find anyone else again—that she must have done something wrong; it's all her fault; or if she had been more talented or good-looking, this wouldn't have happened.

4. Give her the pencil and have her trace around her thumb and each finger.

5. Help her identify a dispute for each one of her irrational beliefs, and have her write these on the fingers of the "helping hand." Some of the disputes she writes may be similar to the following:

   "This isn't the worst thing that can ever happen, and I will probably find someone else I care about just as much."

   "I can't think of anything I did wrong, and relationships involve two people, so how could it be all my fault?"

   "This might have happened no matter how talented or good-looking I am."

6. Discuss with your client how she can use this strategy in the future by mentally putting the disputes on her fingers and closing her fist so no one can take those rational thoughts away from her.

How Low Do You Go?

RATIONALE Adolescents often feel powerless over their depression, thinking they will always feel like this and that they can't stand it. It is very important to help them see that they *can* stand it, and they can do something to help themselves. If they cannot comprehend that there is a way out, there is always the danger that if they continue feeling so helpless, an impulsive suicide attempt may be their way of escaping from the pain they think will last forever.

MATERIALS ▷ A sheet of paper

▷ A pencil

▷ Feelings Chart (p. 133)

▷ Will I Ever Feel Better? story (p. 134)

PROCEDURE 1. When your adolescent client presents with depression, give him a copy of the Feelings Chart and ask him to use a scale of 1 (very depressed) to 5 (not depressed) and rate his depression each hour of the day until his next appointment with you.

2. As he shares his results during the next session, look for any patterns: Were there particular days or times of the day that were especially good or bad? Was each hour of every day very low, or were there also some highs?

3. Because clients usually don't mark down all 1s, it will be helpful to point out to your client that he wasn't very depressed every hour of every day.

4. Help him see that, even though he doesn't like feeling this way, he did tolerate feeling depressed, and he can keep on tolerating it.

5. Have him make a list of what he did during the previous week that helped him get through his depression.

6. Suggest that he post that list somewhere to remind him of things he can do to empower himself.

7. Give your client a copy of the Will I Ever Feel Better? story, which describes another adolescent's experience with depression. After he has read it, invite him to discuss with you how it does or does not apply to his situation.

Feelings Chart

	Sunday	Monday	Tuesday	Wednesday	Thursday	Friday	Saturday
6:00 A.M.							
7:00 A.M.							
8:00 A.M.							
9:00 A.M.							
10:00 A.M.							
11:00 A.M.							
12:00 P.M.							
1:00 P.M.							
2:00 P.M.							
3:00 P.M.							
4:00 P.M.							
5:00 P.M.							
6:00 P.M.							
7:00 P.M.							
8:00 P.M.							
9:00 P.M.							
10:00 P.M.							
11:00 P.M.							
12:00 A.M.							

What Works When with Children and Adolescents © 2002 by Ann Vernon. Champaign, IL: Research Press (800) 519–2707

Will I Ever Feel Better?

I was 14 when I first started to feel depressed. There wasn't anything in particular going on in my life that I was feeling bad about. I had good friends, I got along pretty well with my parents, and I did well in school. Sometimes I fought with my younger sister, but that wasn't the cause of the bad feelings. I could just be sitting in class or hanging out in the lunchroom and I would suddenly feel down. Sometimes those moods would last for the rest of the day, and sometimes I would feel better the next hour. It was confusing.

What made matters worse is that when I felt this way, I sometimes just wanted to snap people's heads off. I'd talk back to my parents for no reason, and they'd get on my case. Or I sometimes went off on my friends. That was really embarrassing, and I didn't understand why I did it. My parents finally decided to have me see a counselor. At first I was really upset about that, and I told them I wasn't going to say anything. I thought that they must think I was crazy because they were making me go. But I had no choice. During the first session, the counselor told me that she understood that I might not like coming to counseling because I might think there was something really wrong with me. The counselor said that she didn't think that was the case, based on what she had learned from my parents, and she explained that feeling depressed and angry during adolescence was very normal. I felt relieved when she said that, but I still wasn't about to say much to this person. The counselor gave me some information about how long this moodiness could last. She suggested that it might go on for several months or up to a year, but that it wouldn't last forever unless it was a chemically based depression, in which case medication could help. She told me she could help me find some ways to manage these moods if I was willing.

I left the first session feeling a little better. At least I knew that I was normal and that I wasn't the only kid who felt this way. I also was glad to know this wouldn't last the rest of my life. I still wasn't all that convinced that anyone could help me manage these moods better. But I figured I might as well give it a try since I had to go. Anything would be better than feeling like I did.

During the second session, I did tell the counselor a little bit more about how I was feeling. I mentioned that when I got depressed, it just seemed like everything was awful. The counselor helped me learn to put things in perspective by showing me a "catastrophe scale." This is a way of rating from 1 to 10 how bad things really are. She also suggested that I make a list of things I liked to do or that helped me feel better so I could refer to this list and try something when the bad moods started. She told me that I might have to force myself to do something to get out of the mood rather than just allow it to keep on developing. I told her this would be hard because sometimes when I felt bad, all I wanted to do was sleep. The counselor told me that was normal, but she said that it is better to stay active because then it is harder to feel depressed. She also told me that some of her other clients said writing in journals, listening to music, or drawing helped them deal with depression.

I continued to see the counselor for a while, and my moods did start to improve. Now I am 16 and much less depressed. I don't get irritated as often, and although I still have bad times, they aren't as frequent as they used to be. Now if I get depressed, I don't think it will last forever, and I know I'm not crazy. Just recently, I noticed that my 13-year-old sister is starting to act the same way I did when I was 14. I heard my mother tell my sister that it was probably just adolescence—and that she'd outgrow it. I think that's what happened with me.

Take a Sad Song and Make It Better

RATIONALE   Adolescents often listen to sad music when they are severely depressed. This tendency, of course, only serves to exacerbate the depression. The following intervention helps them change their "sad songs" into something more hopeful.

MATERIALS   ▷ A sheet of paper

▷ A pencil

PROCEDURE   1. When your client describes the music she listens to when she is depressed, suggest that she write the lyrics to some of her favorite sad songs.

2. Have her highlight the irrational concepts and depressing themes expressed in the lyrics.

3. After discussing these, and as a way to help this adolescent deal more effectively with her depression, encourage her to rewrite the lyrics, using more rational and nondepressing words.

Done with Depression

RATIONALE   Adolescents are often overwhelmed by their depression and think things will never get better; this attitude generally results in their being depressed about being depressed. It is helpful to share stories or poems written by other adolescent clients with similar circumstances so your clients can see that it is possible to become less depressed.

MATERIALS   ▷ 3 poems written by adolescents (pp. 137–138)

PROCEDURE   1. Give a copy of the three poems to your client and, during the session, have him read the first two. Explain that these poems were written by a 16-year-old during a yearlong bout with depression.

2. After the client has read them, discuss how the poems affected him and how the content did or did not relate to his own experiences with depression.

3. Have the client read the third poem. Explain that it was written by a 16-year-old after a yearlong bout with depression.

4. After the client has read the third and final poem, discuss his thoughts about the message conveyed by the author:

   Does the tone of the poem differ from that of the first two?

   If it does present a contrast, how does the client feel about it?

   Does he feel more depressed or less depressed?

   Does he feel more hopeful, more capable of becoming less depressed?

5. Discuss with the client the fact that when you are depressed, you often feel very hopeless, but these feelings eventually change, as illustrated in the last poem. For this reason, it is very important to get counseling; as illustrated in the poem, you do not have to stay miserable forever.

Depression

Disillusioned
Emptiness
Progressing
Rapidly
Entering
Self-regret
Strengthening
Intensity
Over
Never-ending pain

(Untitled)

She looks normal,
on the outside at least,
with her jeans and black sweatshirt.
Her eyes are empty,
something is missing.
She walks in the room
and takes off her sweatshirt
And turns her arms over.
Long, red scars spread across them.
Now she doesn't look so normal.
Normal people don't have arms that look that bad.
Then she pulls a gun out of her pocket
and holds it to her chin,
then she crumbles to the floor
lying there lifeless,
with blood oozing all around her
that matches that on her arms.
Unusual girl, hurt, depressed,
DEAD.

(Continued from page 137)

(Untitled)

Every day the same obstacles.

But now we can overcome.

The shadow upon me is slowly drifting away

To where I can actually see myself and all that lies
*   around me.*

So this will all end and I will finally get my wish,

Of happiness—now and forever.

The following case study illustrates the use of several developmentally appropriate interventions with an 8-year-old boy. The youngster had been referred for counseling by his parents and teacher because of issues relating to perfectionism that often resulted in anxiety, temper tantrums, and self-downing. This session was the fourth in a series of five, and it occurred after a three-week interval.

Counselor: Hello, Phillip. It's good to see you again. How is your summer going?

Client: Oh, fine.

Counselor: What's been happening since the last time I saw you?

Client: Well, I got two trophies from softball.

Counselor: You did? I'll bet you felt proud about that. What were the trophies for?

Client: Well, one was for first place in the tournament, and the other one was for, hmm, I can't remember what it's called.

Counselor: For your team or for you individually?

Client: For my team.

Counselor: For your team. Well, that sounds pretty great. Congratulations!

Client: Thanks.

Counselor: Now if I remember right, weren't you upset a few weeks ago because you thought you weren't doing very well in softball? What does getting some trophies mean about that?

Client: Well, that means I must be pretty good.

Counselor: That's right. Was that a surprise for you?

Client: No, not really.

Counselor: No? But at the time that you were talking to me about this a few weeks ago, I think you were putting yourself down because you thought you'd made some mistakes in softball. Am I right?

Client: Yes.

Counselor: And that's kind of like the problems we started talking about last year, when you first started coming in because of some of the problems at school, right?

Client: Hmm. I remember what the other trophy was.

Counselor: What was it?

Client: It was for sportsmanship.

Counselor: Phillip, that's great! What does it mean to be a good "sportsman"?

Client: Just that you don't, um, that you don't really, um, do anything bad, like, if you miss a ball, like, throw down your glove and get all upset.

Counselor: That's right. So you use sensible behavior; you don't get all upset and think, "Oh, dear, I made a mistake and therefore I am a terrible player and I'll never be good again." You know what? I think it's pretty special that you got this sportsmanship award. Now, let's talk a little bit about how you can get that same kind of sportsmanship award in school next year as a fourth grader. Not that it would be a sportsmanship award, but an award in school for using sensible behavior.

Client: OK.

Counselor: It sounds to me like you got the sportsmanship award partly because when you made a mistake, you didn't get all upset and you didn't throw a temper tantrum, and you didn't think a lot of negative thoughts, right?

Client: Yeah.

Counselor: So let's talk then about what you can do in school as a fourth grader, OK? Help me remember how you behaved last year when you didn't display good "sportsmanship" behavior in school. What did you do when you got upset?

Client: Well, I'd just throw a big fit.

Counselor: That's right. And you were throwing a big fit because what was going on in your head? What were you thinking to yourself?

Client: I was thinking, since I didn't do this good, I'm no good at anything.

Counselor: That's right. That is absolutely right. And you were kind of thinking that same thing about softball earlier in the summer, right? And maybe one of the things the sportsmanship award showed you is that you don't have to be perfect at softball to get some awards and trophies, right?

Client: Hmm, I guess so.

Counselor: Just kinda like in school, maybe? You don't have to do everything perfectly?

Client: Yeah.

Counselor: Like today, I was grading my students' tests, and some of them missed six, and they still got an A.

Client: They did?

Counselor: They did, so they didn't have to be perfect to get an A. Well, let's pretend that I'm your fourth-grade teacher. But before we start, can you remind me what subject you get most frustrated with?

Client: Hmm, well, pretty much math.

Counselor: OK, math. So I'm going to hand back a math paper and put "Math, page 101," at the top of the page. And let's pretend that there are 10 problems on that page, OK? So we have problems 1, 2, 3, 4, 5, 6, 7, 8, 9, 10. *(The counselor takes slips of paper and writes Nos. 1–10 on them.)* I'm going to hand back this paper, and I'm going to have No. 1 be right, No. 2 be right, No. 3 be wrong, No. 4 be right, Nos. 5 and 6 be wrong, and Nos. 7 through 10 be correct. So now I'll hand back this paper, and I want you just to pretend to act like you used to act when you got a paper back that wasn't perfect. OK?

Client: OK.

Counselor: All right. I'll pretend like I'm handing out a few other papers. *(She distributes these "papers" to imaginary clients as well as to Phillip in this role play.)* Shelly, here's your paper; and Brian, here's your paper; Mary, here's your paper; and here's your paper, Phillip.

Client: How come I got those wrong? *(Stomps his feet on the floor, tears up his paper, and throws down his book.)*

Counselor: My goodness, Phillip, what's the problem? What are you thinking?

Client: I don't know how I got those wrong.

Counselor: So you don't know how you got those wrong. You sound confused.

Client: Yeah.

Counselor: It seems to me like you were feeling angry, too, because you tore that paper up and threw it and your book on the floor. Are you saying to yourself that you shouldn't have gotten those problems wrong?

Client: Yep.

Counselor: So you're saying to yourself that you should have gotten every single one of those 10 problems right? And what does it mean about you if you didn't?

Client: That I'm stupid and dumb.

Counselor: Does that mean you're stupid and dumb all the time, every day, in every single thing you do?

Client: *(Nods yes.)*

Counselor: It does? So that every single day you can never miss any? Otherwise, you'll be stupid and dumb? Well, are you stupid and dumb in everything, or do you just think you're stupid and dumb in math?

Client: I'm stupid and dumb in everything.

Counselor: Well, let's just take a look at that. *(The counselor uses a paper-and-pencil exercise to illustrate this point. She draws a large circle and puts smaller circles inside and labels them "Math," "Reading," "Spelling," "Softball.")*

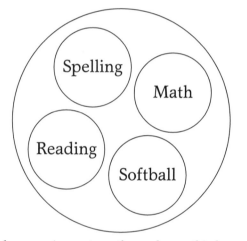

So here we've got math, and you think you're stupid and dumb in math. And let's say we have reading, spelling, softball. What else? What other subjects do you have?

Client: Science, music, um . . . social studies.

Counselor: OK. What about phys ed?

Client: Yeah, and art, too.

Counselor: Anything else?

Client: I don't think so.

Counselor: OK. So here we have this big circle with all these little circles inside. Take a look. Now, you think you're stupid and dumb in math, so we'll put a big *X* on that. Is there anything else you think you're stupid and dumb in?

Client: All of them.

Counselor: All of them? Every single one of them?

Client: *(Nods yes.)*

Chapter 3 • Interventions for Internalizing Problems

Counselor: But I thought I heard you say you got an award in softball, and that meant you were pretty good. So should we leave the softball one in here?

Client: Sure.

Counselor: OK. So now does that mean that every single day in math when you miss one or more that you're stupid and dumb?

Client: No, not really.

Counselor: Not really. And aren't there some days when you do get them all right?

Client: Yeah.

Counselor: So if you get some right some of the time, you can't be stupid and dumb all the time in math, can you?

Client: *[Shakes his head no.]*

Counselor: So should we just put a small *x* on that circle instead of a big one?

Client: Yeah.

Counselor: Now let's talk about science. Do you always do poorly in science, all the time?

Client: Not really.

Counselor: No?

Client: Except for one time.

Counselor: Oh, one time. Wow. Well, listen. Let's pretend that there's a line here on the floor right here in front of us. Let's have this end be "All the Time" and that end right down by the wall be "Never." All right? So I want you to think about the science; think about your last five assignments. That might be kind of hard to think back to, but can you think about some assignments you had in science? And would you say you got all of them perfectly right, none of them perfectly right, or were you someplace along this line?

Client: Along here. *[Points to the place on the line.]*

Counselor: OK. Well, get up and stand on the line and let me see where you are. *[Waits for client to stand on the line.]* So that's closer to getting them all right than getting them not right. Right?

Client: Yeah.

Counselor: So what does that tell you, Phillip?

Client: It means that I'm pretty good in science.

Counselor: That's right. And we've already decided you're pretty good in math and pretty good in softball. So if we kept going through all these circles, do you think that maybe the conclusion we would reach is that you're pretty good in all these subjects most of the time?

Client: Yeah.

Counselor: OK, but let's suppose that for one day or two days, or maybe even for a week, you would blow it completely. Now, what do you suppose would be the likelihood of that happening—that you would just get all F's for five days in a row?

Client: I don't think that would happen.

Counselor: So then do you think it is something you need to worry about, considering your past performance? And don't you suppose that the more you worry about it, the more likely it is you won't do as well?

Client: Yeah.

Counselor: Why is that?

Client: Because I'm worrying about it so hard that I can't think.

Counselor: That's exactly right.

Client: And then I might not get as many right.

Counselor: That's exactly right. The more you worry, the more likely you are to get more problems wrong because you're so bothered about what it is you're trying to do, right?

Client: Yeah, I'm so bothered about thinking that I'm not gonna get all these right that there's not as much brain left to think about the problems.

Counselor: Right. Your brain gets all polluted with all that junky thinking.

Client: Yeah.

Counselor: Well, let's get back to that little role play we did a few minutes ago. Here you have your paper on the floor, and you are feeling angry and confused because you missed some problems and don't know how you could have gotten them wrong. I could tell that you were angry because of your behavior: You threw your book on the floor and tore up the paper. Were you thinking, "Oh, it's awful that I got three wrong. I should have gotten them all right, and because I didn't, that means I am dumb and stupid"?

Client: [Nods yes.]

Counselor: OK. Now let me see if you can change your thinking. I'm going to give you the paper back,

OK? And this time you're going to miss three again. But this time you're going to try to say some different things to yourself, OK? So I'm going to hand out the papers, and we'll see how you act when you think differently. *[Collects the "papers" and hands them out again.]* OK, now here's your paper, Brian, and who else did I have? Mary, here's yours. Shelly—did I have a Shelly?

Client: Shelly, yeah, Shelly.

Counselor: That's my niece. OK, Shelly. And here is your paper, Phillip.

Client: Yeah, I only missed three!

Counselor: So this time you seem happy about missing three.

Client: Uh-huh.

Counselor: Well, it's the same situation. So what were you telling yourself that made you happy about it this time when you were so angry about it before?

Client: Well, three is still an A, so I might as well just say, OK.

Counselor: What if three hadn't been an A? Would that have been the end of the world?

Client: No. 'Cause I could still get all the other ones A's and stuff and get a good grade still.

Counselor: Maybe so. But let's suppose it isn't an A. What does that say about you? Does it mean you are a dumb, stupid, rotten kid? Does it mean you're no good?

Client: Not really.

Counselor: That's right. So is it really the end of the world if you get a B?

Client: No.

Counselor: And why not? If you get a B, does it mean you will always get all B's in everything all the time?

Client: No, probably not.

Counselor: You're right; I doubt that that would happen. So let's suppose that it's next year, and it's fourth grade. How do you want fourth grade to be different from third grade?

Client: I want to have a real good year.

Counselor: Good. And what does having a real good year mean to you?

Client: It means that my mom and dad don't put me in my room.

Counselor: And why did your mom and dad put you in your room in third grade?

Client: Because I got all mad and stuff, about little piddly things.

Counselor: What were some of those little piddly things you got mad about?

Client: Like the math test that we did here.

Counselor: Yeah, right. So you got all upset about things that maybe you didn't need to get all upset about, right?

Client: Yep.

Counselor: So if you could choose what you get upset about, which you can really do, is there something going on in your life now that's worth getting upset about—more than missing some problems on a math paper, for instance?

Client: Not really—not that I can think of.

Counselor: Well, that's good. So last year your parents got pretty bothered because you would get upset over little things. Well, what did you do when you got upset? That's maybe the key.

Client: Uh, . . .

Counselor: When you got upset, did you just kind of walk away with a frown on your face? Is that why they put you in your room?

Client: No, I kind of made a big disaster.

Counselor: Did you? How did you make a big disaster?

Client: In school, I'd just interrupt everybody.

Counselor: Kind of lost your cool, then?

Client: Yeah, I got a bad reputation, so I gotta make it better this year.

Counselor: Have you seen any of the kids from your classroom this summer, Phillip, those you felt that you got a bad reputation with?

Client: Not that I got a bad reputation with.

Counselor: So it wasn't everybody you got a bad reputation with?

Client: Well, no.

Counselor: But it sounds like you were feeling a little guilty and knew you shouldn't have acted the way you did. Well, you know, Phillip, you just needed to learn some new ways of thinking, feeling, and behaving, didn't you? And you needed to learn that you don't have to get so upset if you don't do everything perfectly. And now that you've learned that since we've been working together, you've got an opportunity to change that for next year. And from what you've said, it sounds like you have been doing pretty well this summer.

Client: Yeah, except for that one time with softball.

Counselor: And what was it that was upsetting for you then?

Client: That the coach put me in right field, and I didn't think he should have.

Counselor: So you were angry with the coach for putting you there because . . . ?

Client: Because I wasn't going to be good in right field.

Counselor: But then you ended up getting a trophy, right? So you proved to yourself that even though you didn't think you could do it, you did.

Client: Yep.

Counselor: I'm just thinking back to what you said about wanting fourth grade to be different. If I was a fourth grader, and you had handed this paper back to me, and I'd gotten three wrong—if I was behaving sensibly and wasn't going to throw a fit—what would I do when I got the paper back and saw that I missed three?

Client: The same thing that I did.

Counselor: The first time or the second?

Client: The second.

Counselor: And what do I need to be telling myself so I can be cool about this?

Client: Hey, you only missed three. You still got an A.

Counselor: Well, but I wanted to get them all right. *(At this point, the counselor and the client slip into a role play, with the client playing the counselor.)*

Client: It's still an A, and you don't really have to worry about it. If it was a B, it would have only been a little worse.

Counselor: Is a B a really bad grade?

Client: No, a B isn't even really a bad grade, so . . .

Counselor: So I can get a B and it'd be OK?

Client: Yeah. So you shouldn't get all upset about it.

Counselor: But I think I should get all A's, because my brothers get all A's all the time.

Client: Well, if you keep on getting papers like that, you will. You didn't miss that many.

Counselor: Oh, really? But I think I should get them with everything right.

Client: Do your brothers get them with everything right?

Counselor: Well, sometimes they don't, but I still think I should be better than they are.

Client: Are they older or younger than you?

Counselor: They're older. They're really good in things.

Client: But they have more experience and stuff than you.

Counselor: You mean, you think that'll help?

Client: Yeah. If you get more practice in and stuff.

Counselor: Oh, OK. Maybe you're right.

Client: Practice makes perfect.

Counselor: It does? What if I make mistakes all the time, though? Then it's not perfect, is it?

Client: If you get more practice, then it sometimes will be perfect.

Counselor: Do I have to be perfect? Do I have to get everything right all the time to think that I'm an OK kid?

Client: No.

Counselor: No? So, you think I'm OK even if I don't get perfect grades?

Client: Yes. So you don't have to worry about missing some.

Counselor: OK. But what if I get upset? You know, I'm going into fourth grade, and I know fourth grade is a little harder than third. And what am I gonna do next year when I get a paper back like this and I start feeling upset about it? What can I do so that I don't lose my cool and make a fool of myself?

Client: Well, you could, well, just not do it.

Counselor: Not get upset?

Client: Yeah. Not get upset.

Counselor: Well, so is there something I could think about or something that would help me kind of remember to not get upset and down on myself?

Client: You could, uh, . . .

Counselor: 'Cause, you know, I kind of think that I'm dumb when I make mistakes. And I think that I shouldn't make mistakes.

Client: Well, act like there is like a Nintendo game or something in your head, and it zaps all of those bad thoughts.

Counselor: Oh, that's a good idea. OK, well, I could try that. Yes, I could just kind of pretend like I've got a zapper around my head, and then when I get those thoughts—like I'm dumb and stupid and no good and I shouldn't ever miss any—I could just kind of zap those thoughts.

Client: Yeah. I think that will work.

Counselor: You know, a friend of mine told me that I could kind of pretend like there's a stop sign in front of my face, and then, when I start to get angry and upset with myself, then I can look at that stop sign. Then I can just think, "Stop. It's not the end of the world; I don't have to get everything perfect all the time." Then maybe I can calm down and not act real upset and throw my paper on the floor and everything like that. Do you think that would work?

Client: Uh-huh. I've tried that, and it works.

Counselor: OK. Well, Phillip, I'll stop pretending that I'm you. You did a good job being my counselor! We just kind of slipped into that, didn't we? So what do you think you've learned from what we've been talking about today, Phillip, that will help you in fourth grade so that you don't have the same kinds of problems, getting upset like you did in third?

Client: I've just learned how not to be upset and that you don't have to be perfect.

Counselor: That's right. So now that you think you don't have to be perfect, what if you went to the other extreme? I mean, last time, in third grade, you were way up here, and you thought you had to be perfect. *(Points to the invisible line on the floor referred to earlier in the session.)* What if next year in fourth grade you thought, "Oh, well, what the heck—so what if I get B's and C's and F's? It doesn't make any difference." What would happen? What do you suppose that would be like?

Client: Well, that would almost be worse.

Counselor: So, we shouldn't go to the other extreme and say, "I don't care at all."

Client: No, stay right in the middle. *(Points to the line.)*

Counselor: Right in the middle, or you could even be a little up there, but you don't have to say, "I have to be perfect all the time."

Client: That's about where my brothers are.

Counselor: Really? I thought they were way up there at the other end and never, ever made a mistake. So you exaggerated a little bit about how wonderful and great they are.

Client: Yeah. But I have a wonderful and great family.

Counselor: You have a wonderful and great family, and I'll bet they think they have a wonderful and great soon-to-be fourth grader. And even if that child makes a mistake now and then, do you think it's necessary for him to get all upset and completely lose his cool and have these awful temper tantrums and have to go to his room because he made a few mistakes?

Client: No.

Counselor: No. Would he get the student award, like the sportsmanship award, if he did that?

Client: No.

Counselor: No. So maybe what you and I could do next year is that we can pretend that there is an award like the "good student" award. What behaviors do you think you will have to exhibit in school to get the good student award?

Client: I gotta be right here. *(Points to the middle of the line.)*

Counselor: Meaning what?

Client: That I'm a so-so kid.

Counselor: A so-so kid? Well, you're probably not just so-so, because you do pretty well on most of your work most of the time, right?

Client: Right. I'd be right over here. *(Points to the line, closer to the "Perfect" end.)*

Counselor: Yeah.

Client: But not way over there. *(Points to the "Perfect" end.)*

Counselor: Right. And because you thought you had to be way over there all the time and told yourself that you weren't any good if you weren't, that's when you started to get real worried and . . .

Client: And went back down here. *(Points to the opposite end of the line.)*

Counselor: Yeah. And that's also when you threw the temper tantrums and got put in your room, because you lost control of your behavior, right?

Client: Yeah.

Counselor: So let's just review one more time. What do you have to keep telling yourself so you won't get as upset and angry if you make a mistake or aren't perfect?

Client: That I don't have to get everything right all the time, and I'm an OK kid even if I'm not perfect.

Counselor: Well, it sounds like you know what to say to yourself. I also think you have some good ideas to help yourself. I liked your zapper idea, and I think you've got some good techniques that you can use. We'll get together right after school starts or maybe right before school starts to review again, and I'll bet you can have a good year. What do you think?

Client: I think I'll have a good year.

Counselor: I think so, too. I think it would be a good idea to keep that zapper inside your head and practice reminding yourself that you don't have to be perfect. I'll check to see how that is going when I see you again!

Summary of Case Study

Phillip's homework assignment, to use the zapper technique to remind himself that he didn't have to be perfect, worked well for him. When I met with him shortly after school started, both Phillip and his mother reported that he had been consistently able to relax his perfectionistic standards, which had created anxiety for him, while at the same time maintaining a high level of performance. At this session, we agreed that he seemed to have the skills to deal with this problem but also agreed to schedule another appointment as needed. I did not hear from Phillip again and assumed that things continued to go well.

As this case study illustrates, the use of concrete interventions is essential for young clients. The larger circle drawn around the smaller circles of individual subjects helped Phillip to challenge his overgeneralization that he was bad at everything. The role play and reverse role play, which occurred very spontaneously, were also effective in helping Phillip learn to dispute the self-downing that resulted when he didn't do everything perfectly. He readily grasped the concept of the continuum and applied it within the session. And the zapper technique not only helped him to eliminate irrational thinking, it also proved useful outside of the session as a homework assignment.

CHAPTER 4

Interventions for Externalizing Problems

As we know only too well, aggression and violence driven by anger have become major problems among youth. The repercussions of undiagnosed anger problems include serious consequences such as school shootings, bomb threats, and assaults in the classroom. However, the majority of serious violent crimes involving youth between the ages of 12 and 18 do not occur in schools, according to Riley and McDaniel (2000). Therefore, in addition to concern about school violence, attention to general violence prevention focusing on conflict resolution and anger management is critical. Perhaps it should come as no surprise that youth are responsible for more than half of all violent crimes; after all, the media tout irrational risk taking and violence as ways of coping with anger and frustration.

Although youth violence was previously conceptualized as isolated reactions of temper, it is now considered a potential developmental issue in which situational factors, societal influences, personality characteristics, and biology all play a role (Heide, 1999). Fryxell and Smith (2000) noted that, although violence is a complex issue with multiple causes, one very important variable exhibited is the high degree of anger and hostility, which is a precursor to acting out and aggressive behavior. High levels of anger and hostility are also associated with poor academic performance and a wide range of social and behavioral problems in and out of the school setting (Smith, Furlong, Bates, & Laughlin, 1998). Furthermore, there are indications that high levels of anger relate to increased risk for substance abuse, delinquency, interpersonal and vocational difficulties, and other maladaptive behaviors (Deffenbacher, Lynch, Oetting, & Kemper, 1996).

Given the interrelatedness of problems that all seem to stem from anger, it is clear that we need to increase our efforts to help children and adolescents deal more adaptively with anger and frustration in order to prevent other problems from occurring. We also need to confront problems associated with school failure and motivation if we are to prevent the dropout rate from soaring. The dropout problem, in turn, leads to a multitude of other problems, including teen pregnancy, substance abuse, gang involvement, "fringe" subcultures, and violent crime. In this chapter, four common externalizing disorders are addressed: anger, acting out, procrastination, and underachievement. In addition, specific interventions for children and adolescents are identified and then followed by a case study that illustrates the application of selected REBT techniques.

Anger

The term *anger* can be used to describe a range of emotional reactions, some of which are appropriate and healthy, such as irritation, disappointment, displeasure, and annoyance. These manifestations of anger are moderate in intensity, motivate clients to change, are consistent with reality, and do not interfere with the ability to achieve goals. At the other extreme are unhealthy angry reactions, such as rage, hate, bitterness, contempt, and hostility. These reactions are based on demanding, blaming, and condemning. They interfere with the ability to achieve goals because they result in a great deal of emotional turmoil, often lead to negative retaliatory behaviors, and are almost always self-defeating (Wilde, 1996). In most cases, these angry and hostile reactions exacerbate already difficult situations.

Although we repeatedly hear declarations such as "He made me mad," anger is in the eye of the beholder, according to REBT theory. A stressful or frustrating event does not *cause* people to be angry any more than other people *make* them mad. Rather, it is each individual's perception that results in a particular emotional reaction, because two people can experience the same situation and react differently. Anger is associated with a demand, and it is experienced when we escalate our desires or wishes into absolutes: "I really want that car. Therefore, I *must* have it." If clients only wanted the car, they would be disappointed, naturally, if they didn't get it. But when they escalate the preference into a demand, they are angry when they don't get what they think they must have.

Anger often results when children feel that their personal space has been violated, their rights have been threatened, or they have been treated unfairly. An element of low frustration tolerance ("I can't stand this") is often present. Because of their limited cognitive abilities, young clients often assume that others are intentionally attacking them in some way, when this oftentimes is not the case. Furthermore, their egocentric nature contributes to their belief that others should act in accordance with *their* rules, rights, and reasons.

Anger can be directed at the world, at oneself, or at others. Young people who are angry at the world tend to demand that life give them what they want and that everything be fair and just. Adolescents in particular are very idealistic and often have very rigid ideas about how the world must be and how they must be treated (Walen et al., 1992). Children who are angry with themselves believe that they shouldn't have acted the way they did and therefore are bad or no good. Anger at oneself can lead to feelings of depression and guilt. When children are angry at others, they think their rights have been violated in some way or that others haven't followed their rules. Their anger stems from their belief that others shouldn't have treated them in this manner—it is awful, they can't stand it, and the wrong-doers deserve to be punished.

Unfortunately, far too many children in today's society are growing up in situations in which they have been severely mistreated or have had their rights violated. Of course, this abuse is wrong and should not occur—but it has occurred. Therefore, young clients need to consider whether their anger helps them deal constructively with a situation such as mistreatment, a situation over which they have little or no control.

Because anger can so easily lead to oppositional behavior, verbal and physical aggression, and other forms of acting out, it is important to help young clients identify the irrational beliefs that cause their anger and teach them how to reduce the intensity of their anger through effective disputing. Examples of challenges to anger-related irrational beliefs include the following: "Where is it written that you should always get what you want, that the world must be fair, and that you always have to have your way?" "How is your anger helping you?" "How is your anger hurting you?" Functional disputes, illustrated by the latter two questions, are particularly useful in helping youngsters manage their anger because they may be reluctant to give up their feelings of anger due to a belief that these angry feelings are justified. Anger often empowers them, and so they consequently feel "righteous" and strong in their convictions. Therefore, it is important to elicit both the advantages and the disadvantages of anger and its associated behaviors. By doing so, the therapist can help young clients realize that when they are angry, they often act against their own best interests by yelling at, hitting, or opposing others who have power over them. Results typically include punishments such as being grounded, getting suspended from school and team sports, and getting hurt physically in altercations with peers. It is essential to show them that, by getting angry, they are likely to lose self-control and give their power away. Thus anger actually makes them "weak," as opposed to "strong."

Because children and adolescents usually do not like the idea of giving others control, this realization of empowerment is often a strong motivating factor in encouraging them to work on anger management. It is equally important to teach children that they may not be able to control many aspects of their lives, but what they *can* control are their emotional and behavioral reactions to activating events; these controlled reactions constructively empower them. Finally, it is essential to show children how anger clouds their judgment, as well as their decision-making and problem-solving abilities, and puts them in a "feeling fog."

Included among those irrational beliefs that are associated with anger are the following:

I must have what I want.

The world should be fair.

I must have things go my way.

Other people must treat me the way I want them to, and when they don't, they deserve to be punished.

The following interventions can help children and adolescents identify the demands that result in anger and learn how to manage their anger-related emotions more effectively.

Don't Pop Your Top

RATIONALE   This is a concrete intervention that serves as a reminder to children to keep their anger under control.

MATERIALS   ▷ A small glass jar with a screw-on lid

▷ 10 to 20 strips of red paper

▷ A pencil

PROCEDURE   1. When your client talks about getting angry, ask her to write everything that angers her on individual strips of red paper.

2. Show her the jar and explain that, if she were to put all of these situations in the jar, there would be so much anger built up that the sheer volume could "pop the top."

3. Tell her that you will help her think of ways to reduce the number of strips so there won't be so much anger. Explain that she needs to understand that anger doesn't just happen; it happens because she thinks to herself that everything has to be fair, that she should always get what she wants, or that everything should always go her way.

4. Help her examine her strips to see how such demands apply to her situations.

5. Help her challenge each demand by asking herself questions such as "Does everything have to be fair?" "Can I stand it if it isn't?" "Can I always get what I want?" Explain that, when she asks such questions, her level of anger will drop to irritation, disappointment, or annoyance.

6. As she works through each of her situations and is able to let go of her demands, allow her to tear the strip into bits if she is completely rid of the anger, or in half to indicate a less intense reaction.

7. Once she has worked through her examples and understands the concept of letting go of the demand in order to reduce the anger, have her put the remaining strips or half strips in the jar, emphasizing that they won't pop the top since she reduced her anger.

Stay Cool Is the Rule

RATIONALE This visual intervention is intended to help children differentiate between very intense and less intense feelings related to anger, as well as to reduce the intensity of anger.

MATERIALS
▷ Several ice cubes

▷ A glass

▷ A book of matches

▷ A pencil

▷ Angry Faces worksheet (p. 161)

PROCEDURE

1. As your young client describes his anger, discuss the concept of anger as a "hot" emotion *(light the match)*, in contrast to less intense, "cooler" emotions *(put the ice cubes in the glass)*, such as disappointment, irritation, or annoyance.

2. After asking him to help you identify the negative effects of intense anger (e.g., temper tantrums, yelling, hitting, or kicking), ask him if he thinks it is better to have hot or cool feelings.

3. Show him how to turn the hot feelings into cool feelings by changing what he tells himself.

4. Give the client the Angry Faces worksheet. Ask him to identify something he has been angry about and to write down that thought in one of the thought bubbles around the angrier head.

5. Help the client elicit the thoughts that cause his angry feelings (e.g., "I can't stand the way they treat me; it's not fair. They shouldn't treat me this way. I'll show them!") and have him write his thoughts in some of the other bubbles around the angrier face.

6. On the same worksheet, point out the less angry face to the client. Have him identify something he has been moderately angry about and write down that thought in one of the bubbles around the less angry face.

7. Help the child learn how to dispute his irrational beliefs and replace them with rational thoughts (e.g., "I don't like it, but I can stand it; it may not be fair, but life is not always fair. Even if they

shouldn't do this, I can't control what they do!") and write them in other bubbles around the less angry face as a visual reminder that replacing the irrational thoughts with rational thoughts results in cooler emotions.

8. Encourage the child to remember the matches and ice cubes and to practice disputing his "hot thoughts" to get "cooler emotions."

Angry Faces

The Anger Alarm

RATIONALE   If we can teach children what pushes their anger buttons, we can be more effective at helping them control their anger, as demonstrated in this intervention.

MATERIALS
- ▷ A sheet of drawing paper
- ▷ Crayons or markers
- ▷ 2 envelopes
- ▷ 10 to 15 strips of paper
- ▷ A pencil

PROCEDURE

1. When your client talks about being angry, use the analogy of an alarm to help her recognize what pushes her anger buttons and sets off the alarm that warns her that her anger is building up and that it is time to give up her anger.

2. Have her use the crayons to draw her version of an "anger alarm."

3. Have her think about things she has been angry about recently and write them on separate strips of paper.

4. After discussing the advantages and disadvantages of hanging onto this anger and what it would take to let it go, have the client think about which anger issues she identified that she can let go of at this time, put them in one of the envelopes, and label it "Time to Let Go of the Anger."

5. Have her take additional strips and write down things that trigger her anger.

6. Have her put these in the other envelope and label it "Pushes My Anger Buttons."

7. Discuss what rational things she can say to herself so that what pushes her anger buttons doesn't set off her alarm and cause her to react angrily.

8. Ask her to write her rational responses on the backs of the individual strips in the "Pushes My Anger Buttons" envelope and see if thinking rationally helps her realize that it is time to give up her anger.

Angry Arnie

RATIONALE   Children need to learn the connection between how they feel and how they behave, as well as the negative behavioral consequences of anger and how to deal with them.

MATERIALS   ▷ A sheet of paper

▷ A pencil

▷ Angry Arnie story (p. 164)

PROCEDURE   1. Share the Angry Arnie story with the client.

2. After reading the story, ask the client to write down what he would do if he were Arnie and how he would get over his anger about this.

3. Discuss his response, asking him to describe what thoughts contributed to Arnie's anger and to identify the behaviors that resulted from these thoughts.

4. Personalize the concepts from this story to the client's own experiences with anger. Give the client a copy of the story to keep if you wish.

Angry Arnie

Arnie was so angry, he thought he might just pop his top. He had just come home from school, only to find his room in a complete shambles. It was obvious that his little sister had been playing there for a long time because all her toys were out and scattered over the entire floor. To make matters worse, his sister had also dragged books off the shelf and clothes out of the drawers. Oh, was Arnie mad.

As he marched down the steps into the kitchen, he muttered under his breath, "Wait till I find that little twerp. She is going to get it. How dare she go into my room when I have my Do Not Disturb sign on the door? How could the baby-sitter let her do this? This is terrible, and they both should be punished."

When he got to the bottom of the steps, Arnie started screaming at the top of his lungs, "Don't you ever go into my room again! You can never play with anything of mine again! I can't stand this! You both get up there and clean my room until absolutely everything is back in place, and don't you dare come out until it is done!"

With that, Arnie stomped outside, slamming the door so hard that it broke the glass. He was so worked up, he didn't even notice. He stormed into the backyard and climbed up to his tree house. All Arnie could think about was his bratty little sister and that lazy baby-sitter who probably just sat and watched TV while she let his room get demolished.

So Arnie sat and stewed about his room. Eventually he heard someone calling to him, so he looked down and saw his friend Annabel, who was two years older than he was. "Can I come up?" asked Annabel. "Yeah, but I'm in a pretty bad mood," replied Arnie. "Why? Did something really bad happen?" asked Annabel. "You better believe it," said Arnie, and he explained the whole story.

After Arnie had finished, Annabel told him, "I can see why you were mad, but is it really that big a deal?" Arnie snapped back: "Sure it is. How would you like it if your sister trashed your room?"

"Well, I wouldn't like it, but I don't think I'd get as mad as you are," Annabel replied. Sure, it was wrong to do it, but if you make her clean it up, what's the problem? Is it really worth getting so upset about?"

"You don't get it. She shouldn't have been in my room in the first place, and the baby-sitter wasn't doing her job, or this wouldn't have happened," explained Arnie.

"You're right . . . but it happened; sometimes people don't do what they should. But you can't do anything about that, can you? Do you really think you're going to change anything by staying mad?"

"Probably not," grumbled Arnie. "But it's just not fair. I spent a lot of time this weekend cleaning my room, and now it's a mess. I don't know what to do."

 What Works When with Children and Adolescents © 2002 by Ann Vernon. Champaign, IL: Research Press (800) 519-2707

Anger Is and Isn't

RATIONALE Anger is a very powerful emotion that many adolescents feel power-less to control. This intervention helps them explore some of the myths about anger.

MATERIALS ▷ A pencil

▷ Anger Is and Isn't Checklist (p. 166)

PROCEDURE 1. Have your client rate each item on the Anger Is and Isn't Checklist.

2. After the client has responded to the checklist, discuss with her some of the facts about anger: that repeatedly talking about an angry incident just makes you angrier because you relive the episode again and again; that it is possible to control anger, and that what you think influences how angry you get.

3. Emphasize the connection between anger and aggression. Dispel the myth that you have a better chance of getting your way if you are angry by explaining that, although some people are intimidated by anger, others get angry or controlling in return. Consequently, you often stand to lose instead of gain by trying to get your way through anger.

4. Encourage your client to share examples of her anger not having worked for her and what she needs to do to get rid of the myths she holds that perpetuate her anger.

Anger Is and Isn't Checklist

Rate each item on a scale of 1 (strongly disagree) to 5 (strongly agree).

_____ 1. When people are angry, they become aggressive.

_____ 2. If you're angry, it's good to keep talking about it and rehashing the incident to get your angry feelings out.

_____ 3. It's almost impossible to control anger.

_____ 4. What you think about something that you are angry about influences how angry you are about it.

_____ 5. The things that make some people angry are the same things that make others angry.

_____ 6. You have a better chance of getting your way if you are angry.

_____ 7. It's usually easy to pinpoint what you're angry about.

_____ 8. Getting angry gives you power.

Anger Alert

RATIONALE Many adolescents indicate that their anger comes on suddenly, for no reason, and that this onset is confusing to them. They also feel as if they have no control over it, and they find that frightening. Helping them learn more about anger and how to deal with it is especially important during adolescence.

MATERIALS ▷ A wide rubber band

▷ A sheet of paper folded like an accordion

▷ A pencil

PROCEDURE 1. When your adolescent client describes his anger, ask him to try to identify the way his anger builds up.

2. Give him a sheet of paper folded like an accordion and have him recall a recent incident involving anger.

3. Ask him to identify the thoughts he had about this incident that made him angry and write them on different levels of the accordion sheet.

4. Help him see how he can challenge the thoughts at each level, before they build up, by asking questions such as the following:

    "Does everything have to be fair?"

    "Is it worth getting angry about?"

    "Even though it would be better for others to treat me the way I'd like to be treated, do they have to—and can I control that?"

5. Discuss with your client the importance of using these challenging techniques as soon as he is aware of these thoughts—it will help reduce the intensity of his anger before it builds up.

6. Once he understands this concept, give him the rubber band and have him put it on his wrist and snap it as a way to alert himself that he needs to stop and examine the thoughts that contribute to his anger.

Adios, Anger

RATIONALE Oftentimes, adolescents don't think they can control their anger, and sometimes they don't want to. When adolescent clients present with anger, they may often say they "just can't help it." Although they don't often admit it, some like their anger because it gives them the power to intimidate and control others so they can get their way. To other adolescents, anger is confusing and problematic because they may suffer negative consequences for the acting out that often accompanies anger. This intervention helps adolescents look at how long they want to hang on to their anger and how to weigh the price of doing so against the payoff.

MATERIALS
- ▷ A sheet of paper
- ▷ A pencil

PROCEDURE
1. To help your client look more realistically at this issue, ask her to divide a sheet of paper into four columns.

2. In the first column, have her write down her three most recent experiences with anger; in the second, have her list the positive payoffs of her anger; in the third, have her note the negative prices she paid.

3. Ask her to review the positive and negative columns and decide how long she wants to hold on to the anger—an hour, a day, a week, a month—and list that in the fourth column.

4. Emphasize that she can choose to say adios (goodbye) to her anger by evaluating both the price and the payoffs and by making a conscious decision to stop being angry.

Attack That Anger

RATIONALE   Anger is often related to adolescents' perception that they are not being treated fairly or in the manner they think they deserve. This intervention helps clients learn to challenge this concept of fairness.

MATERIALS   ▷ 2 chairs

▷ A tape recorder and audiotape

▷ A sheet of paper

▷ A pencil

PROCEDURE 1. When your client is angry because he perceives something as unfair or because others haven't treated him as he thinks he should be treated, have him write down all his thoughts associated with this anger-provoking event.

2. With your client sitting in one chair and yourself in the other, assume the role of the client—making sure to be irrational—and verbalize the beliefs that your client identified. (During the first round of this role play, instruct the client to listen to you rant and rave about the unfairness and the injustice of the anger-provoking event.)

3. After you have finished, invite him to give you his reactions.

4. For this next exchange, use the tape recorder so the client can refer to these strategies whenever he wants to attack his anger. Switch chairs with the client, and have him assume his own role and talk about this anger episode while you dispute his irrational beliefs (e.g., "Is everything in the world fair?" "Can you control how others treat you?" "How does being so angry change the situation or help you solve the problem?").

5. Ask the client to identify another anger-provoking event and share it with you. Switch chairs again. Assume the role of the client and role-play his situation while he plays the role of the counselor and practices the disputing process with his own anger-provoking event.

Acting Out

Anger and frustration often lead to various forms of acting out, such as temper tantrums; yelling and screaming; hitting, kicking, and punching; bullying and fighting; stealing; destroying property; or engaging in more serious acts of violence and aggression. Low self-worth may also contribute to acting-out problems such as bullying, in which the bully irrationally thinks that the only way to feel approved of or worthwhile is to be the toughest kid in the neighborhood. Children who steal may feel worthless because they don't get enough love or approval and thus try to compensate for their feelings of inferiority by taking what they want in order to feel better (Bernard & Joyce, 1984). Some children act out as a way to control others or their environment, having learned that parents may give in and let them have their way in order to avoid their own discomfort. Others may behave badly because they lack socialization skills or behavioral self-control.

Underlying most forms of aggression or acting out are the beliefs that I must have my way and that others should give me what I want—and if they don't, I'll figure out a way to get it. It is common to hear children say they "can't help it," as they fail to see the connection between how they think, feel, and act. It is also not surprising, given their tendency to think in the here and now, that they don't consider the possible negative consequences of their behavior; because of their faulty thinking, youngsters may figure they won't get caught or that it's not a big deal even if they do get caught.

It is important to distinguish between acting out and more serious oppositional defiant and conduct disorders. These more serious disorders evince a persistent pattern of conduct that violates the basic rights of others or major age-appropriate social norms.

The following irrational beliefs often accompany aggression or acting out:

> I must have my way, and if I don't, I can't stand it.
>
> Others must be punished if they violate me in any way.
>
> If I don't get what I need or want from others, I'll get it myself.

The following interventions can be adapted, as necessary, to help children and adolescents develop more control over acting-out behavior.

More of the Same

RATIONALE   Because children may not fully understand how their behavior affects them and others, it is sometimes helpful to show them—in an exaggerated way—what the effects look like. This intervention is especially geared toward children who throw temper tantrums.

MATERIALS   ▷ A sheet of drawing paper

▷ Crayons or markers

▷ A large mirror or a video recorder with television playback

PROCEDURE   1. In talking with your client about her temper tantrums, help her understand that what prompts the tantrum is her belief that she has to have her way or can't stand having to do what others tell her to do.

2. Ask the client to show you how she acts when she has the tantrum. (In most cases, young clients will not give you a full-blown version, so you may need to push for more, inviting them to get on the floor and pound their fists and kick their feet, yelling, "I have to have my way! I have to have my way!")

3. Use the mirror or video recorder to help your client see what she looks like.

4. After she has witnessed the event, ask her how she felt about seeing herself behave that way and whether she would like to work on perfecting her technique or changing her behavior. Explain that, in order to change her behavior, she has to tell herself that she doesn't *have* to have her way, she just *prefers* it, and she has to ask herself if it is worth acting like a baby to try to get her way.

5. Invite the client to draw a picture of herself having a tantrum so she can keep it as a reminder of how she looks when she acts this way.

6. Suggest that, if she is proud of this type of behavior, she can make multiple posters and put them up around school or around the house. But if she wants to change her behavior, she can rip up the picture after she has gone a week without throwing tantrums.

Away with Acting Out

RATIONALE This story helps children realize that they can control their behavior by changing their anger-provoking thoughts.

MATERIALS ▷ Away with Acting Out story (p. 173)

PROCEDURE 1. Share the Away with Acting Out story with your client.

2. Discuss what Andre, the main character, would have to do to let go of the idea that he could not always do what he wanted to.

3. Encourage your client to share his thoughts on how this story applies to him. If you wish, give him a copy of the story to keep.

Away with Acting Out

Andre was angry. He desperately wanted to go biking after school, but his mom told him that he couldn't go until he had cleaned his room. "Why should I have to do that?" Andre yelled. "You are so mean. You never let me do what I want. It's not fair. You always let Allie have her way; she never has to do anything, and I have to do all the work and never get to have any fun."

Andre was so angry that, as he went by his sister Allie's door, he ripped her favorite poster off and tore it up. Then he went into his room, slammed the door hard, and started throwing things around as he yelled, "It's not fair that I have to clean my room and can't do what I want! I have to have my way!"

Pretty soon, Andre heard his mom coming up the steps. "Stay away from me!" Andre yelled while trying to push his bed against the door to keep her out. But Andre wasn't strong enough, and his mom opened the door and came in. "Sit down and listen to me, Andre," she said. "No. I don't have to listen to you; you never let me do what I want to do," cried Andre. Then Andre's mom gave him a choice: He could calm down and talk things over, or he could keep ranting and raving and spend the next week grounded to his room. Reluctantly, Andre sat down to talk things over.

Andre's mom explained to him that sometimes things don't seem fair and maybe they aren't, even though people usually try to be fair. She told Andre that all people have to do some things they don't like to do, like clean their rooms—just because that's the way the world is. "Do you suppose I ever have to do anything I don't want to do?" Andre's mom asked him. "No. I thought adults got to do anything they wanted," replied Andre. "Well, I might like to stay home and ride my bike or go hiking instead of going to work, but I have to go to work every day to make money," explained Andre's mom. "I suppose I could throw a fit about it, but that wouldn't stop me from having to go to work. So instead, I just say to myself that there are some things that don't seem fair or that I'd rather not do, but I don't have to upset myself about them. When I think that way, I am less likely to get so mad that I act out. So maybe that's something for you to think about: that you can't always have your way, and you can choose not to act out. Does that make sense?"

Andre pondered this for a while, but it was really hard for him to let go of the idea that he couldn't always do what he wanted or that he could choose not to act out by changing the way he thought about it. It seemed to him that this would really be tough to do. When he explained that to his mom, she told him that it always takes time to change, but if you work on it little by little, it can happen. So Andre and his mom made a deal: Andre would work on it, and if he made progress, they would go biking together.

Act Now, Pay Later

RATIONALE It is important to help children understand the connection between how they act and the consequences of those actions, as this intervention emphasizes.

MATERIALS
▷ A mousetrap and a piece of cheese

▷ A sheet of drawing paper

▷ Crayons or markers

PROCEDURE
1. Show your client the mousetrap and cheese and discuss with her what would happen to a mouse if it wanted the cheese in the trap. Ask her if she thinks the mouse would consider the consequences before it tried to get the cheese.

2. Ask her if she has ever wanted to do something so much that she didn't think about the consequences. Invite her to share an example.

3. Discuss what she could have done to enable her to remember to think before she acted.

4. Give her the paper and crayons or markers, and have her draw a mousetrap on one half of the paper. On the other half, have her write the following as a reminder to think before she acts:

   T—Tempted to do something you want to do.

   R—Remember to think about the consequences.

   A—Act now if it's a smart thing to do.

   P—Plan ahead to avoid bad consequences.

Step into Their Shoes

RATIONALE Use this intervention to help children change their aggressive behavior by looking at things from another perspective.

MATERIALS
- ▷ A large pair of shoes
- ▷ A sheet of drawing paper
- ▷ A crayon or marker

PROCEDURE

1. When you are counseling a young client who insists that he cannot change his behavior—that he has to act mean and behave aggressively because others "made me do it"; or he got blamed for something that wasn't his fault and so he had to retaliate; or something else forced him to behave a certain way—ask him to describe in detail a recent situation in which he had difficulty controlling his behavior and consequently was mean and aggressive.

2. Discuss the thoughts and feelings associated with this incident, as well as the consequences.

3. Have him identify a classmate or sibling who might have been at the scene but who didn't behave aggressively or act out in any manner.

4. Position the shoes in the middle of the sheet of paper and ask the client to step into them and pretend that he is the classmate or sibling who stayed calm and didn't become aggressive.

5. As he is standing in these shoes, have him try to imagine what the classmate or sibling was thinking that helped him or her stay calm.

6. Handing him the crayon or marker, have the client trace around one of the shoes, and then, on the inside of the shoe, write the rational, calming thoughts that he has been imagining.

7. Suggest to the client that he refer to this drawing to help him remember these thoughts whenever he finds his behavior getting out of control.

Actions Speak Louder Than Words

RATIONALE   Many adolescent clients are especially reluctant to discuss their own negative behaviors, let alone change them. This intervention is an indirect way to get them to set personal behavioral goals to overcome negative actions.

MATERIALS   ▷ A sheet of paper

▷ A pencil

PROCEDURE   1. When your client has been referred to counseling because she is acting out in various ways that result in negative consequences, try the following approach:

Rather than ask her about her own behavior, first ask her to think about several negative acting-out behaviors her friends or acquaintances have engaged in, and then ask her to list on the sheet of paper the behaviors as well as the consequences.

Invite the client to discuss whether she thinks these peers thought about the consequences, if they had ever promised to change, and what might have prevented them from following through on their good intentions.

2. Ask her to identify any negative acting-out behaviors she herself has engaged in and what the consequences were.

3. Invite her to speculate as to what might happen if she changed these behaviors and how she might succeed in changing them.

4. After discussing the advantages and disadvantages of behavioral change, ask her to select one of the behaviors she would consider working on and to list the steps she could take in order to change it.

Awesome Actions?

RATIONALE Try this intervention with adolescents to motivate them to change their negative acting-out behavior so that the consequences of their behavior are positive.

MATERIALS
▷ 3 sheets of paper

▷ A pencil

▷ Awesome Actions Cards (p. 179)

PROCEDURE
1. Ask the client to sort through the Awesome Actions Cards, ranking the behaviors in descending order of severity.

2. Have him take a blank sheet of paper and, at the top, label it "Thoughts That Could Lead Me to Do This."

3. Ask him to number this paper from 1 to 8, take the cards in the order in which he ranked them, and identify the thoughts he might have had that would lead him to act as described on each card.

4. When he has completed this step, have him take a second sheet of paper and label it "Consequences That Could Occur as a Result of These Actions."

5. After he once again numbers from 1 to 8, have him take the cards in rank order and identify consequences for the action described on each card.

6. After discussing possible consequences, ask him to go through and cross out the actions he would not consider engaging in because of the consequences of his doing so.

7. Refer to the first sheet and help him dispute the thoughts related to fairness, justice, and demandingness. Help him see how he can change his actions by changing his thoughts and considering consequences.

8. On another sheet of paper, have the client list several of his actions that he or others consider inappropriate.

9. Ask him to identify any irrational beliefs and consequences.

Chapter 4 • Interventions for Externalizing Problems

10. Have him practice disputing the irrational beliefs—a practice that can result in behavior change.

11. As the final part of this intervention, ask the client to commit to changing one behavior.

Awesome Actions Cards

Stealing	Beating someone up
Trashing someone's property	Throwing a fit when you don't get your way
Keying someone's car	Running away
Punching in the door	Threatening someone with a knife

Action Awareness

RATIONALE Adolescents often act impulsively without considering consequences. To help them become more aware, use this intervention.

MATERIALS
▷ A spiral-bound notebook (to use as an action log)
▷ A pencil

PROCEDURE
1. Suggest to your client that she maintain an action log, writing in a notebook all of her actions for several days.

2. When she comes to the next counseling session, provide her with the following codes and have her rate her actions accordingly: *P (positive); N (negative); PC (positive consequences resulted); NC (negative consequences resulted); SC (should change).*

3. When she has finished the coding, discuss the results, emphasizing that no one "makes people do anything"; they are responsible for their own actions.

4. Ask her to identify positive behaviors she wishes to continue and negative behaviors she wishes to change, using her action log to map out an action plan of what will change, how she will do it, and when she will initiate her plan.

Account for Your Actions

RATIONALE   Adolescents are notorious for blaming others for their actions, so it is important to help them be accountable.

MATERIALS   ▷ A sheet of paper

▷ A pencil

▷ A section from a local newspaper listing misdemeanors, arrests, traffic violations, and so forth

PROCEDURE   1. When your adolescent client needs help in being more accountable for his actions, hand him the newspaper section and ask him to look it over to determine who was accountable for the negative actions.

2. Discuss with him what beliefs these people had that might have led to these actions, what the consequences of their actions could be, and other factors that might have influenced them.

3. Have him write down actions *he* has engaged in that he thinks could result in some type of significant consequence. Have him also identify who is responsible for the action, what beliefs he has that influence him to continue this behavior, and possible consequences.

4. Ask him to commit to change one of these behaviors by identifying the following:

Beliefs that need to change (and what those changes would be)

Other factors that are getting in the way of his making the change (such as peer pressure)

How he will deal with the factors he just identified

Positive consequences as a result of changing

How he will reward himself for the change in his actions

Procrastination

Why do children and adolescents procrastinate? Because they don't want to do things they don't like or things they may find uncomfortable or unpleasant. They may not want too much responsibility, are afraid of making a wrong decision or a mistake or not being perfect, or fear others' judgments. Furthermore, they don't think they should have to do things that are too hard or might be a hassle, and they may hope that what they are avoiding will somehow, magically, get done. Knaus (2000) noted that procrastinators experience nagging guilt, self-denigration, and ultimately feelings of hopelessness. They may also feel overwhelmed and consequently become anxious as the workload builds up. To complicate the issue, they are often angry at themselves, thinking that they should be able to get the work done and that they are stupid for allowing themselves to fall into this trap.

According to Knaus (2000), procrastinators believe that the world is too difficult or demanding and that they are inadequate. Some procrastinators are afraid to fail; they feel inadequate because they cannot live up to their unrealistic, self-imposed standards. Consequently, if they put off studying or preparing for an event, they protect themselves from feeling like a failure by telling themselves that they would have done much better if only they had taken the time to prepare.

Although procrastination can have numerous unpleasant consequences, it is not easy to overcome. Procrastinators subscribe to the Scarlett O'Hara philosophy: "I'll think about it tomorrow." Or they rationalize their delay by telling themselves such things as "I'll feel more energized after I take a bike ride." For the time being, they feel less anxious because they have fooled themselves into thinking they will begin the task later. However, as soon as they realize that they have no intention of doing it later, they are angry at themselves for rationalizing their delay tactics.

Often, procrastinators get so frustrated that they just give up or try to find easier ways to complete the task—a strategy that may not work out. Their subsequent failure to succeed only supports their belief that things are too difficult for them. Procrastinators frequently think that things will work out somehow—that even though they put things off until the last minute, they may be able to cram or overcompensate at the last minute in order to accomplish what needs to be done. If they succeed, their success reinforces their belief that there is nothing wrong with their behavior because they managed to complete the task.

Irrational beliefs associated with procrastination include the following:

> I shouldn't have to do things I don't like to do.
>
> It's too much of a hassle to do this.
>
> I can't do things that are too difficult or too demanding.

Put It Off

RATIONALE   This intervention can be used to help children learn that putting things off instead of doing their tasks in a timely manner makes each situation worse.

MATERIALS   ▷ A pile of newspapers

▷ A sheet of paper

▷ A pencil

PROCEDURE   1.   When the child complains about having to get work in on time or do chores when others want them done, have her think back to recent instances in which she just kept putting things off.

2.   Ask her to make a list of these occasions.

3.   Suggest that she help you with an experiment that will help her see the effects of putting things off: Ask her to lie on the floor, and then explain that you are going to read the list of things she put off doing, one at a time.

4.   As you read each one, put a stack of newspapers on the client. Continue to pile them on top of each other as you read subsequent items on the list.

5.   When everything on the list has been read, discuss how she feels with everything "all piled up," and talk about what happens when she allows things to get to this point, as well as what she would have to do to get out from "under the pile" in real life.

6.   Suggest that she tape a piece of newspaper to her desk at school or on her dresser at home to remind her how things pile up when she procrastinates.

Calling All Procrastinators

RATIONALE This intervention forces children to stop and think about the positive and negative aspects of procrastination.

MATERIALS ▷ 2 sheets of drawing paper

▷ Crayons or markers

PROCEDURE
1. Suggest to your procrastinating client that he is a member of the Procrastinators Club, and the club is trying to recruit new members.

2. Have him make a poster that he thinks would convince his classmates to join his club.

3. After he has completed the poster, tell him that there is also a Non-Procrastinators Club, which wants to steal members from the Procrastinators Club.

4. Have him imagine what arguments these non-procrastinators would use to convince others to join their club instead of the Procrastinators Club.

5. Ask him to make a poster to represent this group as well.

6. Ask the client to share what he put on the two posters, engaging in a discussion about the difference between the two "clubs," as well as the negative consequences of procrastinating.

7. Encourage your client to use the posters to remind him that it is better not to procrastinate.

Procrastination Pointers

RATIONALE This intervention gives children a concrete way of remembering what to do to when they realize that they are procrastinating.

MATERIALS None

PROCEDURE 1. Teach the following song to your client (sung to the tune of "Mary Had a Little Lamb"), personalizing the song by using the client's name.

Procrastination Pointers

_____ *had some chores to do, chores to do, chores to do;*
_____ *had some chores to do that she just did not do.*
So her mother chewed her out, chewed her out, chewed her out;
So her father chewed her out and said he'd give her two.
So _____ *knew she had to work, had to work, had to work;*
_____ *knew she had to work or miss out on all the fun.*
So _____ *turned the TV off, TV off, TV off;*
_____ *put her book away and decided not to play.*
Before _____ *knew it, the chores were done, chores were done, chores were done;*
Before _____ *knew it, the chores were done, and then she had some fun.*

2. After your client has learned this song, encourage her to write her own songs, which include other pointers on how to avoid procrastination.

Now or Later?

RATIONALE   When children are asked to do something they don't want to do or that interferes with what they are engaged in, "I'll do it later" is a common response to the request. This intervention addresses the problem of putting things off until later.

MATERIALS   ▷ Game board (from the Appendix or one of your own design)

▷ A game marker (only the client plays the game)

▷ Do It Now and Do It Later Cards (p. 187)

PROCEDURE   1. To begin play, shuffle all the cards (both the Do It Now Cards and the Do It Later Cards) and put them in a pile.

2. Instruct your client to draw a card and decide if it is a Do It Now or a Do It Later Card.

3. For each Do It Now Card, he moves ahead two spaces. If he draws a Do It Later Card, he cannot advance unless he can identify what he could tell himself so he would be more likely to "do it now"—in which case he can advance one space.

4. After the client has finished playing the game, discuss whether there are any advantages to putting things off and what he can do to change his behavior.

Do It Now and Do It Later Cards

Do It Now	**Do It Later**
Your dad tells you to clean your room. You don't want to do it, but figure that it's better to get it over with now so he won't bug you.	Your parents ask you to pick up the sticks in the yard. You think it's a stupid job, and you don't feel like doing it, so you go to your friend's house instead.
Your mom asks you to get the mail from the mailbox at the end of the drive. It's cold outside, and you're watching your favorite television show. Nevertheless, you put on your coat and do as she asks because you don't want her to get mad.	Your dad asks you to take the soda cans to the recycling bin. You think it's too much hassle, and it interferes with something you'd rather be doing, so you put it off.
Your dad asks you to please feed your dog. You're busy playing a video game, but you remember that he has threatened to get rid of the dog if you don't feed it, so you do as he asks.	Your mom reminds you to deliver your newspapers so the customers don't complain. It's freezing cold outside, and you just can't force yourself to leave the warm house, so you put it off until a customer phones to ask about the paper.
Your little sister asks you to help her with her math homework. You don't want to stop what you are doing, but you think about how you'd feel if your older brother refused to help you when you needed it, so you help her out.	Your dad tells you to clean out the gerbil cage before you go to the movie. You're watching television, so you tell him you'll do it at the next commercial. But you end up watching the commercial and keep putting off the job.
Your parents tell you to do your homework. You hate doing homework; it's no fun. You'd rather play video games, roller blade, or ride your bike. But you know they'll make you do it sometime, so you decide you might as well start now and get it over with, and then you can do something fun.	You're supposed to fold the clothes in the laundry basket before your parents get home from work, but you keep putting it off because you've got better things to do.
Your mom asks you to change the cat litter; it's a job you hate because it always stinks. You know that if you put it off, it may smell even worse, so you just do it, even though you don't like it.	You know you should probably study for the social studies test, but you hate that subject. You just keep finding other things to do until bedtime, and then it's too late.

Why Procrastinate?

RATIONALE   This intervention helps clients understand why they procrastinate and serves as one of the first steps in changing this negative behavior pattern.

MATERIALS   ▷ Why Procrastinate? Inventory (p. 189)

PROCEDURE   1. When your adolescent client is self- or other-referred for problems dealing with procrastination, ask her to complete the Why Procrastinate? Inventory.

2. After she has completed the questionnaire, discuss her responses and help her learn to challenge her irrational beliefs with questions such as the following:

"Do things always have to be easy or enjoyable in order to do them right away?"

"Isn't it true that, even though some things are frustrating or a hassle, they are not intolerable?"

"Is life all about only doing things the easy way?"

"Is it really easier to do it later?"

"Are there negative consequences for putting things off?"

"Even if you're not absolutely sure about how to do something, what does it say about you if you don't know exactly how to do it or get it perfect?"

Why Procrastinate? Inventory

Circle your response to each item.

1. I procrastinate because it's easier to do it later.   Yes   No   Sometimes

2. I procrastinate because I really don't want to do it.   Yes   No   Sometimes

3. I procrastinate because I'm afraid I won't do it right.   Yes   No   Sometimes

4. I procrastinate because it's too much of a hassle to do it.   Yes   No   Sometimes

5. I procrastinate because it's too frustrating to do it.   Yes   No   Sometimes

6. I procrastinate because it doesn't matter if I put if off.   Yes   No   Sometimes

7. I procrastinate because I'll feel more motivated later.   Yes   No   Sometimes

8. I procrastinate because I don't know how to do it, so I can't start until I know for sure what to do.   Yes   No   Sometimes

9. I procrastinate because I'm afraid of making the wrong decision.   Yes   No   Sometimes

10. I procrastinate because I'm not in the mood.   Yes   No   Sometimes

Procrastination: Price and Payoff

RATIONALE   This intervention helps adolescents evaluate both the price and the pay-offs for procrastinating and challenges them to change this behavior.

MATERIALS   ▷ A sheet of paper

▷ A pencil

PROCEDURE   1.   As your client discusses problems related to procrastination, have him take a sheet of paper and divide it into two columns, labeling them "Payoffs for Procrastination" and "Price of Procrastination."

2.   Ask him to list in one column all the payoffs (positive results) for procrastinating and, in the other column, the price he pays, or the negative consequences.

3.   Help him analyze his responses and make a value judgment about whether procrastination helps him more or hurts him more.

4.   As a homework assignment, have him identify something he can do to help himself avoid procrastinating.

5.   Suggest that he keep a chart so that each time he completes a task without procrastinating, he can reward himself with something pleasant.

Better Late Than Never

RATIONALE As adolescents grow older, problems associated with procrastination can have more significant ramifications. The habits that adolescents develop now may adversely affect them in the workplace or in higher education, where there is less tolerance for this type of behavior. This intervention helps them to develop awareness and to learn what to do about this behavior.

MATERIALS ▷ A sheet of paper

▷ A pencil

▷ Better Late Than Never Vignettes (p. 192)

▷ PROCRASTINATE Acronym (p. 193)

PROCEDURE 1. Have your client read the Better Late Than Never Vignettes.

2. After the client has read the vignettes and discussed with you the consequences of procrastinating in these examples, have her write several vignettes about her own procrastination problems and consequences.

3. Share the PROCRASTINATE Acronym to give her tips on overcoming this problem.

Better Late Than Never Vignettes

1. Tory's motto was "Better late than never." So when he showed up for work 30 minutes late two days in a row, he was surprised when his boss gave him a warning: "Be late again and you're out of a job."

2. Jaime's motto was "Better late than never." He hated studying for tests, and he always had better things to do. So he kept putting off the studying and flunked the exam.

3. Amanda's motto was "Better late than never," which is why she never started writing papers until the last minute. But she hadn't counted on getting sick the night before a big paper was due, so her grade went from an A to a B in the class because she wasn't able to turn the paper in on time.

4. Jillian's motto was "Better late than never." So when her grandmother told her she would pay Jillian $25 if she would mow her lawn before the weekend, Jillian figured it wouldn't matter if she waited until Sunday. But when she finally went to mow the lawn on Sunday, it had already been mowed, and Jillian was out $25 that she really needed to pay her bills.

PROCRASTINATE Acronym

P—Put distractions aside.

R—Really put forth your best effort.

O—Organize your tasks.

C—Consequences for procrastination aren't good.

R—Really concentrate.

A—Attend to tasks.

S—Stick to it, even if it's hard or a hassle.

T—Try to break tasks into smaller chunks.

I—Initiate the dreaded task sooner rather than later.

N—Never put things off until the last minute.

A—Act as if you want to do this.

T—Try a self-reward when you don't procrastinate.

E—Even if you put some things off, keep trying to improve.

Paralyzing Procrastination

RATIONALE Procrastinators often fall into a vicious cycle of putting things off, becoming overwhelmed and anxious, and then putting themselves down for putting tasks off, all of which leads to further procrastination. To help adolescents avoid becoming paralyzed by procrastination, use this intervention.

MATERIALS ▷ A pencil

▷ Paralyzing Procrastination Checklist (p. 195)

PROCEDURE 1. As your client discusses his problems with procrastination, point out that he doesn't have to perpetuate this behavior.

2. Give him a copy of the Paralyzing Procrastination Checklist and ask him to put an X beside the techniques he has tried and an O beside those he thinks might work. Then ask him to identify two additional techniques he could use in the future.

3. Before he leaves the session, have him select one technique that he will try immediately.

4. Encourage him to set up a self-reward system that he can implement once he completes a task without procrastinating.

Paralyzing Procrastination Checklist

Put an X *beside the techniques you have already tried, an* O *beside the techniques that you think might work, and then identify two additional techniques you could use to overcome procrastination.*

_____ 1. *One step at a time.* Break tasks down into small steps and do one at a time.

_____ 2. *Timer technique.* Set a timer for 15 minutes. See how much you can get done. Then reset the timer and go another 15 minutes. After 30 minutes, take a short break and start the cycle again.

_____ 3. *"Prices I pay" poster.* Make a list of all the negative consequences that can occur if you procrastinate. Post this list to help remind you not to procrastinate.

_____ 4. *Make a bet.* Make a bet with yourself about how long you can work on an unpleasant task. Set a time limit and then challenge yourself to do more.

_____ 5. *When will I start?* When you have a big project coming up, set a date to indicate when you will start. If you don't start by that date, identify something you hate to do, and then do it every day until you start the task.

_____ 6. *Sign a contract.* Enlist the help of a friend, a teacher, or a parent. Outline a plan to accomplish your task. Set reasonable deadlines for when you will start and when you will finish. Sign a contract in the presence of another person, who will agree to monitor your progress.

_____ 7. *Visualize.* When you have a big task to complete, visualize yourself starting the task, working hard on it, and completing it. Practice this visualization every day until the task is done.

_____ 8. *Just do it.* Put "Just Do It" signs in your room, on your mirror, in the car, or in your backpack as reminders to just do it.

Add your own ideas:

_____

_____

_____

_____

Underachievement

Underachievers are capable of better performance, but for several reasons fail to live up to their potential. They may set unrealistically high standards, consider their self-worth contingent on their performance, and fear rejection or condemnation if they fail to perform as they think others expect them to. Underachievers are so consumed with the thought of doing poorly that they are often distracted. They may fear failing so much that they adopt the belief that it is better not to try than to try and fail. Underachievement can also be looked at as a "safe" way to rebel. For instance, well-behaved students who are afraid to act in more unacceptable ways may see underachievement as a way to assert their power and get back at their parents, who have little control over their level of achievement.

It is important to assess parental attitudes toward achievement when working with children and adolescents. In many cases, the parents may demand high performance—or at least that is how their children perceive it. In other cases, children may assume that if their parents show very little interest in their schoolwork or activities, then it doesn't matter how they perform. There are also some parents who put their children down for less-than-perfect performance. Such high expectations often consign their children to underachievement: Not only do these children suffer from anxiety about not being able to live up to perfectionistic standards, but they also become angry at their parents, from whom they are receiving only conditional acceptance.

Sometimes underachievement is related to the irrational belief that things will turn out fine whether they work or not. These underachievers are skilled at delaying and avoiding—two tactics that relate to procrastination. Other irrational beliefs relate to frustration tolerance ("I shouldn't have to do anything that is unpleasant!"). Underachievers holding this belief don't do their work if it isn't entertaining or enjoyable, usually forgetting that often there are negative consequences for poor performance. This belief seems prevalent among today's youth, many of whom can't stand to do anything that is uncomfortable, boring, or compromising in any way. It is not uncommon for adolescents, in particular, to fail a class just because they don't like the teacher or hate the class or develop an "I'll show them" mentality. Furthermore, they may choose to underachieve because it's "cool"—a belief that stems from a fear that their friends may disapprove of them if they do well. Another irrational assumption is that nothing they do in school will ever be of use to them. In other words, if it's not relevant, why do it?

Bernard (2000, pp. 40–41) identified the following irrational beliefs associated with underachievement:

> I must do well and always be approved of, or else I will be a terrible person nobody could love.

Since I will be worthless for doing poorly, I might as well do nothing at all.

My worthlessness will not be obvious, and I won't feel as worthless as long as I don't try.

I shouldn't have to do things I don't feel like doing.

Life should be fun, comfortable, and never boring.

I can't stand the pain of doing what I don't want to do.

No matter how hard I work, I'll never do that well.

Difficult tasks are impossible; they should be easy.

The following interventions can be used or adapted to help children and adolescents challenge the irrational beliefs that result in underachievement and assist them in improving their performance. It should be noted that before using the following interventions, it would be wise to rule out other factors contributing to underachievement, such as learning disabilities; visual/hearing impairments; attention deficits; communicative disorders; exposure to traumatic events (e.g., physical, sexual, or emotional abuse); and, in adolescents, substance abuse.

Poor Performance

RATIONALE   To help younger children deal with issues related to underachievement that seem connected to perfectionism and anxiety, try the following intervention.

MATERIALS   ▷ A jar of bubble solution with wand

▷ A ruler

▷ A small sheet of paper

▷ A pencil

PROCEDURE   1. Begin by asking the child how she would describe the perfect bubble: How big would it be? What shape would it take? How long would it last?

2. Invite her to experiment and try to blow perfect bubbles. Indicate that you will be the judge, measuring the bubble with a ruler and writing down a number from 1 (bad) to 5 (perfect) for each bubble blown.

3. After the child has spent several minutes blowing bubbles, stop the activity and reverse the roles so that your client is evaluating your bubble blowing.

4. Again, after several minutes, stop and compare the ratings:

    Did either you or the client get all 5s? If not, what does that say about you?

    Are you rotten bubble blowers because you didn't get all 5s?

    Are you rotten persons because you didn't get all 5s?

    Would others stop having anything to do with you just because you didn't get all 5s?

5. Discuss how these concepts apply to your client's underachievement and what she can tell herself so her anxiety or perfectionism won't get in the way of her performance.

Understanding Underachievement

RATIONALE Read and discuss the following story as a way to help children understand their issues related to underachievement, such as not wanting to do work because it is boring, takes too long, or calls for too much effort.

MATERIALS ▷ Understanding Underachievement story (p. 200)

PROCEDURE 1. Share the Understanding Underachievement story with your client.

2. Discuss the story with your client. Point out that Ursula's decision to finally do her homework made her feel better because Ursula discovered that she could achieve her goal if she put her mind to it.

3. If you wish, give your client a copy of the story to keep.

Understanding Underachievement

Ursula didn't feel like doing her homework. Social studies was boring, it would take too long to do her math, and she hated the story she had to read for reading lab. It would just be so much more fun to play with her friend Ulysses. She knew her mom would ask her if she had any homework, but she figured she could tell a little lie and get away with it. As she raced down the alley to Ulysses's house, she really wasn't thinking about what would happen tomorrow when she didn't have the assignments done.

She and Ulysses really had fun until Ulysses's dad called him in to do his homework. "I'm not going to do mine," Ursula told Ulysses. I hate school, and I'd rather play. "So would I," said Ulysses. "But you know that the teacher will get mad if you don't do it, and then you'll have to stay in for recess, and we won't be able to play on those new swings. Besides, you'll have to do it sometime. You can't just go through school never doing your work, can you?"

So Ulysses went inside, and Ursula slowly walked home. She thought about what Ulysses had said, but she still wasn't convinced that she wanted to put any energy into doing that boring work. When she turned the corner, she was still deep in thought and ran smack into old Mrs. Uppum, who lived down the street. "Hey, there, Ursula. What are you thinking about that is so important that you can't watch where you're going?" asked Mrs. Uppum. "Well," Ursula replied, "I was just thinking about how I hate homework and don't want to do it. You're lucky that you're old and don't have to do it."

"You're right. I don't have to do homework, but I still have to do some things that are boring or things I don't like to do," said Mrs. Uppum. Ursula looked surprised. "Like what?" she asked.

"Well, I don't especially like to wash dishes, but there's no one else to do them; and if I don't, I'd have to eat off dirty plates, and then I'd get sick. And I really think it is boring to clean the house, but if I didn't do that, I'd never be able to find anything," Mrs. Uppum said.

"Gee, I thought once I was grown up, I would never have to do things I didn't want to do—especially homework," said Ursula.

"Well, I'm sorry to disappoint you, but we always have to do some boring things or some things we don't like to do," Mrs. Uppum said. "And sometimes the more I think about how boring or awful it will be, the more I put it off and don't do it. I remember doing that with my school-work when I was about your age, and the work just kept piling up until I thought I would never get it done. So I guess you have a decision to make, don't you?"

Ursula trudged away from Mrs. Uppum, feeling rather discouraged. She didn't think there was any way she could get out of doing homework forever. It wasn't that it was hard or anything—she just would rather be doing something else. "Oh, well," she thought to herself. "I might as well do it and get it over with. Then I can have my recess time, and the teacher won't yell at me because I didn't turn in the work. Maybe if I dig right in, it won't seem so horrible."

So Ursula did her homework and surprised herself by getting everything done by the time her mom called her down to dinner.

Excuses, Excuses

RATIONALE   This behavioral intervention helps children set small, doable goals en route to accomplishing tasks by not allowing their low frustration tolerance or perfectionistic behaviors to interfere with their achievement.

MATERIALS   ▷ 8 to 10 index cards

▷ A pencil

▷ A trash can for depositing excuses

PROCEDURE   1. When your client is underachieving, discuss what stops her from doing better. It may be that she doesn't spend enough time practicing or doing homework; doesn't prepare for tests or performances; doesn't feel like doing the work; doesn't understand the task and won't ask for help; or has better things to do with her time.

2. As the client thinks of her reasons for not doing better, have her write down each one on a separate index card.

3. Tell her that sometimes these reasons are like excuses—and if she looked at these excuses as if they were trash, she could tear them up, toss them in the trash can, and not have them interfere the next time she has to achieve something.

4. Suggest to the client that she review what she has written on the index cards, think about whether or not they help her accomplish her work, and tear them up and throw them in the trash if in fact they interfere.

5. Tell her that, now that some or all of her excuses are gone, she can set some goals to improve her performance.

6. Ask your client to share a specific area of performance she would be willing to work on to improve, and help her identify several small, doable goals.

7. Write these goals on separate index cards and ask her to prioritize them and then to work on them in that order as a homework assignment.

The Road to Achievement

RATIONALE Underachievers may not know what it takes to improve their performance. This intervention provides them with some direction.

MATERIALS
▷ Game board (from the Appendix or one of your own design)

▷ A small toy car, used as a game marker

▷ The Road to Achievement Cards (p. 203)

Note: If you construct your own game board, you could depict a road, along which the client advances his game marker.

PROCEDURE
1. To play the game, your client takes the car, draws a card, and decides if the behavior written on the card is a good study skill.

2. If it is a good study skill, he moves one space along the Road to Achievement. If it isn't a good study skill, he moves back one space and puts that card in a separate discard pile.

3. If, after all the cards have been drawn, the client is not at the end of the road, he can take the cards from the poor study skills discard pile and suggest a better study skill, thus advancing another space.

4. The activity continues until the client reaches the end of the road.

The Road to Achievement Cards

The assignment looks hard, so you just give up.	The assignment is boring, so you do some of it, take a short break, and then do the rest.
The assignment is so boring, you watch television instead.	You keep your assignment sheet in the front pocket of your backpack.
You lose your assignment sheet.	You are a good listener.
You forget to take home your backpack.	You keep your papers neat and organized in separate subject folders.
You write sloppily and don't proofread.	You study hard for tests.
You don't do your homework.	You take time to proofread your papers and write neatly.
You rush through homework so you can play.	You do all your homework each day so you don't fall behind.
You stuff all your papers in the same folder.	You take your time to do your homework, even though you'd rather be done so you can play.
You don't study for tests.	You usually remember to take your backpack home.
The work looks hard, but you keep trying.	You ask for help if you don't understand something.

Underestimating Underachievement

RATIONALE   Adolescents often don't think about the consequences of underachieving, nor do they see it as a problem. This intervention is designed to help them see how this behavior can affect their life now and in the future.

MATERIALS   ▷ 15 strips of paper (each approximately 1 inch wide and 6 inches long)

▷ A stapler

▷ A pencil

PROCEDURE   1. Introduce this activity by having your client take a strip of paper, identify one consequence of underachieving, and put the number 1 on that strip.

2. Have her take a second strip, number it with a 2, and identify a consequence that could happen as a result of the first consequence.

3. Follow this procedure until the client has exhausted all possible consequences and has numbered each strip.

4. Have her take the first strip, fold it into a ring (making sure that the writing is on the outside of the strip), and staple it. Have her loop the next strip through the first ring and staple it as well. Invite her to continue this process until she has completed a paper chain.

5. After discussing the consequences listed on the rings of the chain, ask the client if she thinks underachieving is a wise thing to do. If she believes that it is, suggest that she wear the paper chain as a reminder of the negative consequences of underachieving.

Why Try?

RATIONALE   This intervention is directed at adolescents who think it is easier not to try than to try and fail. They have set their standards very high, and, because of their tendency to think concretely, they don't see how they are hurting themselves by employing arbitrary thinking.

MATERIALS   None

PROCEDURE   1.   When your adolescent client describes how he doesn't even try and says, "I know I will fail, so what's the point?" engage him in a rational role reversal:

> You assume the role of the student who insists that it's not worth trying, emphasizing how you know you will fail, how it's easier not to try, how it's not a big deal, and so forth. The client, meanwhile, assumes the role of the counselor to help you with this issue.

2.   After several minutes, stop the role play and ask for the client's reaction to what just occurred, discussing how he sets himself up for further problems with his arbitrary attitude and his assumption that he will fail or that his performance won't meet his often unrealistically high standards.

3.   Invite the client to contract with you to change this behavior by identifying rational beliefs that can help him change his feelings. For example, he might ask himself questions such as these:

> "There's no proof that I will fail . . . so, if I try my best, aren't the chances good that I can succeed?"

> "Is it really easier not to try, or is that just an excuse?"

> "Even if I do try and I do fail, does that mean I should never try again or that I will always fail?"

Underachievement Is Unauthorized

RATIONALE   It is not at all uncommon to hear adolescents say it doesn't matter if they do well in school. If they are bored with a subject or don't like the teacher, they just don't do the work. They may choose to under-achieve because trying to achieve takes too much effort, and they would rather be doing something else. This intervention is designed to help them address the low frustration tolerance issues associated with underachievement.

MATERIALS   ▷ A sheet of paper

▷ A pencil

PROCEDURE   1. Whenever your adolescent client appears to be making a con-scious effort to achieve below her potential, determine if this prob-lem is a result of boredom, mild rebelliousness, or the belief that the task is irrelevant or not entertaining.

2. Rather than initially disputing the client's issues that relate to low frustration tolerance, act as if you agree with her, saying such things as "Yes, it must be really hard to do boring work" or "It must be hard to force yourself to do things that seem so meaning-less and irrelevant."

3. Casually emulating the backdoor approach of Lieutenant Columbo (the relentless police sleuth portrayed by actor Peter Falk in the popular TV series *Columbo*), ask if she thinks there are any prob-lems with doing what feels good versus doing what she should do.

4. Suggest that, before she digs herself a hole or has adults climbing all over her back, it might be a good idea to verify her perspective with a short survey:

   The purpose of the survey would be to ask others if they think they should ever have to do boring or uninteresting work or tasks that seem meaningless or irrelevant.

   She would also want to ascertain whether others have found it possible to avoid boring, meaningless tasks all their lives, and if they encountered any negative consequences by avoiding the work they were supposed to have done.

5. During the session, have the client write several questions for the survey and identify at least three adults and three peers she will ask to complete her survey.

6. In all likelihood, she will not complete the survey. However, by constructing the survey with her and raising some of the questions you want her to answer, you will be encouraging her to challenge her irrational beliefs.

To Do or Not to Do

RATIONALE   To do or not to do: This is a key issue for adolescent underachievers who, for a variety of reasons, don't perform well. This intervention teaches them to evaluate decisions about whether or not to put more effort into trying to achieve.

MATERIALS   ▷ A pencil

▷ To Do or Not to Do Questionnaire (p. 209)

PROCEDURE   1. Often when you are working with an underachiever, he is not self-referred and therefore may not acknowledge a problem with his performance.

2. Give the To Do or Not to Do Questionnaire to your client and ask him to complete it.

3. After the client has completed the questionnaire, discuss his responses and reactions.

4. Help him to evaluate carefully the positive and negative consequences of underachieving and how his behavior is helping him and also hurting him. Questions you might ask are these:

   "What are the positive consequences of underachieving?"

   "What are the negative consequences of underachieving?"

   "How is what you are now doing helping you?"

   "How is what you are now doing hurting you?"

5. Encourage him to commit to a behavior change by answering the following question, which serves as a homework assignment: "What would you be willing to change about your performance?"

To Do or Not to Do Questionnaire

Circle your response to each item.

1. I think I'm capable of doing better work.   Yes   No   Uncertain

2. I don't perform better because it takes too much effort.   Yes   No   Uncertain

3. I don't perform better because my friends don't think it's cool.   Yes   No   Uncertain

4. I don't perform better because it doesn't really matter.   Yes   No   Uncertain

5. I don't perform better because it really irritates my parents when I get bad grades.   Yes   No   Uncertain

6. I don't perform better because I don't care if I do well.   Yes   No   Uncertain

7. I don't perform better because I don't like others telling me what I'm supposed to do.   Yes   No   Uncertain

8. I don't perform better because I have better things to do with my time.   Yes   No   Uncertain

9. I don't perform better because I'm stupid and can't do any better.   Yes   No   Uncertain

10. I'd try harder if my parents or teachers just let it be my problem and stopped hassling me about it.   Yes   No   Uncertain

11. I don't perform better because how I do in school doesn't have anything to do with my future.   Yes   No   Uncertain

12. I don't perform better because I don't like to ask for help.   Yes   No   Uncertain

This case involves 17-year-old Kristen, who had problems with anger and suffered from low frustration tolerance. Following a review of her homework from the previous session, in which her anger and frustration were explored in depth, this session focused on Kristen's anger and feelings of worthlessness after she was rejected from the local chapter of the National Honor Society.

Counselor: Last time when we met, you were very frustrated about driving and upset that other people weren't driving the way you thought they should drive. So your homework assignment was to practice using rational coping statements to calm yourself down and to think more rationally. How did that go?

Client: It worked pretty well because once I began to consciously say to myself, "I can't change how they drive, so why upset myself?" I didn't get so angry.

Counselor: Good for you.

Client: I still got a little upset just because I feel like other people should drive better, but I realize that I can't control what they are going to do, so as long as I keep reminding myself of that, then I'm not as frustrated.

Counselor: Well, good. You mentioned that you still got a little upset over this—somewhat irritated, perhaps. It's natural to feel a little irritated, but if you think about this on a continuum, with one end being "very upset" and the other end being "not at all upset," it sounds like you were closer to not being upset—just slightly irritated because people weren't driving the way you thought they should drive. So what are you telling yourself to be able to switch from being very upset, which is where you have been previously, to being slightly upset, as you were last week?

Client: Well, I guess I was thinking that I don't have to like the fact that somebody drives slow, and, although it may make me late for an appointment, it just isn't worth getting so worked up about it since I can't do anything to change the other driver.

Counselor: Exactly. You can't control what they do, but you can decide how upset you want to get over this.

Client: Right.

Counselor: And one of the things we kind of talked about last time is that you've got lots of things going on in your life, and you can decide if this is one of the things you're going to choose to let bother you when there may be more important things to put your energy into.

Client: Yeah, it's not something I should place a lot of value on. It's just driving. So I just leave a little bit earlier now, so I won't have to worry about construction and things like that, and then I know that I've got plenty of time even if I do get caught behind somebody who's driving slow.

Counselor: So you've changed your thinking, but also your behavior. But suppose you were late. Is that the end of the world?

Client: I don't know. I guess because my dad has to be a half an hour early to everything, it's kind of been instilled that I have to be early, too; so for some reason it just bothers me if I'm late.

Counselor: Well, it would be preferable if you were on time, or even if you were there a little bit early—but do you need to get terribly upset if you aren't?

Client: No, I guess not.

Counselor: The world isn't going to come to an end if, once in a while, you are a few minutes late because of circumstances beyond your control.

Client: Right. Especially if it's not a major appointment.

Counselor: And even if it were a major appointment, chances are that it's not going to really be a disaster if you're a few minutes late, is it?

Client: No, I guess not.

Counselor: Well, keep practicing your rational coping statements—and I'm glad to hear that you've made progress. Is there another issue you'd like to discuss today?

Client: Yeah, there is. I didn't get into the National Honor Society, and I was sure I was going to make it.

Counselor: I'm sorry to hear that. How are you feeling about it?

Client: I'm really, really angry. I mean angry to the point where sometimes I can't even talk, I'm just so furious. I'm to the point I don't really know what to do or how to channel my anger. I don't even want to go to school.

Counselor: Let's back up a little and talk about what you are thinking that has resulted in this intense anger.

Client: I guess it didn't surprise me. But the first thing I did was to request a meeting with the advisory board, and I met with them today. I walked out of there even angrier than I was before I walked in. I just wanted to know why I was denied, because in my opinion there is no reason I should have been.

Counselor: So you were rejected and didn't think you should be. Can you identify what it is that you were thinking that has resulted in this anger?

Client: Well, I know that there are a lot of circumstances that surround whether or not you get chosen at this particular school, and a lot of them are very subjective and are based on your parents' social status, which church you go to, what activities you're involved in at school, whether or not the teachers who are on the board like you or not. It's not an objective point of view, based on whether or not I'm academically qualified—it's more about personality and whether or not you're liked.

Counselor: So are you saying that the reason you are so angry about being denied is that you don't think the criteria for selection are fair? That they are too subjective rather than objective?

Client: Yeah, I guess so. When I look at some of the people who are not even in the top 15 percent of my class who got in, I don't think it's fair that I'm in the top 5 percent of the class and got denied.

Counselor: And I'm assuming this is what you discussed with the advisory board?

Client: I did. I told them that I met the academic qualifications, and they said that they also looked at leadership and service. But I still don't get it. I'm on the debate team and speech team. I'm in all kinds of extracurricular activities, and I'm an officer for one of the drama clubs. I work at all the musicals, and the only thing that I'm not involved in is athletics and music, which is a big thing at this school. And I don't go to church, which is probably a strike against me, too. But so what? I shouldn't get rejected just because I don't go to church and am not a jock.

Counselor: So you're angry because you think you met most of the criteria for NHS, and it's not fair that you didn't get in.

Client: Right. When I look at who got in and compare them to me, it's not fair.

Counselor: Well, as you and I have discussed in relation to other issues, there are some things in life that just aren't fair.

Client: I know, but I think the advisory board should be very careful about who they let in, and I think they discriminated against me.

Counselor: And they may have, and it very well might have been unfair. But is there a guarantee in life that everything will be fair?

Client: I suppose not, but I still feel angry about it.

Counselor: That's understandable. But you are telling yourself that it should have been fair—and we just finished establishing the fact that sometimes things aren't fair. But is there something else about this that bothers you other than the fact that the selection process was unfair, in your opinion?

Client: I guess I just feel like a big failure. It's something that should have been a given because I met academic qualifications. But ever since I came to this town, I haven't been on the greatest terms with some people. I came in as an outsider, and nobody has liked me because I came in pretty close to the top of the class. Nobody likes the way I dress, they don't like the way that I do things, they don't like the fact that I'm outspoken; but that's just me as a person, and I can't change that. But it's created a problem in other situations, so I guess that's why in some ways it doesn't surprise me that I got rejected for NHS.

Counselor: I hear you saying several different things: that you are angry at the system that you think was unfair, and that as a result of being rejected for NHS, you feel like a failure. But you are also saying that, in your perception, some form of rejection began when you moved here.

Client: Exactly.

Counselor: But where is the evidence that you are a failure just because you have been rejected?

Client: Well, if I wasn't a failure, I should have been accepted into NHS.

Counselor: Except that we established that the system may have been unfair—and can you honestly say that you are basing being a success or a failure on the fact that you were rejected from the National Honor Society and haven't been accepted well by some others in this community?

Client: Sort of.

Counselor: Let's look at this more carefully. First of all, I heard you say that you hadn't been on the greatest terms with some people when you first moved here—but then I heard you say that nobody liked the way you looked or dressed and so forth. Which is it—some people or everyone?

Client: It's not everybody—I do have some friends and my boyfriend.

Counselor: So everyone hasn't rejected you, but you were rejected from NHS, and as a result, you think of yourself as a failure. Now suppose your boyfriend came to you and said that he was a failure—a loser, so to speak—because he didn't get into the National Honor Society. What would you say to him?

Client: I'd tell him that there's no way he's a failure just because he didn't get in.

Counselor: Exactly. So why can't you do the same thing for yourself? Are you a total failure because you have been rejected from National Honor Society?

Client: I guess not. But I feel like such a loser.

Counselor: And where is the evidence that you are a loser? Let me show you something. Here is a balloon. I want you to blow this up and tie it. Now take this pin and poke the balloon. What happens?

Client: *(Blowing up the balloon and popping it.)* It popped.

Counselor: Right. When it popped, it just disintegrated into nothing. Now, are you like a balloon? Are you really nothing just because you didn't get accepted into one club?

Client: I guess not. But it's hard not to feel like a stupid failure because of this.

Counselor: Yes, but prove to me that you are a failure. You just said that you are in the top 5 percent of your class, you are in all sorts of leadership and service activities—and even if you weren't so talented and so involved, would you be a worthless person?

Client: I suppose not.

Counselor: Absolutely. Just because you exist, you are worthwhile. The fact that you had the academic qualifications and perhaps were well qualified in other areas but failed to get into NHS has nothing to do with your worth as a person. It doesn't mean that you are a failure; it means that you failed to get in. Does that distinction make sense?

Client: I guess so. But the other thing that bothers me is that I won't get any scholarships to college since I can't list NHS membership.

Counselor: I don't understand how not being in this one organization will automatically exclude you from college scholarships. Do you know this for a fact?

Client: Well, I know that the honor society organization has huge scholarship programs, and you have to be a member to get them.

Counselor: So what you are saying is that you won't be eligible for this one particular group of scholarships—not all scholarships in general, correct?

Client: Yes.

Counselor: And in fact, since you are in the top 5 percent of your class and have numerous leadership and service activities to your credit, don't you suppose that you will qualify for other scholarships?

Client: I guess so.

Counselor: So rather than assuming that you will not get scholarships, what do you need to think so you don't get upset about this issue, too?

Client: Just that there are other scholarships. But that still doesn't help the fact that I'm angry about not being accepted.

Counselor: But you're angry because you think it wasn't fair, and we established the fact that it might not have been. But what can you do about that since there are lots of things in life that aren't fair? Is it fair that you could be driving 5 miles over the speed limit and get pulled over, when someone in the next lane didn't get stopped but was driving 10 miles over? Is it fair that you could get picked up for shoplifting the first time you ever tried it, and someone else has done it for years and has never gotten caught?

Client: No. I see your point, and I just need to stop thinking that it should have been fair.

Counselor: Right. And what can you do to stop yourself from thinking that you are a total failure because you didn't get accepted?

Client: I don't know. That's the problem.

Counselor: Let's try an experiment. I am going to pretend that I am you, and I want you to tell me what a total failure I am—what a worthless nobody.

Client: OK. You got rejected from NHS, you won't get a college scholarship from them, people think you dress weird, you don't go to church, and you wear your hair funny.

Counselor: Is that all? How did you feel when you were saying those things?

Client: Sort of stupid.

Counselor: Because?

Client: Well, maybe that's not enough to make me a total loser. I like the way I dress and wear my hair, so I shouldn't have even said that.

Counselor: So what are you saying?

Client: Well, I guess I'm not a total loser.

Counselor: Right. So if we were to take this piece of paper and in one column put "Proof that I'm a failure," and in the other column put "Proof that I'm not a failure," what would you put on each side?

Client: On the failure side I would put NHS, and on the other side I guess I could put top 5 percent of the class, Junior Leadership, scholarship for the Russia Student Ambassador trip, and Junior Achievement.

Counselor: So it looks like the "Proof that I'm not a failure" side outweighs the other, right? And remember that, although these accomplishments are important, they don't make you who you are. You are still worthwhile just because you exist, regardless of how you achieve and perform.

Client: It's just hard to remember that sometimes, and it was so important for me to get into the National Honor Society.

Counselor: Based on what we discussed in today's session, what can you do to keep yourself from thinking that it's unfair that you weren't selected and that you are a total failure as a result?

Client: To help me remember that everything isn't fair, I'm going to visualize myself on the highway trying to keep up with the person in the next lane and see myself as the one who gets picked up going a mile over the limit.

Counselor: And what would you say to yourself if that happened?

Client: It's not fair—but there's not much I can do about it.

Counselor: And what can you do to keep from thinking of yourself as a total failure?

Client: I just have to remember that I wouldn't think of my boyfriend as a total failure if he didn't get into something like NHS, and I guess I'm not, either.

Counselor: Very good. But I know that you sometimes have a difficult time remembering these rational thoughts and consequently upset yourself. Since the rational coping statements seemed to work well for you last time, for your homework assignment I'd like you to make some additional rational self-talk cards that you can keep with you to refer to if you find yourself getting upset about the issues we discussed. How does that sound?

Client: I think that's a good idea because I know I'll keep thinking about this for a while.

Counselor: Thanks for working hard in this session. I'll see you in two weeks, and we can follow up on your homework.

Summary of Case Study

Working with teenagers to help them give up their demands that everything "should be fair" is often difficult, as Kristen's case illustrates. The analogy of the speeding ticket seemed to help her see that some things just aren't fair, as she referred to it later in the session when asked what she could do to remember that unfair things do happen. Asking her what she would have thought of her boyfriend if he had been rejected also proved to be a good way for her to realize she wasn't a failure; but this point was reinforced with the role play and the "proof of failure" lists, because it often takes several different strategies to get the point across.

Not surprisingly, Kristen continued to hold onto some anger about not being accepted into NHS. In the next session, she reverted to how awful it was, because everyone would think less of her, she wouldn't get good scholarships or other sorts of recognition, and this had "ruined" her high school experience. To help Kristen put this matter in perspective, her homework assignment for the following week was to cut out articles from the newspaper that represented what she considered to be "awful" events. When she came in the following week, I wrote her issue (her rejection from NHS) on a card and then put a strip of masking tape on the floor, labeling one end "Truly Awful" and the other end "Not Awful at All." I then had her arrange her articles, including her card, on the continuum. Interestingly enough, her card was not even close to the "Truly Awful" end. In the next session, Kristen announced that I would be quite proud of her because, during a very stressful time at school, her mother had commented on how awful things were for Kristen, to which Kristen replied, "Being stressed out at school is nothing compared to an earthquake where hundreds of people died."

As this case illustrates, it often takes a combination of disputational approaches for the process to work. Kristen continued to work on her anger, self-downing, and low frustration tolerance; after several more sessions, she made good progress.

Interventions for Typical Developmental Problems

In some ways, growing up is very different today than it was even 30 or 40 years ago. Although it used to be that people took drugs if they had a physical illness, today many young people use drugs or engage in self-mutilation to numb their emotional pain. Depression among children and adolescents used to be rare. Now it is almost an epidemic. Years ago, suicide was something that rarely occurred among young people. Now it is the second-leading cause of death among adolescents (Vernon, 1999b).

Yet in many respects, children and adolescents today experience many of the same problems growing up as they would have years ago. To varying degrees, young people always have, and probably always will, deal with issues about belonging, anxiety about their future after high school, and self-consciousness during puberty. Fighting with friends, mourning the breakup of a romantic relationship, and struggling to compete academically or athletically are also problems that cross generational boundaries.

What we must remember, however, is that, even though typical developmental problems haven't changed much over the decades, change has occurred in the cultural and social factors that affect the lives of young people. Children in today's society grow up faster. As Mary Pipher, author of *Reviving Ophelia*, noted, "The protected place in space and time that we once called childhood has grown shorter" (1994, p. 28). Nowadays, children and adolescents have more to contend with, in addition to typical, normal developmental problems. As noted in chapter 1, irrational thinking and developmental limitations affect children's and adolescents' ability to interpret and respond appropriately to both situational and typical developmental events. Consequently, far too many young people react in unhealthy ways.

If our charge as practitioners is to help children and adolescents "grow up without giving up," it is important that we help them understand what is normal and teach them effective ways to deal with typical developmental problems so that life doesn't seem so overwhelming. The purpose of this chapter is to provide REBT interventions for typical developmental problems concerning relationships, performance and competition, self-consciousness, and transitions. Interventions both for children and for adolescents will be provided, followed by a case study that illustrates the application of the concepts discussed.

Relationships

A significant number of the problems that children and adolescents present in counseling involve relationships—with peers, siblings, parents, teachers, romantic partners, or authority figures. Waters (1982) noted that children irrationally believe that it's awful if others don't like them, and adolescents believe that it would be awful to be a social loser and that they must conform with their peers. According to Ellis (1996), two core irrational beliefs relate to relationships: "I absolutely must, at practically all times, be successful at important performances and relationships—or else I, as a person, am inadequate and worthless!" and "Other people absolutely must practically always treat me considerately, kindly, fairly, or lovingly—or else they are no damned good and deserve no joy in their existence" (p. 13).

It is also important to look at relationships from a developmental perspective. According to an expert on child stress (Youngs, 1995), issues involving relationships begin as early as the first and second grades, at which time children identify worries related to peer ridicule, teacher disapproval, or separating from parents. By the third grade, a key stressor is the disappointment in not being chosen for a team, and this problem continues to be a major source of stress through the eighth grade. Fear of losing a friend, being ridiculed or unpopular, or being disliked by a teacher are also significant issues in elementary school. In middle school and high school, adolescents worry about being unpopular or rejected. Romantic involvement, family relationships, and conflict with adults over role definition are pertinent issues for this age group as well.

It is important not to underestimate the anxiety, frustration, anger, and self-downing that occur in response to relationship difficulties. For this reason, it is imperative to identify effective interventions to address typical relationship problems.

Tuning Out Teasing

RATIONALE   Like it or not, most children cannot escape getting teased. Although most children want to make the teaser stop teasing, the reality is that oftentimes that doesn't happen. It is far more empowering to help them learn to tolerate (not to like) the teasing.

MATERIALS
- ▷ A sheet of paper with the letters A, B, and C printed down the left side
- ▷ A pencil
- ▷ A shoe box
- ▷ Construction paper
- ▷ Scissors
- ▷ Crayons
- ▷ Glue
- ▷ Tuning Out Teasing Strategy (p. 224)

PROCEDURE
1. When your client complains about being teased or being called names, ask him for a specific example and have him write it on the sheet of paper beside the letter A (activating event). If necessary, write this and subsequent examples for the client.

2. Ask him to identify how he felt and how he responded when this happened and to write this beside the C (emotional and behavioral consequences).

3. Help him identify what he was thinking when he was called these names, listing these thoughts beside the B (beliefs). Generally, when children are teased, they feel either angry ("They shouldn't do this—it's not fair") or frustrated ("I can't stand this") or depressed and down on themselves ("They are right about me").

4. After some discussion about his beliefs and emotional and behavioral reactions, help him see the difference between not liking to be called names and thinking he can't stand it.

5. Also ask him how likely it is that he will change the teaser and what strategies he has tried so far that have or haven't worked.

---

6. Indicate that you will teach him a strategy he can use to tune out teasing so that he doesn't have to get as upset.

7. Instruct him to cover the shoe box with construction paper and draw dials on it to make it look like a radio.

8. Using the analogy of tuning a radio to a different station if he does not like what he is hearing, refer to the Tuning Out Teasing Strategy and review the concepts with him. Invite him to cut out the Strategy and glue it to his "radio" (the shoe box) as a visual reminder of what he can do to tune out teasing in the future.

9. For further reinforcement and practice, ask him to explain the concept of tuning out teasing to peers or siblings.

Tuning Out Teasing Strategy

When someone calls you a name, here is what you do:

1. You listen to it.

2. You think: "Am I what they say I am?"; "Can words really hurt me if what they are saying about me isn't true?"; "And even if what they say about me is true, does that mean I am a horrible kid?"

3. You ask yourself: "Do I want to give them the satisfaction of getting upset?"; "Can I change them?"; "What are my choices?"

4. You "tune out the teasing" by changing the channel on your radio after thinking carefully about these questions.

5. You realize that you aren't happy about being teased, but you can tolerate it.

6. You also know that what they are saying about you maybe isn't even true—and even if it were true, it wouldn't make you a horrible kid.

7. You know that you have some choices about how to react and that you probably can't change the teaser, so you are better off changing how you think and react.

Fights with Friends

RATIONALE   It is unlikely that anyone escapes from middle childhood unscathed by fights with friends. As common an occurrence as this is, it still can seem devastating to children, often interfering with their ability to concentrate in school. In many cases, fights result from assumptions that children make about each other, as well as from their lack of effective communication or coping strategies.

MATERIALS   ▷ Blank index cards

▷ A pencil

▷ Tic-Tac-Toe Board (p. 226)

▷ Fights with Friends Assumptions and Coping Strategies Cards (p. 227)

PROCEDURE   1. Before starting the game, talk about what assumptions are and how they can cause problems in friendships.

2. Invite the client to play a game that will help her deal with these issues.

3. To play the game, take turns with your client drawing an Assumptions Card and a Coping Strategies Card.

4. During each turn, each player has to decide whether the child in the situation is thinking rationally (i.e., not making assumptions) and is demonstrating effective behavioral coping strategies. If not, the player has to identify what the assumptions or ineffective coping strategies are and discuss how to change them before putting an *X* (by the client) or an *O* (by the counselor) on the board. The game is over when one player gets three marks in a row.

5. Play the game again to reinforce the concepts.

6. After you have finished playing the game for the second time, debrief with your client by asking her how she can stop herself from making assumptions.

7. Offer your client the blank index cards and invite her to make a new set of cards, using her own examples, and play the game again.

Tic-Tac-Toe Board

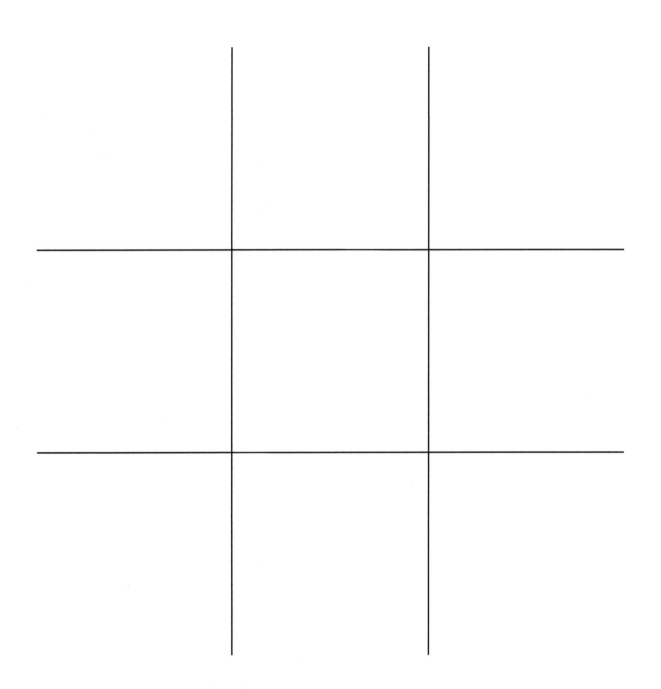

Fights with Friends Assumptions and Coping Strategies Cards

Assumptions	Coping Strategies
You see your best friend sitting next to someone else at lunch. You assume that she doesn't want to be your friend anymore.	You are playing kick ball, and someone calls you a cheater. You immediately throw the ball at that kid so hard that he starts to cry.
You and some friends are sitting at the lunch table. Another student walks by, and one of your friends starts saying bad things about this person. You politely tell this friend that you don't think those things are true and you don't want to listen to them.	Several of your friends are playing jump rope. You ask if you can play, and they say no. You wish they had let you play, but you just go and invite someone else to start a game with you.
Two classmates are sitting on the bus. When you start walking up the aisle, they start whispering. You assume they are saying bad things about you.	One of your friends says bad things about you on the way to school, but you just ignore the remarks because you know you aren't stupid and ugly.
Someone bumps into you while you are lined up to go down the slide. You assume he did this on purpose, so you get mad and push him out of the way.	You want to play one thing, and your friends want to play something different. You get so mad when they won't play your game that you stand by the fence and pout.
You want to play with your friend after school, but she says she is going to someone else's house. You're disappointed, but you just decide to ask someone else over to play.	You get invited to a pizza party with a classmate you don't especially like. You don't really want to go, but you think that it might hurt his feelings if you don't go, so you say yes and end up having a good time.
You don't get asked to a birthday party, and you feel so left out that you stay in your room all day long and refuse to speak to anyone.	You ask a classmate to play soccer with you during recess, and she says she doesn't want to play. You assume she doesn't like you.

Rejected, Dejected

RATIONALE Being rejected from a team, a sleepover, a party, or a club can seem catastrophic to some children. However, because most children experience rejection at some point in their lives, it is important to teach them effective ways to deal with it.

MATERIALS ▷ Several sheets of paper

▷ A file folder

▷ A pencil

▷ The song Rejected, Dejected—Oh, That's Me (p. 229)

PROCEDURE 1. When your client comes to counseling feeling upset about a recent rejection, share this song with him as a way of introducing positive ways to cope. If you wish, give him a copy for himself.

2. After teaching the song to the client, you can both sing it together. Then discuss how the child in the song dealt with being rejected: by finding something else to do and not thinking there was something wrong with him because the others didn't want to play with him.

3. Invite your client to write his own songs about how to deal with this problem. He can keep his songs in a file folder or on his desk at school as a catchy reminder of how to cope with rejection.

Rejected, Dejected—Oh, That's Me
(Sung to the tune of "Jingle Bells")

Dashing to the team
With a lot of steam;
Over the hill I go,
Laughing all the way.

But when I got to school,
Oh, the kids were cruel;
They told me that I couldn't play,
And that was their final rule.

Oh, sad I am, sad I am,
I really wanted to play;
But if these kids are mean to me,
I don't want to stay, so—

I will go, find some fun, something else to do;
Just 'cuz they don't let me play doesn't mean that I'm no good, so—
Off I go, off I go, dashing through the woods;
I can find something else to do that might be just as good.

Words Will Never Hurt Me

RATIONALE   Every child is familiar with the saying "Sticks and stones may break my bones, but words will never hurt me." Unfortunately, this is usually not the case: Children *do* let words hurt them. The purpose of this intervention is to teach them how not to let this happen.

MATERIALS   ▷ A pair of earmuffs or earplugs

▷ A sheet of paper

▷ A pencil

PROCEDURE   1. When your client comes to counseling complaining because someone has said something about her that hurt her feelings, ask her to repeat this saying: "Sticks and stones may break my bones, but words will never hurt me *unless I let them.*"

2. Discuss the idea of not *letting* others hurt her feelings.

3. Ask her to make a list of hurtful things others say to her and then put on the earmuffs or the earplugs.

4. Explain that you are going to read the hurtful things one by one, but because she will have on the earmuffs or earplugs, she is to assume that she just can't hear these words. In short, as you read the words, your client is to ignore you.

5. After you have finished reading the list, ask how it felt for her to ignore you, as if she couldn't hear the words.

6. Discuss the fact that, although in real life she will hear what is said, she can pretend that she is wearing earmuffs or earplugs to block out the words, therefore not letting those words hurt her.

7. Discuss other ways of not letting the words hurt: One way is to challenge whether what others say is true or to think about what good it will do you to get upset.

8. Engage the client in a reverse role play that puts her in the situation of calling someone (in this case, you) names.

9. As she hurls insults at you, pretend you don't hear them, and then utter some rational coping statements aloud, such as "These are just words, so they can't hurt me"; "What they say isn't true, so why upset myself?"; "Why give them the satisfaction of showing them that I'm upset when I can choose to ignore them?"

10. Reverse the roles so your client has an opportunity to practice rational coping statements.

Fickle Friends

RATIONALE   Especially in early adolescence, "fickle friend" issues are common. Because young teens are so emotionally vulnerable, these on-again, off-again relationships can be a major source of stress. It is very important to equip young adolescents, in particular, with some emotional muscle to help them through these troubling times.

MATERIALS   ▷ A pencil

▷ Fickle Friend Worksheet (p. 234)

PROCEDURE   1. Give your client the worksheet and have him finish each sentence.

2. After the client has completed the unfinished sentences, discuss the feelings he identified.

3. Assuming he listed negative feelings such as anger, hurt, depression, or upset, work with the client to identify the irrational beliefs he holds about several of the examples.

> For instance, if he was angry because he didn't get invited to a party, he might think that it wasn't fair, that others shouldn't reject him, and that he should have been invited.

> Furthermore, if he was hurt or depressed, he might be thinking that no one likes him, that it's horrible to be left out, and that he won't ever get invited to a party.

4. Using the example of a friend's bad-mouthing him, help your client see how he can build emotional muscle by changing how he thinks. First, have him identify the irrational beliefs associated with his friend's insults.

5. After the client has identified these irrational beliefs, teach him how to dispute them:

> "Where is the evidence that you are what they say you are?"

> "How does it make sense that you are stupid if you are on the honor roll?"

> "How does it help you to be so upset about this if you can't change what comes out of your friend's mouth?"

6. Encourage discussion about how disputing the irrational beliefs results in less upsetting emotions.

7. After working through several of the unfinished sentence examples with your client, have him select a real-life issue and identify the irrational beliefs and how to dispute them.

Fickle Friend Worksheet

1. If a friend suddenly stops speaking to me,

   I feel _____.

2. If a friend starts bad-mouthing me,

   I feel _____.

3. If a friend starts being best friends with someone else,

   I feel _____.

4. To me, losing a best friend

   is _____.

5. If some of my friends go somewhere and don't call me,

   I feel _____.

6. If a friend ignores me at school,

   I feel _____.

7. If I don't get invited to a party,

   I feel _____.

8. If a friend starts flirting with someone I like,

   I feel _____.

Relationship Realities

RATIONALE By nature, adolescents seem to operate with tunnel vision—especially when it comes to relationships. When problems occur, they are often blindsided and devastated. All too often, their irrational thinking results in self-defeating behavior. This intervention is designed to help them look realistically at romantic relationships.

MATERIALS ▷ A pencil

▷ Inside/Outside Squares (p. 237)

PROCEDURE 1. When your adolescent client describes problems in her romantic relationships, she more than likely does not understand that love *doesn't* conquer all.

On one hand, she may find herself paired with a partner who ignores her, treats her disrespectfully, or is abusive—but she tolerates it because she is "in love."

On the other hand, her partner may treat her as royalty but may also be involved in illegal or other sorts of negative behaviors that eventually could have a detrimental effect on the relationship and her.

2. A graphic way to help your client see the situation more clearly is to give her a copy of the Inside/Outside Squares. Then have her do the following:

In the inside square, she should list all the positive traits about the relationship and the individual with whom she is involved.

In the outside square, she should list all the negative realities represented in the relationship.

3. After the client has finished writing, process her observations by discussing (a) the realities she may have been ignoring because of her tunnel vision and (b) the positive aspects of the relationship that she wants to maintain.

4. Because there is no guarantee that her partner will change, brainstorm with her about what she personally might be able to do to improve the relationship.

5. Following up on what she identified in the boxes, have your client weigh the pros and cons to help her determine whether or not to stay in the relationship.

Inside/Outside Squares

Negative Realities

Positive Traits

Problems with Parents

RATIONALE With few exceptions and to varying degrees, adolescents have problems with their parents. They frequently have difficulty seeing things from their parents' perspective and feel entitled to do things their way. These feelings are often reflected in their anger and aggressive communicative styles.

MATERIALS ▷ 3 sheets of paper

▷ A pencil

PROCEDURE 1. When your client describes problems related to a conflict of interests over issues involving independence, ask him to put his name at the top of a sheet of paper and list what he thinks he *should* be able to do that his parents are resisting.

2. Have him write the heading "Parents" at the top of the second sheet and identify what he thinks his parents' perspective is on these issues.

3. After you have an understanding of your client's issues, engage in a reverse role play with the client that should proceed as follows:

> The client plays the part of the parent, who is responding to what the adolescent (played by you) wants.

> First, role-play your "requests" in an angry, demanding manner to elicit the parent's possible reaction.

> Replay the same scenario, but this time be more assertive than aggressive.

> Discuss with your client the differences between the two approaches and ask him which method he thinks will give him a better chance of getting what he wants.

4. After the reverse role play, point out to the client that his anger and aggression come from his beliefs that he *should* be able to do whatever he wants and that it is awful if he doesn't get his way.

5. Urge him to examine the difference between *strongly preferring* or *wanting* to do something and *demanding* that he get his way.

6. Because your client may tend to overgeneralize, claiming that he *never* gets to do what he wants, draw a continuum on a sheet of paper, labeling one end "Never" and the other end "Always." Have him identify where his parents are on the continuum by asking, "Is it really true that your parents *never* let you do what you want?"

7. After discussion, ask the client to reevaluate his list of independence issues and identify the most important issues for him, given that he might not get everything he wants.

8. Practice the role play again, but this time instruct the client to play himself and also to use assertive communication.

9. Debrief the role play by focusing on the advantages of the assertive style and telling your client that, to be assertive, he needs to change his demands to preferences.

Romantic Relationships

RATIONALE One of the major sources of stress for adolescents is the romantic relationship, mainly because adolescents tend to awfulize, catastrophize, and overgeneralize. They don't realize that romantic relationships in high school are probably not going to last a lifetime, and yet they mourn a breakup as if it were meant to last forever. Because their sense of time is so immediate and their pain is often very intense, it is critical to help them deal rationally with romantic involvement so that they don't overreact—a response that can result in serious negative consequences.

MATERIALS ▷ Romantic Relationships story (p. 241)

PROCEDURE 1. Give a copy of the Romantic Relationships story to your client and have her read it.

2. After your client has read the story, discuss with her how it might apply to her own romantic relationship, emphasizing that overgeneralizing and catastrophizing can have a negative impact on how she perceives things. Some general questions to ask include the following:

   "Will it really be the end of the world if you break up with your boyfriend?"

   "Is it beyond the realm of possibility that you will never find someone else?"

   "Even though breaking up can be painful, is it really the worst thing that could ever happen to you?"

Romantic Relationships

Maria was very upset. Her parents had just informed her that they were moving at the end of the month to a town about 100 miles away. Maria couldn't imagine having to leave the place she had grown up in. But more important, how could she leave her boyfriend? All she could think about is that she would never get to see her José, that he would find someone he liked better, and that they would break up. The more Maria thought about this scenario, the more depressed she became—to the point that her parents sent her to see a counselor.

Maria told the counselor that she didn't want to live. This relationship meant too much to her, and she couldn't stand the thought of not being able to see José every day. She knew the relationship couldn't last if they lived so far apart, and she didn't know what she would do without him. They did everything together, and she swore she would never find someone as great as José—and she didn't even want to think about that. She told the counselor she'd rather die than have to move away from him.

First, the counselor acknowledged that this relationship must be very important to Maria. Then she asked her if she had been in any previous relationships that she considered serious, and she indicated that she had. The counselor asked Maria to describe how she had gotten over those relationships when they ended, and Maria said that initially she had just stayed very busy and done a lot with friends—and then she eventually found someone to date. When the counselor asked her why that approach wouldn't work for her this time—if in fact this relationship couldn't withstand the long distance—Maria had to think a bit. She finally said that this relationship was more serious than the other two, and that's why she didn't think she could get over it.

The counselor then challenged Maria by asking her if she thought her previous relationships would be long lasting, and she said yes. The counselor then asked her to think about what would happen if it turned out that this relationship wasn't "the one," either, because relationships during high school are usually not long lasting. She emphasized that, although at this moment it may seem like a very special relationship, there is a good chance it might not always be that way—and if Maria killed herself, she would never have another chance to find someone who might be even more special.

Maria admitted that this was a possibility she hadn't thought about. She and the counselor discussed other assumptions she was making (for example, the fact that she was only moving 100 miles away but thought she would never again see her boyfriend was probably an overexaggeration). There wasn't any guarantee that either of them would find someone else. There also was no proof that she absolutely couldn't stand it if they broke up; after all, she had been through this type of situation before and had survived. In reality, Maria would be very sad. But would there literally be nothing worse than breaking up with José? After she thought about these things, she admitted that she might have been overreacting to this particular situation. She agreed to stay alive, take one step at a time, and remember that she could stand it if things didn't work out—even though they might not have worked out the way she had wanted.

Performance and Competition

As children enter school, their social arena expands, and they become more aware of themselves in comparison to others. This awareness often becomes a source of anxiety as they strive to perform well and compete for leadership positions in groups, starting spots on athletic teams, scholastic recognition, and overall popularity. Waters (1982) noted that one of the irrational beliefs for children is that "I must win" (p. 572). Ellis (1996) identified a core belief as "I absolutely must, at practically all times, be successful at important performances and relationships—or else I, as a person, am inadequate and worthless!" (p. 13).

The pressure to perform and compete is often deliberately or inadvertently reinforced by parents and teachers. Sometimes children assume that adults expect high performance, and this assumption may cause children to place unreasonably high standards on themselves. Whatever the source, the anxiety over performance can create physical (e.g., somatic complaints, stress-related illnesses) and behavioral (e.g., avoidance, compromised performance) problems. The following interventions specifically address the performance and competition issues that children and adolescents can learn to deal with in healthy ways.

I Have to Win

RATIONALE   This is a story that can be used with children who think they have to win.

MATERIALS   ▷ I Have to Win story (p. 244)

PROCEDURE   1. Read the I Have to Win story to your client. If you wish, give your client a copy of the story as well.

2. After you have finished, discuss the issues Jorge was dealing with and how his friend helped him realize that he didn't always have to win or be the best at everything.

3. Ask your client for examples of how he can apply this lesson to his own life when he struggles with the pressure of thinking he has to win.

I Have to Win

Jorge was trying out for the soccer team. He and some of the other kids in the neighborhood were really excited about it. The night before the tryouts, Jorge's older brother told him that if he didn't make the A team, he'd be a real loser. Jorge went to bed that night with a knot in his stomach: He didn't want to be a loser, but there were lots of kids trying out, and some of them were a lot older and probably better than he was. He wasn't sure he could make the A team.

On the day of the tryouts, Jorge was really nervous. His brother was on the sidelines watching; once, he even walked over to where Jorge and his friends were waiting and said, "Hey, wimps. . . . You'd better make the A team or me and my friends won't give you the time of day." Jorge was embarrassed, and all he could think about was how he would be able to face his brother if he didn't do well.

Pretty soon it was Jorge's turn to try out. He was already so nervous because of his brother's taunting that, by the end of tryouts, he knew he hadn't done very well. He was wishing he hadn't even thought about going out for the team in the first place. He must have looked pretty sad, because one of his friends came over and asked him what was wrong.

"Well, you heard what my brother said—that he and his friends wouldn't speak to us if we didn't make the A team," said Jorge. "He said we'd be wimps and losers if we didn't get picked."

"Hey, man," said Adam. "I can't believe you are letting that get to you. Your brother thinks he's a big guy, but so what if we don't make the A team? We're not losers. There are lots of really good players trying out, and if we don't make the A team, we'll still get to play on the B team— it's not that big a deal. Just ignore what he says. He's just trying to get to you."

"I hadn't really thought of it that way, and I guess you're right," Jorge said. "I hate it when he says that stuff; and then I feel like I need to win, and I get so worried about it."

"Well, that's just one kid talking," Adam replied. "And even though it would be great to make A team, we're not losers if we don't, right?"

"Right," said Jorge, who remembered this conversation with Adam later that day, after his brother taunted him because he failed to make the A team. "You think you always have to win, but I don't," Jorge said to his brother. "So just leave me alone! I'm not a loser just because I'm on the B team."

Making the Grade

RATIONALE   Many children feel pressured to get top grades. Although this pressure often results in perfectionism, it also can cause children to feel compelled to compete with peers or siblings and to think they are "less than" if they don't perform as well. The anxiety that results from classroom spelling or math drills, comparing report cards or test scores, or reading aloud can be significant. This intervention helps address these issues.

MATERIALS   ▷ A 2 × 3–foot sheet of clear, heavy plastic or paper, divided into six squares, each square shaded or marked with a different color: red, blue, black, green, yellow, and purple (see sample on p. 246)

▷ A pencil

▷ Making the Grade Scenarios (p. 247; for you to record the client's responses)

Note: This game is played like Twister.

PROCEDURE   1. One by one, read the Making the Grade Scenarios to your client and ask her to respond verbally to each.

2. As the client responds to each question, she moves on the sheet of plastic as directed by the scenario.

3. Record your client's responses to each scenario, and, at the end of the game, debrief by discussing what she said to herself when she felt pressured to perform well. Examples might include the following:

    "Others might think I am dumb."

    "They shouldn't do better than I do."

    "I will let others down if I don't do well."

4. Discuss feelings she may have had—such as embarrassment, anxiety, worry, or confidence—that depended on what she was thinking.

5. Point out the connection between thoughts and feelings. If the client typically has negative emotions in situations such as those discussed in this intervention, help her see how she can become less anxious or embarrassed by using rational self-talk.

---

6. To make this concept of rational self-talk more concrete, use one of the scenarios (e.g., the spelling drill) as an example and verbalize what your client could tell herself that would be more rational: "I hope I spell the words right and don't have to sit down, but just because I miss a word doesn't mean I am a stupid kid. I might be a little embarrassed, but it's not that big a deal."

7. Have your client select from the various scenarios, or encourage her to use her own examples to practice rational self-talk.

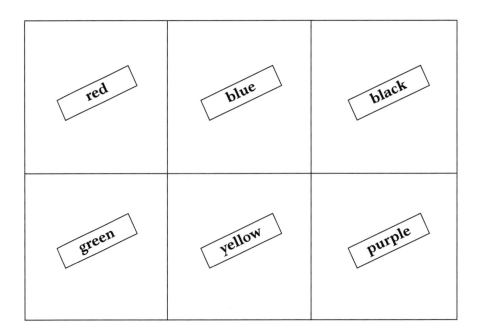

Chapter 5 • Interventions for Typical Developmental Problems

Making the Grade Scenarios

1. Your teacher asks you to read aloud. You feel _____ because you are thinking _____ (left foot on red).

2. During a math lesson, your teacher divides your class into teams, which take turns doing timed problems on the board. If you miss your problem, you have to sit down. You feel _____ because you are thinking _____ (right foot on blue).

3. During a spelling lesson, your teacher has everyone stand up, divides your class into teams, and then gives the students words to spell. Those who misspell a word must sit down. The team that has the most people left standing doesn't have to take the final spelling test. You feel _____ because you are thinking _____ (right hand on green).

4. All week long, you have been studying for a history test. Your dad told you he'd give you $5 if you got every single question right. You feel _____ because you are thinking _____ (left hand on purple).

5. The teacher says all the students will read their short stories aloud and then vote on the best one. You thought your story was good, but someone else got the most votes. You feel _____ because you are thinking _____ (left foot on black).

6. One of your friends asks to see what you got on your report card. You are afraid he got better grades than you did, and you feel _____ because you are thinking _____ (right foot on yellow).

7. The student with the best grades for the week gets to be the line leader. You thought you would get to be the leader, but someone else did. You feel _____ because you are thinking _____ (left hand on blue).

8. The student sitting next to you asks to see how many questions you got right on your reading test. You got 75 percent correct. You feel _____ because you are thinking _____ (right hand on purple).

Not a Complete Failure

RATIONALE To help ease their anxiety over performance and competition, children need to remind themselves that they are not complete failures if they don't do everything well in performance situations.

MATERIALS ▷ A pencil

▷ Not a Complete Failure story (p. 249)

PROCEDURE 1. Have your client read the Not a Complete Failure story, or read the story to him.

2. When he has finished reading, have him write or dictate his own rational ending.

3. After your client has an ending to the story, discuss how he can avoid thinking of himself as a complete failure on the basis of only one poor performance.

4. Have him relate this concept to his own performance situation.

Not a Complete Failure

Bobby was pouting. He had just finished his piano lesson, and the teacher told him he wasn't playing one of the songs very well. Bobby started to cry. "I can't play anything right," he sobbed. "I just want to quit because I'll never be as good as my sister. I'll just make a fool of myself in the recital, and I can't stand having you always tell me that I'm no good." The teacher just looked at Bobby and said, . . .

_____

_____

_____

_____

_____

_____

_____

_____

_____

_____

_____

_____

Doing the Best I Can

RATIONALE   Children need to remind themselves that doing the best they can is important. They should also keep in mind that, if they fail to achieve as well as someone else or get the top score, they don't gain anything by putting themselves down.

MATERIALS   ▷ A jump rope or a basketball

PROCEDURE   1. Have your client jump rope or bounce a basketball in time to the chant.

2. Tell her that jumping rope or bouncing the ball in time to the chant will serve as a quick and easy reminder to her just to do the best she can in situations where she is trying to achieve.

3. As she jumps rope or bounces the ball, teach the client the following chant, personalized with her own name.

Down at the school, where the sun shines in,
There sits _____ with her hand on her chin.
Along comes the teacher and taps her on the hand,
And tells _____ just to do the best she can.
So _____ starts thinking and does her best.
How many did she get right? Can you guess?

The client should keep count as she jumps rope or bounces the ball until she misses.

4. Debrief this activity by asking the client to describe what it means to do the best she can.

5. Show her how she can avoid putting herself down, even when she really tries hard and does her best but still doesn't do well. She could tell herself things such as these:

"I'm doing the best I can, and I'm not a failure if I miss something."

"Even if I miss things this time, I can maybe be better next time."

6. Invite the client to make up additional chants along this same theme.

Best of the Class

RATIONALE By the time students reach high school, pressure begins to mount to be at the top of the class if they plan to compete for scholarships, get accepted to good colleges, or be competitive in the job market. Clients often think that if they aren't the best, then they are the worst. This intervention—bolstered by the use of a continuum that helps them to gain a better perspective—is designed for clients who think it is awful not to be the best.

MATERIALS ▷ A strip of masking tape and a marker

▷ A sheet of paper

▷ A pencil

PROCEDURE 1. Place the strip of masking tape across the floor, labeling one end "The Best of the Class" and the other end "The Worst of the Class."

2. Ask your client to stand at a place on the continuum that most realistically represents where he thinks he is now and mark that with an *X*.

3. Ask him to stand on the spot where he thinks he will be at the end of the year.

4. Tell him that, if he isn't at the very top of the continuum, it doesn't automatically mean he is at the very bottom.

5. Ask him to identify in writing his beliefs about being at the very top and the very bottom and about being where he is now (assuming he isn't already at the top or the bottom).

6. Homing in on the beliefs he identifies, help him to dispute his self-downing messages ("I'm no good if I'm not the best"); his catastrophizing ("It's awful if I'm not the best in the class; I won't get good scholarships or any recognition if I'm not the best"); and his low frustration tolerance ("I can't stand not being the best").

Pressure to Perform

RATIONALE   Although the pressure to perform comes from a variety of sources, for high-achieving students, the strongest pressure frequently comes from self-set expectations. Clients frequently experience symptoms of stress and identify shame, embarrassment, anxiety, and guilt as common emotional consequences of that stress. This intervention is intended to help adolescents reduce the performance pressure they put on themselves.

MATERIALS   ▷ A pencil

▷ Pressure to Perform Sentence Stems (p. 253)

PROCEDURE   1. When your client discusses problems she is having with feeling pressure to perform, invite her to complete the unfinished sentences in the handout.

2. Review your client's responses to the unfinished sentences and help her dispute any irrational beliefs related to performance that would be reflected by negative feelings or self-downing.

3. To help the client understand the disputing process in another way, ask her to imagine that her best friend is thinking it is the worst thing in the world not to be a high achiever, berates herself when her performance falls short of her expectations, and is totally devastated if her class rank drops a point.

4. Engage in a role play in which you will be the best friend who is complaining about these issues; meanwhile, the client's role is to "counsel" you about it.

5. After the role play, discuss whether the client agreed with the friend about how awful it was and—if not—what it is that makes it so difficult to follow the same advice or line of thinking that she gave to the friend.

Pressure to Perform Sentence Stems

1. When I don't get the top grade, I feel _____.

2. When someone else does better than I do at music, sports, or academics, I feel _____.

3. If my class rank goes down one point, I feel _____.

4. The best thing about being a high achiever is _____.

5. The worst thing about being a high achiever is _____.

6. When I don't do as well as I think I should, I feel _____.

7. If I'm not the best, it means I'm _____.

8. I beat myself up most over my performance in _____.

Winning Isn't Everything

RATIONALE Adolescents naturally lack some degree of perspective on their lives and assume that their whole future will be affected if they are not the best player on their team or the best musician or the top student. You can use this intervention to help them perceive their performance realistically.

MATERIALS
▷ Several obituaries from a local newspaper

▷ A sheet of paper

▷ A pencil

PROCEDURE
1. When your client awfulizes about such things as his failure to be the best student, win every game, or be awarded the most prestigious scholarship, ask him to read the obituaries.

2. When he has finished reading, have him comment on whether reference is made in any of the obituaries to the deceased's performance in high school.

3. Ask the client to write his own obituary, stressing that he must write in detail about all his shortcomings or failures as an athlete, musician, student, actor, and so forth.

4. When he has finished, discuss how he felt writing his own obituary and whether he thinks his high school performance is really going to matter years from now.

5. Help him focus on how he can stop taking himself so seriously by not dwelling on every imperfection or perceived failure.

Pick Me

RATIONALE   As adolescents look ahead toward graduation, the competition for scholarships, honors, and awards can be a major source of stress for those in the running. It can also result in feelings of inferiority and shame for those who do not make the grade. This intervention shows adolescents how to deal with the stress caused by competition.

MATERIALS   ▷ A pencil

▷ Pick Me Scenarios (p. 256)

PROCEDURE   1. Give your client a copy of the Pick Me Scenarios and have her answer the questions that follow each scenario.

2. After your client has shared her responses, help her replace any irrational beliefs with more rational ones by using rational emotive imagery in the following manner:

   Have her pick one of these scenarios—or one of her own choosing, if none of these applies to her.

   Have her close her eyes and vividly imagine the rejection.

   You may help her along by painting the following picture for her: "You receive the bad news in front of lots of other students and parents, hear people applaud because you didn't get it, and see the television news cameras focusing on the winner."

   Have her get in touch with how she would feel if she experienced this.

   Once she has envisioned her feelings, ask her to imagine that, instead of feeling devastated, she feels disappointed that she didn't receive this honor.

   Have her focus on what she had to tell herself to experience the more moderate, appropriate feeling of disappointment instead of the feeling of devastation.

3. Debrief by discussing the client's own experiences with competition and how she can deal with her feelings if she does not live up to her own expectations.

Pick Me Scenarios

1. *You really wanted to be elected to the National Thespian Society, but you didn't make it.*

   If this happened to you, how would you feel? _____

   _____

   What would you think? _____

   _____

2. *You were hoping to get elected captain of the basketball team, but one of your teammates got the vote over you.*

   If this happened to you, how would you feel? _____

   _____

   What would you think? _____

   _____

3. *You applied for a $1,000 scholarship that you thought you had a good chance of winning, but you lost.*

   If this happened to you, how would you feel? _____

   _____

   What would you think? _____

   _____

4. *You thought you would win first place in the state speech contest, but you finished second.*

   If this happened to you, how would you feel? _____

   _____

   What would you think? _____

   _____

Self-Consciousness

With society's strong emphasis on people's physical image and their comparisons to fashion models and star athletes, it should come as no surprise that many young people are very self-conscious about the way they look and act. In some circles, children feel left out and different if they are not wearing designer clothes that their families might not be able to afford. In other instances, children as young as 9, or even 8, years of age are beginning to watch what they eat for fear of getting fat. As they reach puberty, many adolescents become obsessed with how they look. This obsession accounts for the many hours they spend in front of the mirror, making sure that every hair is perfectly in place or agonizing over a minuscule pimple that, in their minds, is gigantic. In the overall scheme of things, these physical imperfections are minor issues; however, self-consciousness remains a key source of anxiety for children and adolescents.

Some of the issues related to self-consciousness are also related to self-acceptance. Additional interventions are included in this chapter because they address more specific developmental aspects of this issue.

I Feel Strange

RATIONALE   Younger children often feel self-conscious about being different from others. As they begin to mature, often at rates that don't correspond with those of their peers, they may feel self-conscious about their activities. By age 10, some children still want to be kids and play with toys, whereas others want to act more grown up and put away their playthings. This intervention helps children learn how to deal with this issue.

MATERIALS   ▷ A sheet of paper

▷ A pencil

▷ I Feel Strange scenario (p. 259)

PROCEDURE   1. Give your client a copy of the I Feel Strange scenario to read, or read it to him.

2. Discuss with him why the fifth grader in this story didn't want his friend to know he was playing school and how he knew that his friend would have considered it babyish.

3. Ask the following question: Although he might have been assuming that his friend thought it was babyish to be playing school, even if his friend thought so, what was wrong with his playing what he wanted to?

4. Ask your client if there is anything about this scenario that applies to him.

5. Ask your client to take either this scenario or one from his own life and write or dictate an ending to it in which the boy doesn't feel so self-conscious—and what he would need to think or do differently to make that happen.

I Feel Strange

You are 10 years old and still like to play school with your younger sister and her friend. Yesterday one of your fifth-grade friends called, and you nearly died of embarrassment when you heard your dad tell him that you were playing school. You wondered why he didn't call you to the phone, but you just went on playing. A few minutes later, your friend poked his head in the playhouse that was set up as a schoolroom. You said hi and began to stammer, saying that you were really bored and didn't have anything better to do. You were afraid to ask him if he wanted to join you, so you just stood there awkwardly.

Keep My Mouth Shut

RATIONALE Wearing braces is something children are apt to feel very self-conscious about. The same can be said about wearing glasses or anything else that sets them apart from their peers. This intervention should help children put their concerns into perspective.

MATERIALS ▷ A toy microphone (or a tape-recorder microphone)

PROCEDURE
1. When your client discusses feeling self-conscious about wearing braces or glasses or even having a new haircut that she doesn't like, try the following role play:

    Tell her that you are a news reporter who is very excited to learn that there are kids in this town who wear braces (or glasses, etc.) and that you want to interview them about this phenomenal personal characteristic.

    Tell her that you will give her a few minutes to think about how important she feels, the advantages of having or wearing this item or having this hairstyle, how cool it is, and how unique and special she feels as a result.

    Conduct the interview, using the microphone to make the role play seem more realistic.

2. After completing this role play, ask the client how she felt when she took what she had considered a negative and turned it into a positive.

3. Debrief this intervention by talking specifically about what your client feels self-conscious about and challenging her assumption that everyone is probably looking at her, that she will always feel strange, or that she can't stand the discomfort of looking the way she does.

4. Discuss what *reframing* is—turning something negative into a positive or looking at it in a different way—and emphasize how the client can apply this concept to her personal situation.

Being Shy

RATIONALE   Children often feel shy about performing in front of others. This intervention gives them some suggestions for how to overcome their shyness by using a limerick that illustrates various issues related to shyness.

MATERIALS   ▷   A sheet of paper

▷   A pencil

▷   Being Shy limerick (p. 262)

PROCEDURE   1.   Read the Being Shy limerick to your client, personalizing it by using the client's name. If you wish, give him a copy.

2.   After reading the limerick, discuss the meaning of the phrase "Being shy is just in your head."

3.   Emphasize how thoughts such as how awkward he thinks he is, how nervous he is about performing, and how terrible it would be to make a blunder cause him to feel shy in front of an audience.

4.   Invite your client to write his own limerick or an advice column to others about how to overcome shyness.

Being Shy

_____ was so shy;
In front of a group he would usually cry.
One day his favorite teacher said,
Being shy is all in your head.
To which _____ replied, "Oh, my; oh, my; oh, my."

So next time you stand in front of a crowd,
Let your voice ring out, clear and loud.
There's no need for fears,
They're just between your ears;
So hold your head high and act very proud.

Well, _____ did what the teacher said;
He remembered that being shy was just in his head.
When it was his turn,
His stomach did churn;
But he did just fine—there was no dread.

 What Works When with Children and Adolescents © 2002 by Ann Vernon. Champaign, IL: Research Press (800) 519-2707

Ugly Duckling

RATIONALE   As a result of teasing or their own perceptions, some children feel like ugly ducklings. This often self-imposed label only contributes to feelings of self-consciousness. This intervention helps children sharpen their perspective on this matter.

MATERIALS   ▷ A sheet of paper with the following words (or categories) written on separate lines: *hair, skin, eyes, nose, mouth, ears, hands, fingers, feet, height,* and *weight*

▷ A pencil

PROCEDURE   1. When your client describes feeling ugly or self-conscious about her appearance, urge her to join the Ugly Duckling Club.

2. Explain that, to be a member of this club, there must be something terribly wrong or ugly about her *entire* appearance: hair color and length; eyes, nose, mouth, and ears; skin color; height and weight; and size of hands, fingers, and feet.

3. Give the client the sheet of paper with the words written on it and indicate that this is an application form. Tell her that, to apply to the club, she has to list something wrong about herself in *each* category.

4. If your client lists something in every category, challenge her perceptions by examining her exaggerations.

5. If she is unable to complete the application, help her see that, although she may not be totally satisfied with some of her features, clearly not everything about her appearance is horrible.

6. Discuss what, if anything, she can change about her appearance if she is dissatisfied, but emphasize that she should accept herself regardless.

Chapter 5 • Interventions for Typical Developmental Problems   **263**

In the Mirror

RATIONALE   Young adolescents construct what Elkind (1998) has called the *imaginary audience*. Because of this belief on the part of adolescents—especially young adolescents—that others are as interested in them as they are interested in themselves, they often fantasize about how others will react to them and become supersensitive and overly concerned about their appearance. Some clients will readily describe to their therapists the anxiety they feel about their appearance, whereas others may exhibit a tendency to respond behaviorally (e.g., by not participating in extracurricular activities or social functions). This intervention, which requires clients to complete sentence stems, is designed to help adolescents reduce their high level of sensitivity, which can contribute to their social anxiety.

MATERIALS   ▷ A magnifying glass

▷ A mirror

▷ A pencil

▷ A sheet of paper

▷ In the Mirror Sentence Stems (p. 266)

PROCEDURE   1.   Have your client complete the sentence stems.

2.   After your client has completed the sentences, he may find it reassuring if you explain the concept of the imaginary audience, emphasizing that it is not uncommon to be overly sensitive about one's appearance at this age. Point out, however, that if this sensitivity interferes with his life, it is important that he deal with it.

3.   Ask the client to pick out the one aspect of his appearance that he finds most bothersome.

4.   Using the mirror and the magnifying glass, ask him to focus on this particular feature and describe what he sees.

5.   Discuss the idea of assuming that everyone else sees him through the magnifying glass and ask him if, in reality, this is actually the case.

6.   Explain the term *tunnel vision*, which means looking at only one aspect of a situation and ignoring all the others.

7. Tell your client that, because he is so intent on focusing on what he dislikes about his appearance, he has forgotten that he also possesses likable and positive features and characteristics.

8. Introduce the idea of *self-talk* as an effective way to deal with feeling supersensitive. For example, if your adolescent client thinks his pimples are so noticeable that everyone will stare at them, he could say to himself, "Lots of other kids my age have pimples, too. I don't pay that much attention to theirs, so why should they pay that much attention to mine?"

9. Work with your client to identify other examples of self-talk he can use when he feels overly self-conscious.

In the Mirror Sentence Stems

1. When I see myself in the mirror,

   I think _____.

2. The part of my body I'm most self-conscious about

   is _____.

3. When I look in the mirror, I'm embarrassed

   to see _____.

4. I hate my _____.

5. I wish I could change my _____.

6. What I like best about my appearance

   is _____.

So Ugly

RATIONALE These words—*so ugly*—are frequently uttered by adolescents who are dissatisfied with their appearance. Their tendency to overfocus on their appearance prevents them from seeing themselves in a more comprehensive light.

MATERIALS
  ▷ A paper bag
  ▷ A sheet of paper
  ▷ A pencil

PROCEDURE
1. When your client complains about how ugly she is, hand her the paper bag and tell her to put it on, emphasizing that she should not be caught dead walking the streets looking the way she does. Carry the exaggeration further by suggesting that she also figure out a way to cover up the rest of her body, consider hibernating for periods of time, and so forth.

2. Ask her to forcefully convince you that she is ugly and disgusting in *every* way, shape, and form. What is it about her appearance that is so horrific?

3. Debrief by asking your client what she learned from the exaggeration activity and whether it had any impact on how she sees herself. Is she really as ugly and disgusting as she made it seem?

4. Encourage her to identify her positive attributes.

Zoom In

RATIONALE This intervention is intended to help adolescents deal with self-conscious feelings about their appearance, particularly during puberty.

MATERIALS ▷ A sheet of paper

▷ A pencil

PROCEDURE
1. When your client describes being unhappy about his looks, ask him to imagine that someone else has a camera with a zoom lens that emphasizes what the client is most self-conscious about.

2. Explain that the process of "zooming in" is actually only in his mind because, in reality, people don't scrutinize others that closely.

3. Suggest that he write a newspaper column to all adolescents who think everyone notices all the flaws in their appearance, offering advice and suggestions for overcoming self-consciousness.

4. As a homework assignment, ask the client to implement one of his own suggestions.

Fitting In

RATIONALE Whether they admit it or not, many adolescents feel that they don't fit in, which consequently makes them feel self-conscious around their peers. This intervention arms them with some coping strategies.

MATERIALS ▷ A sheet of paper

▷ A pencil

PROCEDURE 1. As your client describes feeling that she does not fit in with her peers, ask her to make a list of what she thinks is different about herself.

2. Suggest that she first identify those peers who seem to fit in and then describe what she thinks those peers do that is different from what she does—even observing the peers' behavior more carefully, if necessary.

3. As a homework assignment, ask the client to act "as if"—trying out some of the peer behaviors she thinks makes these individuals fit in. (If some of these behaviors involve illegal or unhealthy activities, help your client evaluate the price she might have to pay to fit in.)

Transitions

Transitions often signify a change in one's roles, routines, relationships, and assessment of oneself. Children and adolescents inevitably experience a variety of transitions as they grow up, and their thoughts about these transitions have a great deal to do with how they feel about them. Common transitions about which children may have varying degrees of anxiety are school related (e.g., changing schools, starting school for the first time, moving to the next grade). Others are family related (e.g., adjusting to parental divorce or remarriage, negotiating their place in the family as a new big brother or sister, coping with the death of a close relative). Still another major transition is that of leaving a familiar environment (e.g., moving to a different school, house, neighborhood, or city and adjusting to new surroundings).

For adolescents, typical transitions include graduating from high school and leaving home, entering the job market, and spending less time with same-sex peers and becoming involved in an exclusive romantic relationship. As with younger children, family-related transitions, such as parental divorce and remarriage or loss associated with death or illness, continue to be very difficult for adolescents to handle. Although anxiety—to varying degrees—may be a common denominator in all transitions, other emotional and behavioral reactions to developmental transitions also are prevalent. They, too, are addressed in this section.

Moving On

RATIONALE   Moving to a new locale is a transition that many children experience during their early school years. While some children are happy and excited about a move, others feel quite the opposite. This intervention helps them understand how their thoughts affect their feelings about the move and how to adjust to the transition.

MATERIALS   ▷ Game board (from the Appendix or one of your own design)

▷ 2 game markers

▷ Moving On Cards (p. 272)

Note: If you are constructing your own game board, you could use photographs or drawings of two different houses, placing them at opposite ends of the board. You could then connect the houses with the spaces on which you and the client advance your game markers.

PROCEDURE   1. To begin play, have your client select a marker, while you also select one.

2. Take turns with your client, each of you drawing a card, moving your marker the number of spaces designated on the card, and discussing how thoughts contribute to feelings about the scenario described on the card.

3. Work with him to identify his thoughts and feelings about the scenarios, challenge any assumptions he may be making about these situations, and help him to see that he may have both positive and negative feelings about transitions of this nature.

4. Discuss the ideas your client has about how to cope with transitions that may be difficult.

Moving On Cards

You're moving across town to a new neighborhood and a different school. You feel _____ because you are thinking _____. (+1 space)

You are moving from your house to an apartment. You feel _____ because you are thinking
_____.
(+1 space)

You are moving to a different state. You feel _____ because you are thinking _____. (+2 spaces)

You are moving to another country for two years because your parents got jobs there. You feel _____ because you are thinking _____. (+2 spaces)

You are moving to a brand-new house in a different neighborhood and a different school district. You feel _____ because you are thinking
_____.
(+1 space)

You are moving in with your grandparents. You feel _____ because you are thinking _____.
(+1 space)

You are moving from the country to town. You feel _____ because you are thinking
_____.
(+2 spaces)

Make up your own scenario.
You feel _____ because you are thinking
_____.

You are moving from a small town to a big city. You feel _____ because you are thinking _____.
(+2 spaces)

Make up your own scenario.
You feel _____ because you are thinking
_____.

What Works When with Children and Adolescents © 2002 by Ann Vernon. Champaign, IL: Research Press (800) 519–2707

Family Changes

RATIONALE   Welcoming a new sibling into the family is sometimes a difficult transition for younger children. They often assume that their special place in the family is gone forever and that their parents no longer love them. This story introduces a more rational perspective.

MATERIALS   ▷ A sheet of paper

▷ A pencil

▷ Optional: A tape recorder and audiotape

▷ Family Changes story (p. 274)

PROCEDURE   1. When your client discusses her feelings of anger and jealousy caused by the arrival of a new sibling, have her read the story, or read it to her.

2. Have your client write an ending to the story and discuss her "solutions" to the problems imposed by this transition. If you wish, have her dictate the story's ending into a tape recorder.

3. Normalize her feelings of anger and jealousy, but also help her see how her perceptions and exaggerations contribute to the problem.

Family Changes

Sara was sassy—or at least that was her parents' opinion. In Sara's eyes, she had every right to be sassy, snippy, or whatever. She was so sick of not getting any attention except when one of her parents yelled at her to be quiet so as not to wake up the baby. This baby was the cause of all of Sara's problems.

Before Susie was born, Sara was the center of attention, and she did not have to be sassy. But things had changed, definitely for the worst, according to Sara. Sometimes Sara was so upset that she wished her sister had never been born. She even asked her mother to give Susie to another family, but her mother just scolded her for even thinking such a thing.

One day when Sara was sulking, her mother sent her to her cousin Sally's house, hoping that would make Sara happy. Wouldn't you know it? The first thing Sally said when Sara walked through the door was, "Oh, Sara, you must be so excited about your new baby sister. You are so lucky."

"Lucky? I don't think so," said Sara. "She's the *only* one who gets *any* attention at my house now. My parents couldn't care less about me. I'm sure that if I never went back home, they wouldn't even miss me."

"Sara, that's the dumbest thing you've ever said," Sally replied. "Of course they would miss you. They just have to pay more attention to Susie now because she's too little to take care of herself like you can. I'll bet they treated you just like that when you were a few weeks old."

"I suppose you're right, but they don't pay *any* attention to me," Sara said.

"What do you mean?" Sally asked. "Don't they feed you or talk to you? Don't they read you a bedtime story or kiss you good night? Don't they take you to school?"

"Yeah, they do that stuff. But they must not love me anymore, because they spend so much time with the baby," Sara whined. "I'll bet they wish I'd just stay in the park all night, and then they wouldn't even have to bother with me."

"Come on. Do you *really* think they don't love you or wouldn't miss you if you stayed out all night? Where's your proof?"

"Well, I guess I don't have any proof. It just feels that way."

"I know. I remember when my brother was born. I felt mad and jealous just like you," Sally admitted. "But pretty soon I realized that they weren't going to get rid of him, and I really didn't want that, anyway. So I just had to figure out a way to get over feeling mad and jealous."

"What did you do?" Sara asked.

"Well, I . . ."

Next Grade

RATIONALE Children usually have many different feelings about moving to the next grade. This intervention helps them to identify these feelings and also shows them how to constructively address them.

MATERIALS ▷ A feelings cube, made from the bottom half of a milk carton. (Cut the carton in half horizontally on three sides, leaving the fourth side longer to fold over and form the top of the cube.) Cover the cube with paper, and write a different feeling word on each side (e.g., *scared, excited, nervous, happy, unhappy, upset*).

▷ Next Grade Cards (p. 276)

PROCEDURE 1. To initiate this activity, place all but the "Write your own example" cards in a row, facedown.

2. Ask your client to roll the cube. The feeling word that ends up on the top of the cube is the feeling that he will match up with one of the situations on the cards.

3. After the client has identified the feeling, have him turn over the cards until he finds a situation that could represent that feeling for him personally.

4. Encourage him to discuss what it is about that situation that causes that particular feeling, helping him to clarify any existing assumptions or overgeneralizations.

5. Repeat the procedure after taking out the card he identified and turning the rest facedown.

6. After several rounds, have your client jot down, on the "Write your own example" cards, three or four school-related situations involving the next grade and have him place these cards in the row with the remaining cards, playing again as described in the earlier steps.

Next Grade Cards

You've been assigned to a class with lots of new kids, not your old friends.

Your classroom will be on the top floor of the building.

You've heard that the teacher you have been assigned is strict.

You will have to change clothes for physical education.

You think the work will be harder.

_____

_____

Write your own example.

You switch teachers several times each day.

_____

_____

Write your own example.

You have a longer lunch period but no recess.

_____

_____

Write your own example.

You will not be in the same building you were in last year.

_____

_____

Write your own example.

Dealing with Divorce

RATIONALE   Children must learn to deal with several major transitions when their parents divorce. Throughout the initial adjustment process, they often lack information or make assumptions that cloud their thinking. Furthermore, because their sense of time is so immediate, it is often difficult for them to imagine life in the future or see how things could ever get better. The story in this intervention introduces a rational perspective.

MATERIALS   ▷ A sheet of paper

▷ A pencil

▷ Dealing with Divorce story (p. 278)

PROCEDURE   1. Give your client a copy of the story and have her read it, or read the story to her.

2. After your client has read or listened to the story and the two of you have discussed the concepts mentioned in it, ask her to write or dictate her own rational story about a personal loss of hers.

Dealing with Divorce

Antonio was so upset. His parents had just told him that they were getting a divorce. He would be living with his dad in an apartment, and his mom was moving to a different apartment. He would see her on weekends. Antonio was mad—this shouldn't be happening to his family. He thought they had been happy. It wasn't fair that his parents were doing this to him.

Antonio was also very unhappy about having to change schools. He worried about making new friends and hated that he had to leave all his good friends in the neighborhood. He didn't understand why he had to move, but his parents told him that neither one of them could afford to live in the house. He'd rather live anywhere instead of in some tiny apartment where he probably couldn't even have his bike. And the notion that he would see his mom only on weekends was almost more than he could stand to think about.

The next day at school, Antonio was really quiet. He could not concentrate on his schoolwork because all he could think about was how terrible he felt and how awful things were. When he started to cry during math class, his teacher asked him what was wrong, so he told her the whole story.

"Antonio," she said, "I know this is really hard for you, and I'm so sorry this is happening to your family. Maybe it would help if you talked to Amaya about this. Her parents were divorced several months ago." Antonio thought this was a good idea, and the two of them met during recess in Mrs. Amado's office.

Amaya asked Antonio to tell her what was happening, and after he finished, she told him that she could understand how he felt. "I was so sad when my parents got divorced that I thought I would never feel better," Amaya said. "I cried all the time, and I didn't even feel like playing with my friends. But now I'm a little more used to it, and I'm not as sad all the time."

"But isn't it terrible that you just get to live with one parent?" Antonio asked.

"Yeah, I don't like that," Amaya said, "but at least they live in the same town, so I get to see my dad every week and talk to him on the phone. My friend Angela only gets to see her dad during the summer because he lives a long ways away. That would really be awful."

"That's for sure," Antonio said. "But I am really mad that I have to go to a different school and live in an apartment."

"I had to change schools, too, and I hated it at first," Amaya said. "But I made new friends almost right away, so now it doesn't seem bad at all. My mom still lets me invite my old friends over, so now I have a whole lot more friends than I ever did."

"I hadn't thought about that," said Antonio. "I guess it'd be OK if I could still see them sometimes. I just don't want to move."

"Who knows?" Amaya said. "Maybe you'll like your new neighborhood."

"Well, maybe, . . . but it just seems like everything is changing, and it's awful," Antonio whimpered.

"I know. I felt like that, too," Amaya said. "But now it doesn't seem like everything is so awful. I guess I'm just getting used to it."

After talking to Amaya, Antonio felt a little better, and things didn't seem quite so awful. He still wished things were different, but he knew he couldn't do anything about that. As Amaya said, he just had to remember that things wouldn't always seem so bad.

 What Works When with Children and Adolescents © 2002 by Ann Vernon. Champaign, IL: Research Press (800) 519–2707

Preparing for the Future

RATIONALE   Preparing for the future can be both exciting and anxiety provoking. This intervention is especially intended to help high school seniors understand how their thoughts influence their feelings.

MATERIALS   ▷ A pair of eyeglasses

▷ A sheet of paper

▷ A pencil

PROCEDURE   1. When your client discusses his future, have him put on the eyeglasses and instruct him to "look" past high school graduation to the immediate (6 to 12 months) future, listing everything he "sees," along with a corresponding feeling.

2. Encourage him to be very specific (e.g., if he is going to college, he might list "Having to make new friends and feeling somewhat anxious about it").

3. After he has completed his list, take several of his examples and ask him to identify specific thoughts that influence how he feels (e.g., maybe everyone will ignore him or he won't find anybody to connect with or he may just have to sit in his room all year while everyone else socializes).

4. Explain to the client how these assumptions create anxiety and how to challenge them:

    "What are the chances that *everyone* will ignore you?"

    "Do you think that, out of thousands of students, you won't find *anyone* to connect with?"

    "How realistic is it to think that you will sit in your room all year and never have *anyone* to socialize with?"

5. After you have demonstrated the disputing process, help your client work through other examples that he has had negative feelings about, and then identify strategies he can use to help him deal with these issues.

Times Are Changing

RATIONALE   As young people get older, their peer relationships often change. Friendships that once were strong may become less so as interests and values change—or as romantic relationships consume time once devoted to platonic relationships. This intervention helps clients learn to deal with these changes.

MATERIALS   ▷ Several small strips of paper

▷ A pencil

▷ Several balloons

▷ Optional: stationery and stamps; a journal

PROCEDURE   1. When your client expresses feelings about relationships that are changing, help her see that this is a normal phenomenon by asking her to name two or three childhood friends whom she no longer associates with and explain why.

2. Point out to her that she probably is not still "mourning" the loss of those friends because so much time has passed.

3. Have her list the names of people she has been close to in recent years, but is no longer as connected to. Ask her to describe how she thinks these relationships have changed and what she misses most about them.

4. Help her deal with any irrational beliefs, such as "Things shouldn't change" or "Friends shouldn't value their romantic interests more than our relationship," by acknowledging her loss but asking her what power she has over other people's choices. Ask her whether it helps her move on to new relationships by staying stuck in the "It shouldn't be this way; my relationship shouldn't change" mentality.

5. Suggest that she list, on separate pieces of paper, things she misses from these former relationships and that, each day, she "let go" of one by putting it in a balloon and literally sending it off into space.

6. If you wish, encourage her to write letters—which she may or may not send—or make entries in a journal as a way to deal with her feelings and express her thoughts about the loss of a friendship or the change in a relationship.

What's Next?

RATIONALE   What's next after high school is a major issue that all adolescents face. This intervention helps them assess their options.

MATERIALS   ▷ What's Next? Sorting Board (p. 282)

▷ What's Next? Cards (p. 283)

PROCEDURE   1. As your client begins to discuss his plans for after high school, ask him to look at each of the What's Next? Cards.

2. Have him think about whether the option presented on the card is something he is very likely to do, somewhat likely to do, or not at all likely to do. (Two cards allow the client to write his own examples.)

3. Instruct him to place each card in the appropriate column on the sorting board.

4. After he has finished, discuss what he sees as the most likely options for him; what obstacles he may have to overcome and how he would overcome them; and how he feels about these options.

5. Work with him to clarify assumptions and misperceptions, and dispute irrational beliefs where appropriate.

What's Next? Sorting Board

Very likely	Somewhat likely	Not at all likely

What's Next? Cards

Full-time job away from this community	Part- or full-time college in this community
Full-time job in this community	Trade or technical school—part time
Part-time job away from this community	Trade or technical school—full time
Part-time job in this community	Trade or technical school away from this community
Two-year college—part time	Trade or technical school in this community
Two-year college—full time	Getting married and living away from this community
Four-year college—part time	Getting married and living in this community
Four-year college—full time	_____ Write your own example.
Part- or full-time college away from this community	_____ Write your own example.

Get a Job

RATIONALE   Getting a job can be a major transition for high school students. Time management is often a problem, as they attempt to juggle home, school, extracurricular activities, and work responsibilities while still having time for friends and dating relationships. By having less free time and more disposable income, they may face the inevitability of family conflicts because they are less likely to help with household chores and may make decisions about how to spend their money that don't meet with parental approval. In addition, the stress of the job itself and the anxiety that is often associated with assuming a new role with unfamiliar responsibilities can seem overwhelming. This intervention addresses the stress and anxiety associated with job-related transition.

MATERIALS   ▷ A pencil

▷ Get a Job Worksheet (p. 286)

PROCEDURE   1. When your client describes the stress and anxiety she experiences as she incorporates work into an already busy schedule, give her the Get a Job Worksheet.

2. Ask her to write down in the circles the stressors she feels as she juggles her responsibilities.

3. After discussing these stressors, help her identify any irrational beliefs and ask her to write them in the small squares linked to the circles. Her irrational beliefs might resemble the following:

"I have to do it all perfectly."

"It shouldn't be so hard to find time for everything."

"I can't stand the pressure."

"Even if I'm tired and in a bad mood, I shouldn't be impatient with others."

"I should be able to find time for everything, and if I can't, it means I'm totally inadequate."

4. After talking through her irrational beliefs, teach the client how to dispute them by asking herself questions like these:

> "Who says I have to do it all perfectly? Is that humanly possible?"

> "Where is the evidence that I can't stand the pressure? Aren't I standing it, even though it is sometimes pretty hard to do?"

> "Where's the proof that I'm totally inadequate if I'm having trouble finding time for everything?"

5. After disputing her irrational beliefs, work on a stress management plan. Ask her to target *one* area (e.g., school, extracurricular activities, work, family responsibilities) and identify two things she could do to reduce stress. For example, if she selects work, she might (a) reduce her hours or work only on weekends if possible or (b) consider dropping an extracurricular activity in order to work after school and relax on weekends.

6. Ask her to follow through on what she identified as her target area for the stress management plan and identify other areas to work on as well.

Get a Job Worksheet

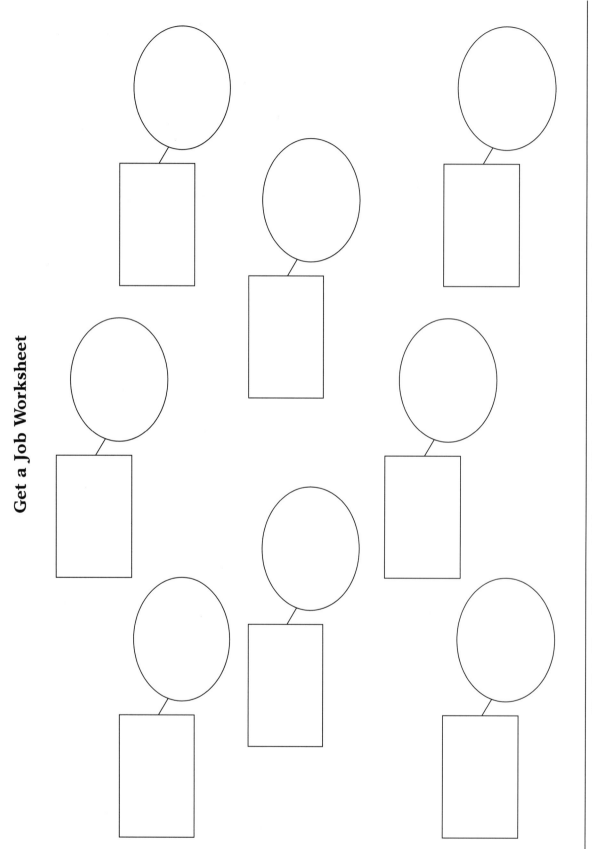

What Works When with Children and Adolescents © 2002 by Ann Vernon. Champaign, IL: Research Press (800) 519–2707

CASE STUDY

This case study illustrates the typical developmental issues of 13-year-old Lisa, who was referred for counseling by her parents. In recent months, Lisa's grades had declined, and she had become quite disrespectful and somewhat defiant. Although they did not think Lisa's problems were terribly serious at this point, her parents wanted to get help now before things escalated.

Counselor: Hello, Lisa. I understand from my brief phone call with your mother that you do not want to be here. I can appreciate that, because lots of kids your age feel much the same way when they come for the first time.

Client: My parents are the ones who need to be here—not me.

Counselor: Well, my guess is that I'll end up seeing them, too. But before I see them, I really wanted to hear about the situation from your perspective. That way, when I meet with them, I will have heard your side of the story. Just remember that you are my client, and what you tell me stays between us unless you are planning to hurt yourself or someone else. Is that your plan?

Client: No way! I'm not that dumb. I'm just mad at them.

Counselor: Well, why don't you tell me what it is about them that makes you mad?

Client: It's just everything. They are so dumb.

Counselor: Do you suppose you could think of a specific example?

Client: Um . . . oh, yeah. I wanted to stay overnight with my friend, and they actually called her parents to make sure they were going to be home. That was so stupid. I just didn't get the point. They said they just wanted to make sure I would be OK—like I'm some 2-year-old or something.

Counselor: Sounds like it might have been embarrassing for you.

Client: You got that right.

Counselor: So they embarrass you and make you mad. Can you give me another example of something they've done?

Client: Sure. Last week they grounded me for no reason, and I can't do anything for three whole weeks.

Counselor: You definitely sound mad about that—and you said they did this for no reason?

Client: Well, they said it was because I snuck out of the house one night when I was supposed to be in bed. I don't see what the big deal is about that. If they would let me stay out later, I wouldn't have to sneak out.

Counselor: So you think they are too strict and that it's actually their fault that you are behaving this way?

Client: Yeah—all my friends get to do whatever they want, and I am the only one who has these stupid rules.

Counselor: So you resent the rules and try to find creative ways to work around them. Are you usually successful, or do they catch you like they did when you snuck out?

Client: They usually catch me.

Counselor: And are the consequences usually as bad as being grounded for three weeks?

Client: It just depends. I don't think there should be consequences, and if they let me do what I wanted to, I wouldn't have to break their stupid rules.

Counselor: Right, but what do you think the chances are of changing your parents?

Client: Zip. They'll never change. They like being this way.

Counselor: And it sounds like you don't like being grounded, but end up being in that position quite a bit. So— how is what you are doing helping you?

Client: I guess it's not, when you put it that way. But they shouldn't be so strict; they never let me do anything.

Counselor: They really don't ever let you do anything? Help me understand this. If, on a 1 to 10 scale—with 1 being never and 10 being always—you'd say that they would always be at the 1 rating, which means that they never let you do anything?

Client: *(Laughs.)* Well, not always. I mean, they let me do some stuff.

Counselor: So if it isn't a 1, where would you say they would be?

Client: Oh, probably a 3.

Counselor: And you'd like them to be at a 10?

Client: Exactly!

Counselor: Well, what do you think makes the difference between the times they let you do things and the times they don't? Is there anything you do that you think influences their decision?

Client: I don't think so.

Counselor: I know some kids your age who have noticed that if they get good grades or do their chores without being told or don't mouth off to their parents, they find that their parents usually let them do a little more. I don't know if that would work for you or if you'd be willing to try it.

Client: I don't know. I hate studying and doing chores.

Counselor: I understand that. But do your parents bug you about it?

Client: All the time. They're always on my case about those things.

Counselor: So what I am suggesting is that it might not hurt to try changing in those ways to see if it might make a difference. It's up to you, but it could be worth considering.

Client: But why should I have to change? They are the ones who should change. They shouldn't be treating me like I'm 2 years old.

Counselor: I hear what you're saying about them needing to change. I think most teenagers would say the same thing. But do you really think you can make them change? I mean, it doesn't really sound like what you've been doing has been getting you anywhere except grounded, has it?

Client: No. But I can't stand the way they are, and it's not fair that I have to change and they don't.

Counselor: I'm sure you think it would be great if there was a law about parents being less strict with their teenagers, but I don't know of one, do you?

Client: No.

Counselor: And since there is no law that says parents should be more reasonable, . . .

Client: I get the point. But I can't stand them the way they are now.

Counselor: Well, if you want them to change, you may just have to be the one to take the first step, because it sounds like your parents can be pretty stubborn. Are you willing to do that?

Client: I suppose.

Counselor: I was just thinking that if you were willing to try an experiment—maybe you could actually get them to change a little.

Client: Like what would I have to do?

Counselor: You mentioned that your parents bug you about getting better grades, doing your chores, and mouthing off. So I was thinking that if you were willing to work on one or two of those things that it might help. And if not, we can always think of something else.

Client: I don't know. I hate doing chores and homework, and when they bug me, I can't help but talk back to them because they make me so mad.

Counselor: I know it's a pain to do things you hate to do, but if there is the possibility of a gain—that they would start to change—it might be worth considering, especially since you have admitted that what you are doing now isn't helping you get more freedom.

Client: I guess I'll try it.

Counselor: As I said, you probably won't like it, but it might pay off in the long run. See you in two weeks, and good luck!

Summary of Case Study

Although this client stubbornly held on to the irrational belief that her parents should change, she eventually realized that this belief and her rebellious behavior were not helping her achieve her goal. The functional disputes ultimately prompted her willingness to try a behavioral experiment that did help modify her parents' behavior to some degree. Subsequent sessions with this young client and her parents focused on effective communication and problem-solving skills. The sessions also helped the parents better understand adolescent development and how to live with a teenager.

CHAPTER 6

Applications for Parents and Teachers

Few would argue that being a parent is sometimes as frustrating and challenging as it is rewarding. The same can be said for teaching. Both at home and at school, parents and teachers often struggle in their attempts to nourish happy and productive young people. Unfortunately, this task has become increasingly difficult, given the growing number of children who could be considered "at risk" and whose social-emotional needs often interfere with their ability to learn and develop in healthy ways.

Parents and educators alike cannot help but be alarmed and disheartened by current child-related concerns such as homicide, suicide, street violence, substance abuse, eating disorders, academic underachievement, depression, conduct and attentional disorders, and promiscuous sexual behavior. Not only do these issues make parents' and educators' jobs increasingly difficult, they also heighten the awareness that now, more than ever, parents and teachers need skills that increase their effectiveness as educators, role models, and nurturers of young people. At the same time, we must recognize that adults living and working with children have issues in their own lives that can interfere with their competence. Furthermore, adults frequently exhibit negative emotional and behavioral reactions that are based on irrational beliefs; it is those negative reactions that contribute to a deterioration in the adult-child interaction.

Although parents and teachers might wish for ready-made answers or cure-all approaches that will "fix" the child, such methods often do not work. The reason they don't is that the adults themselves frequently have negative feelings about the youngster or the problem that can sabotage their ability to deal calmly with the situation. After all, parents and teachers are human, and sometimes when they get angry and upset about a child's behavior, they act out as well. Suppose Johnny has been throwing temper tantrums at home as well as at school. Both his parents and his teachers are at their wit's end trying to figure out what to do. As Johnny is on the classroom floor, kicking and screaming, his teacher is trying to keep 28 other children quiet, is

291

frustrated beyond belief, and is screaming at him to stop. When he does the same thing at church, his father is so angry, he brusquely grabs Johnny by the arm and practically drags him down the aisle. In both instances, emotions clouded these adults' ability to think clearly and caused them to overreact, in turn likely resulting in their feeling guilt and embarrassment.

Although traditional approaches to teaching and parenting offer practical suggestions for dealing with problems, rational emotive behavior therapy (REBT) goes beyond that. It is a skills-based approach that offers solutions and, more important, helps adults identify irrational beliefs that cause the ineffective emotional and behavioral reactions that interfere with good parenting and teaching. REBT proposes that there are actually two types of problems in dealing with children: *practical problems*, such as determining which rules to apply or how to communicate effectively with youngsters, and *emotional problems*, such as feeling angry when children don't follow rules or becoming depressed about their physical disabilities. Working with both types of problems is essential for long-lasting solutions.

This chapter explains how negative emotions prevent parents and educators from implementing effective strategies with children. It then goes on to discuss how practitioners can teach these adults to identify and dispute irrational beliefs—which will have a positive impact on how adults relate to children. The chapter also presents beliefs that are specific to parents and teachers and describes the effects these beliefs have on parenting, teaching styles, and approaches to discipline. In addition, it describes effective communication and discipline strategies and offers suggestions for solving practical problems. The chapter concludes with a case study that illustrates how these principles can be applied to parents.

PROBLEM ASSESSMENT

When parents or teachers seek assistance from helping professionals about a problem they are having with a child, it is, of course, necessary to gather information about the child. This information should relate to the nature and severity of the problem; the onset of the problem and when it typically occurs; any significant changes or transitions or traumatic events that may have precipitated the problem; and other relevant data regarding the intensity of the problem. Equally important is that practitioners ask about the role the parents or teachers play, specifically searching for how they have dealt with the problem—which strategies have or have not worked well and how the child responded to these interventions. Eliciting parents' or teachers' feelings about the problem or how they have dealt with it—as well as discovering their irrational beliefs—is essential in problem assessment.

To form a comprehensive picture of the problem, it is helpful to use the BASIC ID, a multimodal approach developed by Lazarus (1976). BASIC ID is an acronym for behavior, affect, (physiological) sensation, imagery, cognitions, interpersonal relationships, and drugs/biology/health. Keat (1979) adapted this model for use with children. His HELPING model includes the following dimensions, which spell out the HELPING acronym: health; emotions; learning/school performance; personal relationships; imagery; need to know; and guidance of actions, behaviors, and consequences. These assessment models emphasize a holistic approach that involves parents and teachers in the data-gathering process, as illustrated in the following example of the BASIC ID:

> Mr. Chen, a fourth-grade teacher, sought the assistance of the school counselor because he was having difficulty with Jesse. According to Mr. Chen, Jesse was constantly fidgeting in his seat or wandering around the classroom when he was supposed to be working at his desk. When he was up and about, he bothered other children, thus disrupting the classroom. At times he was very defiant. He also blurted out answers on the rare occasions when he was paying attention, made careless mistakes in his work, and was totally disorganized.

> After determining that the problem had been ongoing throughout the school year and that various interventions had been tried, albeit unsuccessfully, the counselor asked Mr. Chen first to describe Jesse's behaviors (B) in more detail, including how *he* behaved in response to Jesse's actions. The counselor then asked Mr. Chen if he had any ideas about Jesse's affect (A): Did he exhibit any anger, for example, in response to Mr. Chen's attempts at discipline? Was Mr. Chen able to identify any other emotions this child might be experiencing? And what about his *own* emotional reactions to Jesse? By asking Mr. Chen to discuss the child first and then gently leading him into a discussion of his own behaviors and emotional reactions, the counselor lessened Mr. Chen's resistance and yielded important information. After describing Jesse's attentional behavior problems in detail, this teacher said he had tried numerous behavior management techniques that had not worked very well. "I'm at my wit's end," he said. "These techniques work with other children—I can't figure out why Jesse isn't responding. I'm so frustrated—and then I feel guilty because I sometimes get angry and take this out on the other children, who don't deserve it. It's Jesse who is the problem. He just drives me up a wall."

> "Obviously," the counselor said, "his behavior is having a negative effect on you, and I envision us working

together to find better ways for you to respond to Jesse, which in turn should bring about behavior change.

"Getting back to our assessment, let me ask if you have had any physiological sensations (S) or know of any that Jesse might be having. I'd also like to know how this affects your image (I) of yourself and how you think Jesse sees himself." Mr. Chen was not able to identify anything in the sensation category, but he did see himself as ineffective and thought Jesse saw himself as powerful.

"And when you feel angry and frustrated and see yourself as ineffective, what thoughts (C) go through your head?" the counselor asked this teacher. Mr. Chen responded that whenever he tried something that didn't work, he found himself thinking that Jesse *should* respond—that these techniques worked for other children, and they should work for him, too. He also said that, on days when Jesse's behavior was exceptionally bad, Mr. Chen left school telling himself that he was in the wrong profession—that he was totally ineffective and couldn't do anything right. The counselor continued to elicit more cognitions from Mr. Chen before moving on to the final two areas of assessment: interpersonal relationships (I) and drugs/biology/health (D). Mr. Chen said that Jesse had very few friends because of the way he behaved. He reiterated that he felt he was taking out his frustration with Jesse on the other children, a response that he thought had a negative impact on his relationship with the entire class. Mr. Chen was not aware of any health-related problems that Jesse was having, stating that he was not on medication but probably should be. As for himself, Mr. Chen often left school with a tension headache.

This example shows how the BASIC ID helps practitioners systematically gather relevant data, including an assessment of irrational beliefs. Identifying parents' and teachers' irrational beliefs relative to the child's problem is an essential first step in problem resolution.

IDENTIFYING IRRATIONAL BELIEFS

Because the ultimate goal in working with parents and teachers is to help them be more effective with children, it is essential that we improve parents' and teachers' stability so they are able to achieve *their* goals. Parenting and teaching are stressful jobs, and, although educators receive more training than parents, both parties are often not as well prepared as they would like to be to handle daily challenges.

Like children, adults think that the *activating event* (A) causes their emotional and behavioral *consequences* (C), and they work hard to change this activating event. According to REBT theory, although activating events may serve as important contributors to the consequence, the *beliefs* (B) about the A actually cause the C. Four general categories of irrational beliefs that interfere with effective parenting and teaching are (a) uncertainty (anxiety), (b) self-condemnation, (c) demanding, and (d) low frustration tolerance:

Uncertainty (anxiety). It is not at all uncommon for parents and teachers to lack parenting and teaching skills, because children do not come with operating instructions. Unfortunately, there is often no "best way" to handle certain situations, and it is hard to predict outcomes. Many parents and teachers think they *should* know what to do and what the outcomes will be, feeling anxious and uncertain because they don't have access to a crystal ball. Part of the true test in working with children is for adults to do their best without ever knowing for sure what is right.

Self-condemnation. When children have problems at home or in the classroom, the adults in their lives are often quick to blame themselves. If children score poorly on basic skills tests, teachers assume it is because they themselves were inadequate and didn't do enough to prepare their students. If children turn to drugs and alcohol or become troublemakers at school, parents blame themselves, thinking that if their children turn out poorly, then they are bad parents. In reality, teachers and parents are not the only influences in youngsters' lives. Furthermore, adults won't always do the right thing, but they are worthwhile people regardless.

Demanding. When parents and teachers believe that children *must* turn out a certain way but don't, they think it is awful, and they fall into the trap of demanding. It is perfectly normal to *want* children to develop certain traits or abilities, and it is important to encourage this development. Demanding parents and teachers, however, have little tolerance for children who do not always put forth their best effort; consequently, they feel angry and resentful about the children's inadequacies. Furthermore, these relationships often become controlling and conflictual when absolutistic demands are placed on children always to perform in specific ways.

Low frustration tolerance. Parents in particular, especially in today's society, may think that children should not have to endure hardship or discomfort. Parents who believe that children should never be frustrated are constantly rescuing them, interrupting their own busy schedules to take gym clothes or lunches to school because their youngsters forgot them; they do not want their children to be punished for this negligence, nor do they want them to experience any discomfort. Parents with low frustration tolerance are the ones who immediately take their son or daughter out of a class if the child complains that the teacher is "mean," or deliver the child's newspapers when he or she complains about having to get up early in the morning to do the job. Furthermore, parents often think that they themselves cannot stand to be uncomfortable. They avoid dealing with problems because they do not want conflict. This same phenomenon can apply to classroom teachers as well. Because these adults want children to like them, or because they think they cannot tolerate confrontations with their students, they fail to establish or enforce rules and consequences.

Bernard and Joyce (1984) identified specific irrational beliefs of parents, categorizing them according to emotional reactions: anger, depression, discomfort anxiety/low frustration tolerance, anxiety, and guilt. These beliefs are described as follows:

Anger

My child must always behave the way I want her to behave.

It is horrible and awful when children do not behave well.

My child must do as I say.

My child must be fair to me at all times.

It should be easier to help my child.

My partner should always be in agreement with me.

Children should always do well and behave correctly.

Children who act badly must be punished.

Depression

I am a worthless parent because my child has so many problems.

I am a terrible parent for being annoyed with my child, who cannot help having the problem.

My worth as a parent depends on the performance of my child.

If others think I'm a poor parent, I'm worthless.

If my child misbehaves frequently, it is awful, and I'm a failure as a parent.

If my child does not love me or approve of me, I am worthless.

When I don't perform as I think a good parent should, I am a complete failure as a person.

If you really want others to know that you care for them, you must become upset over their problems. If you're too calm, you don't care.

Unkind words, gestures, and behaviors from kids can just hurt us emotionally.

If you are not an outstanding parent, or if you make mistakes, it is awful, and you are worthless.

My child's problems are all my fault.

When my child misbehaves, he is doing it because he doesn't love me.

Discomfort Anxiety/Low Frustration Tolerance

I can't stand it when something bad happens.

I can't stand my child's behavior.

I can't stand my child's attitude.

If something is frustrating or difficult, it must be avoided.

It is best to avoid dealing with difficult issues for as long as possible.

Anxiety

I couldn't bear it if something bad or painful happened to my child.

The world is a dangerous place, and you must be aware of this at all times.

Painful experiences must be avoided at all costs.

I *must* worry about my child (I can't help it).

Worrying is a sign of good parenting.

Guilt

If I make a mistake, it will always affect my child.

I am the sole cause of my child's problems.

I could have and should have done something to prevent my child's disability/problem.

I am totally responsible for everything that happens to my child.

Because of my own inadequacies, my child will always suffer.

It is awful for my child to suffer, and I must prevent it at all costs.

I must never do anything wrong to my child.

Although many of these irrational beliefs pertain to teachers, Bernard, Joyce, and Rosewarne (1983) also identified beliefs specific to teachers:

Students should behave properly at all times.

You can judge the worth of students by their behavior.

I generally need someone's advice at school to help me overcome problems with students.

I must have my students' approval.

I should know how to solve all the problems I encounter with my students.

I should have the power to make my class do what I want.

It is easier to avoid problems or difficulties than to confront them.

I can't stand it when students are being unpleasant.

Students should not be frustrated.

My worth as a teacher is determined by the effectiveness of my students.

I must have control of my students at all times.

I should have the respect of my students at all times.

I shouldn't have to perform unpleasant tasks at school.

I should be a perfect teacher.

Parents should do a better job of raising their children.

When parents and teachers think irrationally and are intensely emotional about a problem they are having with a child, the practitioner must resist the temptation to offer practical solutions to the problem instead of identifying and disputing irrational beliefs. The following personal experience illustrates the practitioner's dilemma:

I clearly recall working with a mother who was overwhelmed by the multiple responsibilities she had caring for her three children. She was experiencing a great deal of stress and felt very guilty about taking it out on her children by nagging, yelling, and occasionally spanking. As she talked about her role as a parent, it became evident that Connie was one of those parents who felt she had to "do everything" for her children in order to qualify as a "good mother." However, in her case, the price she had to pay was getting to be too much, even though she was reluctant to look at it that way.

Because she wanted to reduce her stress, I asked her to describe how she spent her time, focusing specifically on the activities she did with and for the children.

When she explained that she spent an hour each day with each of her three children, helping them practice the piano, I could see why she was overwhelmed: This task alone took up so much of her time. However, rather than helping this client identify her irrational beliefs that good parents always help their children with homework, lessons, and so forth—that her worth as a parent depended on her children's performance; that if she did not spend time helping them, she was being selfish; and that if her children did not perform well, others would certainly think she was a bad parent, and that would be awful—I mistakenly jumped to what I thought was an ideal solution to relieve her stress.

"Connie," I said, "why not just practice with one child per day? You would free up 2 hours a day that you could use for relaxation or enjoyment to help relieve your stress. By doing that, you would be less likely to feel so overwhelmed and frustrated and take this out on your children." At the time, this client agreed that she could try this, but I should have known she would not be successful because I had failed to dispute the irrational beliefs about being a good mother that were preventing this client from changing her behavior.

As this example illustrates, effective problem resolution must address what it is that is perpetuating the problem. Sometimes, however, parents and teachers are reluctant to look at themselves, and therefore they become defensive. Their resistance may relate directly to their guilt and shame about not being perfect because they can't "fix" the child's problem themselves. It is important to address this issue by pointing out that teaching and parenting can be very challenging and that there is no such thing as a perfect parent or teacher (or a perfect child). On the other hand, informing them that their job may be easier if they learn to handle *their* feelings about the child's problem often facilitates self-disclosure, which in turn helps them to identify irrational beliefs.

To reduce resistance further, it is also helpful to educate parents and teachers about how their negative emotions, such as anger, depression, guilt, discomfort anxiety, and the like can affect their behavior. Strong feelings such as anger, for example, transform the most reasonable adults into mean-spirited people who say things they don't mean and do things they wish they hadn't done. Parents or teachers with high degrees of discomfort anxiety fail to establish reasonable rules and don't follow through on consequences, and this failure only perpetuates problems. Guilty parents who feel responsible for their children's unhappiness may overindulge them and later have to deal with the negative results, as their spoiled, manipulative children assume the upper hand.

Recognizing that parents and teachers have other stressors in their lives besides the children they live and work with is also a good way to establish a solid working alliance. These are not easy roles, and there are no easy answers. Dispelling myths is also effective (Vernon & Al-Mabuk, 1995). For some reason, there is an assumption that parents have an innate ability to know what to do and can intuitively solve whatever problems their children are having. Although this myth does not apply as strongly to teachers, we often hear that "good teachers are born, not made." In either case, intuition can play a role, but there is more to these roles than innate ability.

Another common myth is that, once adults have figured out how to parent or teach properly, it will be smooth sailing from then on. Realistically, that is not the case, because there are always new challenges to face. Additionally, many parents and teachers believe that their jobs should be easy, that they should not have to work so hard to find the right strategies. Unfortunately, children do not automatically respond appropriately, and there will be failures and setbacks that necessitate renewed efforts. Finally, it is important to dispel the myth that what works with one child will work with another. Because children have different temperaments and personalities and also have different needs at various developmental stages, the "one size fits all" approach does not work, and this reality makes teaching and parenting more difficult.

DISPUTING IRRATIONAL BELIEFS

Helping parents and teachers understand the connection between their thoughts and feelings and behavioral consequences (the B–C connection) is an important step in identifying, and consequently disputing, irrational beliefs. Although some adults stubbornly hold on to the notion that the activating event (e.g., a child's refusal to do her homework or follow rules) causes them to feel upset, the practitioner can correct this misunderstanding by pointing out that two sets of parents or teachers each could be faced with the same problem (e.g., Annie refusing to comply with the rules). Whereas the first set of teachers or parents is extremely frustrated and angry about this lack of compliance—because these adults believe that Annie should follow rules, and they cannot stand it when she doesn't—the second set of individuals is more relaxed about it. Although the more laid-back parents or teachers would like her to behave differently, they just keep trying different approaches and do not let their irritation about her behavior rule their lives. These two sets of individuals respond differently because of what they are telling themselves about this child's behavior.

Adults, like children, often minimize the strength of their emotional reactions, so it is helpful to ask them how they behave when they have negative feelings about something concerning a child. Once the intensity of the feelings has been correctly identified, it is not difficult to uncover the irrational beliefs, because anger relates to demanding;

guilt or anxiety relates to discomfort anxiety and low frustration tolerance; and guilt and depression relate to self-downing. The following
case illustrates how to help parents see the B–C connection and identify and dispute irrational beliefs:

> Jim and Donna came to counseling seeking help with
> their 16-year-old, whose behavior was troubling them.
> Since their daughter, Tara, had started dating Ben, she
> had become more defiant and secretive. Against her
> parents' wishes, she had dropped out of two extracur-
> ricular activities so she could spend more time with
> her boyfriend. Furthermore, Tara had begun lying to
> them, something she had never done in the past.
>
> When I asked how Jim and Donna felt about these
> recent changes, they immediately replied that they
> were very angry and worried. I also asked what they
> had tried to do to address the problem. They said that
> Tara was not allowed to see Ben more than once a
> week and that her car had been taken away indefinite-
> ly because she had lied about her whereabouts. In
> addition, they were monitoring her phone calls and
> had threatened to ground her for three weeks if they
> caught her doing anything she wasn't supposed to do.
> Considering what Jim and Donna had shared about
> Tara's behavior, I thought their reactions were a bit
> extreme. Certainly, most parents are somewhat con-
> cerned about problems such as these, but the strength
> of both their emotional and their behavioral responses
> was a clear indication that their irrational beliefs were
> having a pronounced impact on their actions.
>
> I pointed out that because their feelings were so
> intense, it would be helpful to me if they could share
> more of what they were thinking about their daugh-
> ter's changes and Ben's influence on her. They said
> that they knew Ben had smoked pot and that they wor-
> ried that he would convince Tara to do the same, even
> though she had always claimed to be adamantly
> opposed to it. Because he had just graduated from high
> school, they also worried that he might persuade her to
> drop out of school or become less involved than she
> already was so they could spend more time together.
> Furthermore, he came from a "broken family" and was
> not the kind of boyfriend they had envisioned for their
> daughter. They also were concerned that she would
> become sexually active and might end up pregnant.
>
> Although the parents readily shared their thoughts,
> feelings, and behaviors, it was clear that they wanted
> me to "fix" their child. I thought it would be helpful to

meet Tara in order to gain a better understanding of the situation and to verify my assumption that the parents were overreacting. After what the parents had shared, I was prepared to see a defiant teen headed for destruction. In contrast, a very neatly dressed, polite young woman walked into my office and proceeded to talk about her feelings toward Ben and how her parents were totally misconstruing the situation. She admitted that she had lied occasionally because they never let her do anything with him, and that, although Ben had been a pretty heavy pot smoker, she did not approve of it and had no intention of starting. Furthermore, she was certain that Ben was no longer smoking because he had just had a drug test that was required for his new job. Not surprisingly, from her perspective, her parents were the problem, and she wanted me to "fix" *them!* I did share with her that her parents thought Ben was a very negative influence on her. I asked Tara if I could see a picture of him so I could know if in fact he looked like the monster her parents had portrayed. From what they had shared, I had expected to see a shaggy-haired, stoned young man with tattoos and multiple body piercings. Instead, I saw a clean-cut, attractive adolescent with one pierced ear. My observation further confirmed my assumption that the parents were probably overreacting and, as a result, creating more problems.

In the next session with Tara's parents, I indicated that they seemed to have done a good job raising their daughter because she was polite and appeared to have a good head on her shoulders—even though she might be making some questionable decisions at this particular time. I used a continuum to help them put Tara's behavior in perspective, explaining that on one end are the teenagers I frequently see who are regular drug users; who have dropped out of school or whose grades have fallen dramatically; who associate with a bad crowd of peers; who refuse to comply with any rules; who have either run away or threatened to do so; or who are pregnant. On the other end are the perfect teens, who do not exist. I asked the parents where they would realistically place Tara on this continuum. Donna admitted that Tara was probably closer to the end representing the perfect teen, but she was afraid her daughter would shift to the other end. Jim reluctantly agreed with his spouse, but kept insisting that Ben was closer to the other end and therefore would convince Tara to change her behavior as well.

After validating their concern, I explained the difference between concern and anxiety, pointing out that their anxiety about how things *might* turn out was having a negative impact on how they were presently handling the situation. I also told them that it is normal for adolescents to be somewhat difficult at certain times during their development. However, I stressed the importance of keeping things in perspective—not automatically jumping to the conclusion that just because their daughter is dating someone they do not consider appropriate means she will end up marrying him, or that just because Ben is no longer in school does not necessarily mean that he wants Tara to drop out, especially considering he completed high school himself. I challenged them to look for evidence based on her past behavior: Had she normally been readily influenced by peers? Had she ever threatened to drop out of school? Had she ever experimented with drugs or alcohol? I also used functional disputes: What good does it do to assume that their daughter will dramatically change her behavior, get pregnant, or drop out of school? How does their anxiety and anger interfere with their ability to deal with this problem effectively? Do their strict rules and angry attacks on her choices help prevent emotional upset for all parties involved?

By continuing to challenge their irrational beliefs and help them see the connection between their feelings and behaviors, I found that Tara's parents were ultimately able to reduce their emotional upset and apply more developmentally appropriate rules and consequences. Reading *Surviving and Enjoying Your Adolescent* (Barrish & Barrish, 1989) and *What Growing Up Is All About: A Parent's Guide to Child and Adolescent Development* (Vernon & Al-Mabuk, 1995) also helped them deal more effectively with this issue.

As this case illustrates, being overly anxious or angry did not help these parents solve their problems and in fact prevented them from functioning effectively. Although it was normal for them to be concerned and dislike the situation, they could accomplish more by calmly and realistically assessing the problem. These parents finally learned that exaggeration is self-defeating and that the more they exaggerated, the more likely they were to become angry or anxious and to catastrophize. Consequently, their ability to problem solve was adversely affected.

These same disputing principles apply to teachers. Bernard and Joyce (1984) identified the following examples for several commonly held irrational beliefs:

1. Teachers who think they must be in total control of their classes at all times can challenge this irrational belief by recognizing that they will never have total control—and to insist on it will be counterproductive. Students are different; some will behave, and others will not.

2. Teachers who avoid unpleasant or uncomfortable tasks and interpersonal situations can learn that life isn't easy; that their effectiveness will decrease by avoiding these situations; and that they can tolerate these situations, even if they don't like them.

3. Teachers who believe that students who misbehave must be severely punished can dispute this belief by seeing that children sometimes misbehave out of ignorance and that severe punishment usually does not work, but instead only exacerbates the problem.

4. Teachers who think they have to be perfect, can never make a mistake, and must know how to handle every problem can challenge these beliefs by understanding that there is no such thing as a perfect teacher, that all teachers make mistakes, and that one mistake does not mean that they are total failures.

5. Teachers who believe that children should know better and should never misbehave need to challenge this thinking by realizing that, although it would be nice if all children knew how to behave, this certainly is not always the case. Besides, even if all children did behave themselves, they would still make mistakes or poor choices.

Irrational beliefs not only contribute to the way parents and teachers respond emotionally to children, they also influence how these adults behave and how they relate to youngsters. Different styles of teaching and parenting affect the way youngsters are treated.

TEACHING AND PARENTING STYLES

Two characteristics that help identify teaching and parenting styles are warmth and control (Vernon & Al-Mabuk, 1995). High control and low warmth are associated with an *authoritarian* style, whereas low control and high warmth are related to a *permissive* style. A reasonable degree of warmth and a reasonable degree of control reflect an *authoritative* style.

Authoritarian Style

Authoritarian parents and teachers believe that children should not misbehave or disagree with them and that bad behavior should be punished. They also see themselves as having the power to make children do what they want them to do. Furthermore, they think that children must do well without needing praise and rewards. Because these parents and teachers mistakenly assume that getting angry is an effective way to modify others' behavior, they often discipline through punishment, some of which is very harsh (Bernard & Joyce, 1984).

Although children may respond to this style of parenting or teaching by being well behaved and outwardly compliant, the relationship between child and adult is often very tense, and little respect or caring is evident. These children tend to be inhibited and fearful. Although they may not express their anger directly, this anger simmers beneath the surface and is commonly displayed as general unhappiness. Children who have been subjected to authoritarian parenting or teaching have self-esteem problems, looking to authority figures for "right and wrong." They also lack spontaneity, fail to take initiative, and have poor social and communication skills.

Permissive Style

Permissive parents and teachers have low frustration tolerance. They believe that children should never be frustrated, that they should be free to do what they want, that it is easier to give in than to argue, and that all punishment is wrong (Bernard & Joyce, 1984). They see conflict as bad and consider it something that just creates more problems. In their minds, it is easier to let things go so that everyone can be happy. Adults who adopt this laissez-faire style make unclear and inconsistent rules—an approach that results in anxiety on the part of the child. And because children need parameters in their lives, they often act out in varying degrees to reestablish an appropriate hierarchy of authority.

Children who live in permissive homes or have permissive teachers know that, if they misbehave, their behavior will often be overlooked; they know that threats of consequences and punishment are just that—threats. They know that if punishment is in fact meted out, it won't last long. Although at first glance we might think that this situation is what children want, this is not the case: They need structure, and when it exists, they experience relief, even though they may initially rebel against it. The permissive style has a negative impact on children in that they tend to lack self-control, may have difficulty accepting responsibility for their actions, and can be immature.

Authoritative Style

Parents and teachers who practice the authoritative style have rational beliefs. They know that children will sometimes make mistakes and misbehave, but they do not become extremely upset about it or allow their anger to overrule their reasoning ability. They recognize that children need to learn to be independent—that as fallible human beings, they will occasionally make poor choices. Authoritative parents and teachers set reasonable limits and rules; they have clear expectations and are prepared to hand out appropriate consequences. Children in these environments are competent, confident, self-reliant, and responsible. They are less likely to be rebellious and self-destructive because their parents and teachers demonstrate that they respect them and care about them and work collaboratively with them to solve problems.

Practitioners working with parents and teachers can help them become more effective by teaching them how to identify and dispute the irrational beliefs that affect their teaching and parenting style. Once practitioners have succeeded in doing this, it is much easier to work on the practical problem by teaching parents and teachers various discipline and communication strategies that can also improve their relationships with children.

SOLVING THE PRACTICAL PROBLEM

Years ago, Hauck (1967) noted that, when parents encounter emotional problems with their child, it is not a good idea to work on resolving the child's emotional problems first and reducing the parents' emotional upset later. Instead, it is much wiser to help parents use cognitive strategies to calm themselves first and then work on helping the child. Hauck also stated that, in many cases, children will not change until their parents do. This sound advice, which is also applicable to teachers, still holds true today. Not until adults are more rational can practitioners introduce practical problem-solving strategies that will have a positive effect on children's behavior.

If you were to poll parents and teachers, many would admit that a majority of the problems they have in working with children relate to discipline or communication. Out of frustration or a lack of knowledge or skill, some revert to what they experienced as children at home or in the classroom, employing techniques that their own parents and teachers used. Unfortunately, these methods were often strict and harsh and could be classified as authoritarian. Teaching today's parents and teachers more appropriate strategies will help resolve current as well as future problems both at home and in the classroom.

Nelsen and Lott (1991, 2000) identified long- and short-range parenting and distinguished between the two, stating that long-range parenting is farsighted and results in responsible children who have skills that will serve them well throughout life. On the other hand, they noted, short-range parenting results in children who become codependent, unhealthy, and rebellious. Although Nelsen and Lott described these methods as they related to parenting, they seem equally applicable to teaching.

The goal of the long-range approach is to develop responsible children. It involves listening but not "fixing it for them," providing structure and follow-through, and allowing for mistakes. In practicing this approach, parents and teachers offer encouragement to children and teach them how to make their own decisions as well as how to live with the consequences. They also give children an opportunity to share their own perspectives, thus fostering open communication.

The short-range approach does not teach children the skills they need to become independent adults. By doing things for or to children, parents and teachers try to "fix" their problems instead of encouraging them to do so themselves. In this approach there are arbitrary rules with little or no follow-through, and the adults are in control. There is no room for mistakes. Rewards, but more likely punishments, are the main forms of behavioral control.

Basing their work on these approaches, Nelsen and Lott (1991) developed two lists of practices—one that will work with children and one that will not.

Practices That *Will* Work

Appreciation and respect

Logical consequences and follow-through

Reasonable structure

Consistent rules, including limits and routines

Joint problem solving and compromise

Support and validation

Talking with (instead of talking more); listening more

Letting go of anger and resentment; not taking things personally

Empowering, encouraging, and letting children assume responsibility

Practices That *Will Not* Work

Sarcasm and disrespect

Punishment

Permissiveness

Arbitrary rules and lack of follow-through

Control and too many noes

Put-downs, criticism, and name-calling

Lecturing, not listening

Hanging on to issues, resentments; personalizing problems

Overprotecting, doing for

These two categories identify discipline and communication techniques that parents and teachers can employ (or not employ) to increase their effectiveness with children. Many of the suggestions refer to logical consequences (as opposed to punishment).

Logical Consequences

The logical consequences approach to discipline was developed by Dreikurs, who believed that all misbehavior is the result of children's mistaken assumptions about how to fit in and gain status. Dreikurs and Soltz (1964) identified four goals of misbehavior: (a) to get attention, (b) to gain power, (c) to seek revenge, and (d) to use disability to avoid doing something.

When children's goal is to gain attention, they think they count only when they are being noticed. If their goal is to achieve power, they dominate and manipulate because they think this is the only way they matter. Vengeful children think they are unlikable and have no power, but they also think they have the right to hurt others because they have been hurt. Children who adopt the goal of inadequacy think they cannot do anything right and that it is easier not to try at all.

For adults to employ logical consequences effectively, it is first imperative to identify the child's goal. One way to do this is to ask parents or teachers to consider how they feel when the child does something they think is inappropriate. According to Dreikurs and Soltz (1964), if adults feel annoyed, the child's goal is probably attention. If they are angry and frustrated and feel that they are in a win-lose situation, the youngster's goal is most likely power. If they feel hurt and attacked, the child's goal is usually revenge. If they feel hopeless and discouraged, the child's goal is probably avoidance through inadequacy.

It is also helpful for parents and teachers to observe children's reactions when they are corrected. For example, if their goal is to get power, youngsters will overtly defy the rules and utter, "You can't make me," under their breath. If their goal is to get revenge, youngsters may continue the misbehavior and become violent when adults attempt to stop it. Yelling, screaming, and threatening, as well as hitting and kicking, may occur because the children want to inflict physical or emotional hurt.

Logical consequences do not constitute a form of punishment. Rather, they are behavioral interventions directly related to the misbehavior, and they help children recognize their misbehavior as a mistake. These interventions teach children how to be more responsible by allowing them to make choices so they can avoid negative consequences. They also do not involve threat or coercion and deal only with current behavior; they do not involve punishment, which is often a response to the accumulation of all past wrongdoings by the children. In employing logical consequences, it is important to be kind and firm and to avoid argument. Follow-through is critical.

Adults should present the concept of logical consequences as a choice between continuing to behave inappropriately or changing the behavior. For example, if a child is messing around with her food at the table, the parent might say, "You can either stop playing with your

Chapter 6 • Applications for Parents and Teachers

food or excuse yourself from the table. If you choose to leave, you cannot have anything to eat until breakfast." If the child chooses to stay, but in a few minutes resumes the behavior, the parent can say, "I see that you cannot stop this behavior, so you need to leave now." In the classroom, when several children are whispering and not listening to a story, the teacher can say something like "I don't like it when you whisper and interrupt the story. You can choose to stay and listen or go back to your seats. What is your choice?"

Logical consequences are interventions that teach children how to change their behavior and learn from their mistakes. This approach helps avoid power struggles and, for this reason, is very effective with adolescents, who naturally seek power. Adolescents who consistently come home past curfew can be given the choice either to adhere to the curfew or to come in earlier the next night. Those who conveniently "forget" to do their homework can choose to bring it home and do it during the week or not go out on weekends because they will need to study.

Communication Techniques: What Doesn't Work and What Does

Although most parents and teachers do not intentionally block communication, it is easy to fall into such ineffective habits. Gordon (1970, 2000) identified the following communication roadblocks.

Ordering, directing, and commanding. "Do it because I said so" often provokes anger and resistance. Ordering, directing, and commanding put children on the defensive and invite argument.

Warning, admonishing, and threatening. "If you don't stop that, you will have detention for a week." Certainly, those who misbehave need to be advised of the consequences of their actions, but there are better ways to communicate this idea, such as stating, "I want you to stop disrupting the classroom, and if you don't, you will need to serve detention."

Moralizing, preaching. "You should know better than to skip class." Children probably already know this, and most often they will tune out the preaching and moralizing because it is demeaning. It is far better simply to state that there are consequences for skipping class.

Advising, giving solutions or suggestions. It is impossible for parents and teachers not to advise, but heavy doses of it can interfere with youngsters' ability to learn problem-solving techniques. If adults advise too much, children may become overly reliant on the advice or blame the advice giver if things do not turn out as they wished. Obviously, problem-solving ability improves with age, so it is more appropriate to give advice in limited doses to younger children.

Lecturing, making logical arguments. "If you had done what I told you to, you wouldn't be in this mess now." To say that children resent lectures and logical arguments is probably an understatement. Because adults usually end up inviting resentment when they use this tack, they would be better off to zip their lips whenever they are tempted to deliver a lecture. Besides, the lecture usually does not effect positive behavior change and may in fact do the opposite.

Judging, criticizing, disagreeing, and blaming. It is impossible not to disagree with some things children do, but when adults do, they can express their disagreement in the form of an opinion rather than a judgmental, critical, blaming comment. Note the difference between "That was a stupid thing to do" and "I don't think spending all your allowance on candy was the best choice you could have made."

Praising. At first glance, it seems as though this might be a good strategy, but actually it is not helpful, because no amount of praise will make children feel confident if they are uncertain about their abilities. It is better, for example, to offer encouragement that separates children from their behavior: "I have confidence in you" or "I like what you did" versus "You did a good job" (because if the next time the children do not do a good job, it confirms, in their minds, their incompetence).

Name-calling, ridiculing, and shaming. No one likes to be demeaned, and these types of communication can result in problems with self-esteem, humiliation, and resentment for the child on the receiving end.

Interpreting, analyzing, and diagnosing. "You're just dating that boy because you don't feel good enough about yourself to find someone better." A statement like that will only lead to a counterargument. Rather than utilizing these techniques, express your concern in a straightforward manner: "I worry that you are dating him because maybe you don't feel good about yourself."

Reassuring, sympathizing, consoling, and supporting. This is another case in which, at first glance, the techniques employed might seem useful. However, reassurance can backfire. There is no guarantee that telling children they will do well on an exam will make it happen; if they fail, they might feel worse. Sympathy implies a "You poor thing" attitude. (Empathy works better because you are feeling *for* the children rather than feeling sorry for them.) Consolation and support are appropriate as long as they do not make children feel inadequate and incapable of dealing with the problem.

Probing, questioning, and interrogating. "Why didn't you do your homework?"; "Why weren't you home on time?"; "Why were you with them?" "Why" questions put youngsters on the defensive and may provoke arguments. Adolescents in particular resent being bombarded by questions and will be less likely to converse under those circumstances.

Withdrawing, distracting, diverting, and being humorous. Although these may be temporary solutions, when children are upset, it is best to deal with the problem as soon as it arises. Humor can sometimes be taken the wrong way, particularly by younger children, and distracting and diverting techniques sometimes convey the message that you do not think they are capable of handling the problem.

✳ ✳ ✳

The most effective communication technique involves "I" messages—nonjudgmental statements based on feelings. "I" messages are intended to invite open communication and cause less resentment than "you" messages, which are accusations or evaluations of someone's behavior, attitudes, or motives (Gordon, 1970, 2000). Unfortunately, "you" messages are easy to deliver and very familiar: "You should study for tests" or "You should come home on time." Children usually know they are being evaluated negatively, and these messages invite defensiveness. A typical example of "I" versus "you" messages in a classroom might sound like this:

> "Justin, I would really appreciate it if you would stop talking to Jerry."

> "Justin, you had better stop talking to Jerry and get to work *now!*"

The adult's tone of voice is an important ingredient in delivering messages to children. "I" messages should be stated in a calm, firm, but friendly tone, whereas "you" messages are often conveyed in an angry, demanding tone. To deliver an effective message, adults have to set aside their tendency to judge, assume, and blame. They need to stay calm. A simple formula that adults can use to improve the way they send a message to a youngster involves stating a feeling and then following up by describing the bothersome behavior. The message should be delivered in a nonjudgmental manner. Sharing the effects of the behavior and making a request for a change complete the formula. Adults should be specific in describing the behavior, and they should not exaggerate. Instead, they should be objective and brief, as in the following example:

> *(Parent to child)* I am feeling frustrated because I have asked you several times to clean your room, and it still has not been done. It is hard for me to get the laundry done when your dirty clothes are still on the floor. I

would like you to have it cleaned by tomorrow night, and if not, you will not be able to go out with your friends until it is done.

Contrast that approach with the one used in the following classroom example:

> *(Teacher to class)* You had all better shut your mouths and pay attention during this lecture, or you'll all be sent to the principal. Your behavior disgusts me, and I have had enough of it.

Clearly, the second example will do nothing to enhance the relationship the teacher has with these students and will more than likely result in frequent power struggles and a more disruptive classroom.

RATIONAL EMOTIVE EDUCATION

Obviously, as you consult with parents and teachers about problems they are having with children, you are in the business of educating them. This form of consultation is ordinarily done on a one-to-one basis and serves to remedy an existing problem. In addition to this type of intervention, REBT can be offered in the form of *prevention* to parents and teachers through educational programs. In these sessions, which can occur in either small- or large-group formats, participants learn the principles and practices of REBT and how to apply them both to themselves and to children. An important part of this education should also be information about child and adolescent development. Educators and parents need to know how development affects children's ability to conceptualize and respond to situational and developmental tasks, as well as what typically to expect from children at various stages of their development. Practical suggestions related to communication and discipline are also helpful, along with age-appropriate modifications. In addition, teachers can be taught how to apply these principles in the classroom with children through *rational emotive education* (REE).

Because of the educational nature of REBT, its principles can easily and systematically be incorporated into a classroom or a small-group setting. When REBT is utilized in this manner, its primary emphasis is on prevention. REE is a systematic, curricular approach to emotional education, with the goal being to teach rational thinking skills so children can gain emotional insight and learn sensible coping strategies to apply to current as well as future problems.

In the classroom setting, REE is typically implemented through a series of structured emotional education lessons that are experientially based, allowing for student involvement and group interaction. Several programs have been developed (Bernard, 2001; Knaus, 1974; Vernon, 1989a, 1989b, 1998a, 1998b, 1998c) that typically incorporate the following components into their lessons.

Feelings. Understanding the connection between thoughts, feelings, and behaviors is a critical component of REE lessons. It is also important to develop a feeling vocabulary, learn to deal with emotional overreactions, assess the intensity of feelings, and identify appropriate ways to express feelings. Recognizing that feelings change according to how one thinks is a core concept.

Beliefs and behaviors. REE lessons teach children to differentiate between rational and irrational beliefs and to understand how beliefs affect emotions and behaviors. Distinguishing facts from assumptions, disputing irrational beliefs, and developing appropriate behavioral responses are important skills that are included in REE curricula.

Self-acceptance. REE lessons stress the concept of unconditional self-acceptance rather than self-esteem because the latter implies a rating of self. Core ideas in the curricula include developing an awareness of personal strengths and weaknesses; accepting imperfection; learning not to equate performance with self-worth; and understanding that children, like all humans, are fallible and will make mistakes.

Problem solving. Teaching children to think objectively, tolerate frustration, examine the impact of beliefs on behaviors, and learn alternative ways of problem solving are critical components. These goals are achieved in REE by teaching children to challenge irrational thoughts and employ more effective behavioral strategies.

※ ※ ※

REE lessons begin with a short age-appropriate stimulus activity, such as reading a rational story, completing a problem-solving task, participating in a simulation game, or completing a worksheet or art activity. This stimulus activity is designed to introduce the objectives of the lesson and is followed by a directed discussion about the concepts introduced in the stimulus activity. The discussion is the most important part of the lesson and is organized around two types of questions: (a) content questions, which emphasize the cognitive learnings from the activity, and (b) personalization questions, which help students apply the learnings to their own experiences.

REE concepts can also be presented in a small-group format. There are two types of REE groups: (a) problem centered, in which members raise their current concerns and are taught to apply REBT principles to problem resolution, and (b) preventative groups. The approach taken by the preventative groups is similar to that taken by the REE classroom groups, except that the process occurs in small groups of 6 to 10 members. The smaller preventative groups offer a better opportunity for members to interact and deal with the concepts introduced in the lessons on a personal level.

By participating in classroom or small-group sessions, children learn rational thinking principles, presented in a creative manner, that invite group participation and discussion. This approach enables children to apply these principles to current problems; even more important, it equips them with skills they can use to deal with future problems—and to reach new understandings and resolutions. For specific activities, consult Bernard (2001), Knaus (1974), and Vernon (1989a, 1989b, 1998a, 1998b, 1998c).

CASE STUDY

This case study illustrates the application of REBT concepts by a single parent concerned about her 16-year-old son. The boy is failing in school, and his mother suspects he has substance abuse problems. The following conversation is from the counselor's first session with this client.

Counselor: Hello, Mrs. Goman. It's nice to see you. What brings you to counseling?

Client: Well, I'm really worried about my son, Jeremy. He's 16 and has been having a lot of problems lately, and I don't know what to do.

Counselor: What sorts of problems is he having, and when did you first become concerned?

Client: I've been noticing little things for about a year. He started getting moody and argumentative, and at first I just figured it was a teenage thing, but this year he has been having major problems at school. He never wants to go and is always trying to get me to write excuses for him. He is really smart, but now he is failing almost all his classes. He has also started hanging out with a different bunch of kids. I don't know them well because he doesn't bring them to the house much, but I am pretty sure they are into drugs and alcohol.

Counselor: And are you thinking this is something your son does, too?

Client: I think so. I noticed a big behavior change around the time he started hanging out with these new friends. And, although he was moody and argumentative last year, lately it has been much worse. He is very disrespectful and disobedient. I know he lies. Nothing I say or do seems to have any effect on him.

Counselor: It sounds like you have noticed some major changes that are of concern. How are his problems affecting you?

Client: Where do I start? First of all, I feel guilty. I just wanted him to grow up happy and healthy, and now things are such a mess. I don't know what I did wrong.

Counselor: So you are blaming yourself for your son's problems?

Client: I must have done something wrong, or he wouldn't be this way.

Counselor: So it's all your fault that he is flunking his classes and smoking dope?

Client: I don't know. Something went wrong. Maybe it's because his dad and I got a divorce, and I didn't have a lot of money, so he couldn't have the kind of clothes he needed to fit in. I don't know.

Counselor: It's certainly possible that the divorce could have affected him, but do all children from divorced families have problems like this? Or do all kids who don't have the right kind of clothes act like your son?

Client: I don't think so, but I keep feeling that this is my fault.

Counselor: So you feel guilty, and you are telling yourself that you should have done things differently. And it could be true—maybe there were things you could have done differently. But did you deliberately do things that you knew were hurtful and damaging, or did you do the best you could at the time?

Client: I did the best I could. It isn't easy being a single parent, especially when my ex-husband hardly helps out at all and acts like he doesn't even care about his son.

Counselor: Well, it is obvious that you care about Jeremy, but I want you to get past this notion that you are a failure as a parent. Just because your son has problems, how does it figure that you failed? Certainly, what you do influences him, but are you the only influence in his life?

Client: No, I'm sure I'm not.

Counselor: And even if you failed, are you a rotten person?

Client: It sometimes feels that way.

Counselor: But are these feelings of guilt and depression helping you help your son?

Client: No.

Counselor: So what can you tell yourself so you don't continue to beat yourself up about this?

Client: I guess I can just say that I did the best I could to raise him, and now he has problems that aren't all my fault.

Counselor: That's better. Now, tell me how you have responded to Jeremy's problems.

Client: Well, I try to get him up to go to school, and he just yells at me, so I back off and write a note to excuse his absence. Then I'm mad at myself for doing that. And I have talked to him about his friends and how I think he is using drugs, and he just goes ballistic and threatens to move out.

Counselor: You mentioned that you feel angry with yourself for backing off. And you back off because you think you can't stand to hear him yell and threaten to leave home?

Client: Right. I just don't know how to respond.

Counselor: I'm sure it is uncomfortable when he behaves this way, but do you really think you can't stand it?

Client: If you put it that way, I can stand it—I just don't like it. It seems easier to back down.

Counselor: But when you back down, you then get angry with yourself. So it doesn't sound like either alternative is great. But in the long run, will you be doing him any good by backing down because you think you can't stand the discomfort?

Client: I don't think so. But it's so hard, because when he's angry, he calls me names, and that hurts so much.

Counselor: Yes, but you must be telling yourself that words can hurt. Of course, it isn't nice to hear someone you love say these things, but do you really think that he means everything that he says to you when he is angry?

Client: Probably not; I know I just let it get to me.

Counselor: To keep yourself from becoming more depressed about this, you need to develop some "emotional muscle" so his words don't hurt as much.

Client: And how do I do that?

Counselor: By remembering that "sticks and stones may break my bones, but words will never hurt me unless I let them." In other words, you have to ask yourself: "Am I what he says I am? Where is the proof that I am an awful, horrible, mean mother?" And even if you were some of those things, would that make you a totally worthless person?

Client: No.

Counselor: Of course, you won't be happy about what he says, but you don't have to be so hurt and devastated.

Client: You're right—it's just hard to do.

Counselor: Parenting is hard work. But as we have been discussing today, there are things you can tell yourself to take some of the emotional distress away and thus increase your effectiveness. I just noticed that our time is up, but before we close, I'm wondering if this has been helpful and what made the most sense to you.

Client: I do feel better. You helped me see that I did the best I could to raise Jeremy and that I can't take on all the responsibility for his problems. I might have done some things wrong, but I'm not a bad parent.

Counselor: That's right. And it certainly isn't helping you to deal with his problems when you feel guilty and depressed. For a homework assignment, I would like to recommend that you make a list of all the things you have done for Jeremy over the years. You can then refer to this list whenever he berates you so you can keep yourself from being hurt by his words.

Summary of Case Study

As this case illustrates, parents' emotional problems about their children's problems affect their behavior and can compound their emotional upset. Dealing with this mother's guilt and depression by disputing her irrational beliefs about her bad parenting and helping her develop more emotional muscle to handle her son's verbal attacks was a major, positive step. As a result of this counseling, Mrs. Goman eventually got to the point where she was able to become less enabling and insist on counseling for Jeremy. After a few more sessions and months of therapy, including substance abuse treatment for Jeremy, this family's relationship improved.

Game Board

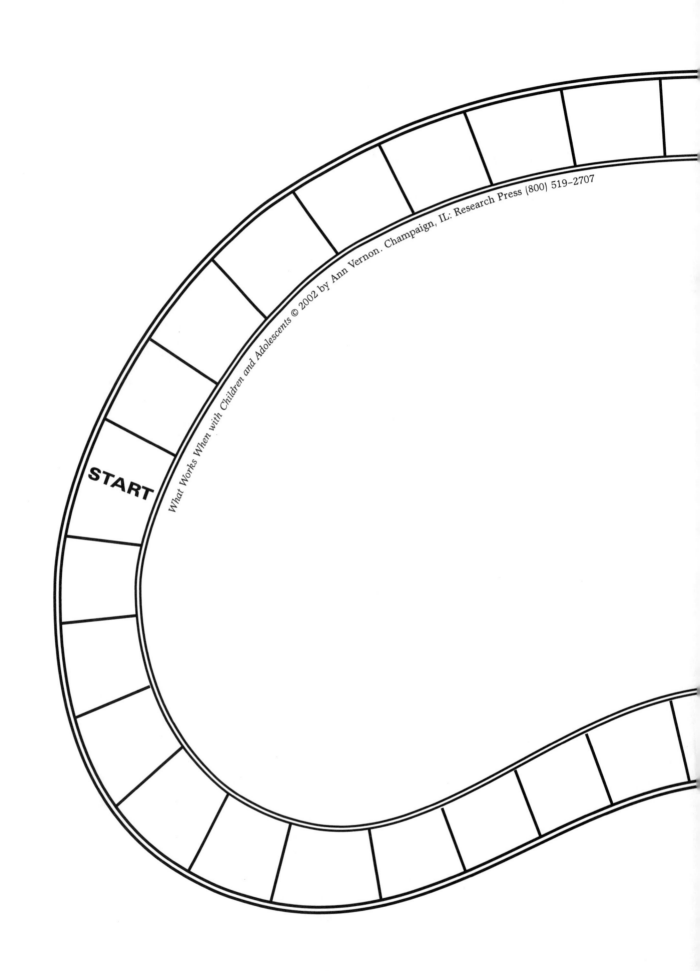

START

What Works When with Children and Adolescents © 2002 by Ann Vernon. Champaign, IL: Research Press (800) 519–2707

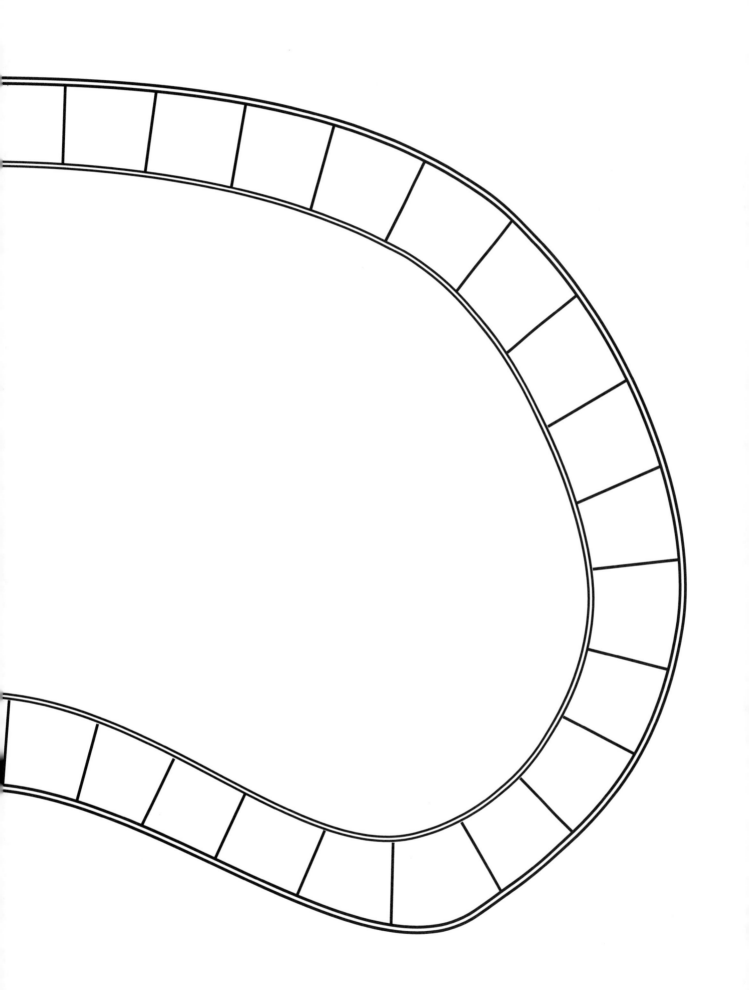

References

Barrish, H. H. (2000). Overcoming perfectionism. In M. E. Bernard & J. L. Wolfe (Eds.), *The REBT resource book for practitioners* (2nd ed.). New York: Albert Ellis Institute.

Barrish, I. J., & Barrish, H. H. (1989). *Surviving and enjoying your adolescent.* Kansas City, MO: Westport.

Beck, A. T., Rush, A. J., Shaw, B. F., & Emery, E. (1979). *Cognitive therapy of depression.* New York: Guilford.

Bedford, S. (1974). *Instant replay.* New York: Institute for Rational Living.

Bee, H. (2000). *The developing child* (9th ed.). Needham Heights, MA: Allyn & Bacon.

Berger, K., & Thompson, R. (1991). *The developing person through childhood and adolescence.* New York: Worth.

Berk, L. E. (2001). *Awakening children's minds.* New York: Oxford University Press.

Bernard, M. E. (1981). Private thought in rational-emotive psychotherapy. *Cognitive Therapy and Research, 5,* 125–142.

Bernard, M. E. (Ed.). (1991). *Using rational-emotive therapy effectively: A practitioner's guide.* New York: Plenum.

Bernard, M. E. (2000). Irrational beliefs associated with underachievement. In M. E. Bernard & J. L. Wolfe (Eds.), *The REBT resource book for practitioners* (2nd ed.). New York: Albert Ellis Institute.

Bernard, M. E. (2001). *Program Achieve: A curriculum of lessons for teaching students how to achieve and develop social-emotional-behavioral well-being,* Vols. 1–6. Laguna Beach, CA: You Can Do It! Education.

Bernard, M. E., & Joyce, M. R. (1984). *Rational-emotive therapy with children and adolescents: Theory, treatment strategies, preventative methods.* New York: Wiley.

Bernard, M. E., Joyce, M. R., & Rosewarne, P. M. (1983). In A. Ellis & M. E. Bernard (Eds.), *Rational-emotive approaches to the problems of childhood* (pp. 415–466). New York: Plenum.

Broder, M. S. (2001). Dr. Albert Ellis—in his own words—on success. *Journal of Rational-Emotive and Cognitive Therapy, 19*(2), 77–78.

Cicchetti, D., & Toth, S. L. (1998). The development of depression in children and adolescents. *American Psychologist, 53*, 221–241.

Cobb, N. J. (2001). *Adolescence: Continuity, change, and diversity* (4th ed.). Mountain View, CA: Mayfield.

Cole, M., & Cole, S. R. (1996). *The development of children* (3rd ed.). New York: Freeman.

Coley, R. L., & Chase-Lansdale, P. L. (1998). Adolescent pregnancy and parenthood: Recent evidence and future directions. *American Psychologist, 53*(2), 152–166.

Deffenbacher, J. L., Lynch, R. S., Oetting, E. R., & Kemper, C. C. (1996). Anger reduction in early adolescents. *Journal of Counseling Psychology, 43*, 149–157.

DiGiuseppe, R. (1999). Rational emotive behavior therapy. In H. T. Prout & D. T. Brown, *Counseling and psychotherapy with children and adolescents: Theory and practice for school settings* (pp. 252–293). New York: Wiley.

Dreikurs, R., & Soltz, V. (1964). *Children: The challenge*. New York: Duell, Sloan, and Pearce.

Dryden, W. (1996). Rational emotive behaviour therapy. In W. Dryden (Ed.), *Handbook of individual therapy* (pp. 306–338). London: Sage.

Dryden, W. (1999). *Rational emotive behavioural counselling in action* (2nd ed.). London: Sage.

Dryden, W., & Ellis, A. (2001). Rational emotive behavior therapy. In K. S. Dobson (Ed.), *Handbook of cognitive behavioral therapies* (pp. 295–348). New York: Guilford.

Dusek, J. B. (1996). *Adolescent development and behavior* (3rd ed.). Upper Saddle River, NJ: Prentice Hall.

Elkind, D. (1984). *All grown up and no place to go: Teenagers in crisis*. Reading, MA: Addison Wesley.

Elkind, D. (1988). *The hurried child: Growing up too fast too soon*. Reading, MA: Addison Wesley.

Ellis, A. (1957). *How to live with a "neurotic": At home and at work*. New York: Crown.

Ellis, A. (1991). Using RET effectively: Reflections and interview. In M. E. Bernard (Ed.), *Using rational-emotive therapy effectively* (pp. 1–33). New York: Plenum.

Ellis, A. (1996). *Better, deeper, and more enduring brief therapy*. New York: Brunner/Mazel.

Ellis, A. (1998). *How to control your anxiety before it controls you*. Secaucus, NJ: Carol.

Ellis, A. (2000). Rational emotive behavior therapy. In R. J. Corsini & D. Wedding (Eds.), *Current psychotherapies* (pp. 168–204). Itasca, IL: Peacock.

Ellis, A. (2001a). *Overcoming destructive beliefs, feelings, and behaviors.* Amherst, NY: Prometheus.

Ellis, A. (2001b). *Feeling better, getting better, staying better.* Atascadero, CA: Impact.

Ellis, A., & Bernard, M. E. (1983). *Rational-emotive approaches to the problems of childhood.* New York: Plenum.

Ellis, A., & Blau, S. (1998). Rational emotive behavior therapy. *Directions in Clinical and Counseling Psychology, 8*(4), 41–56.

Ellis, A., & Dryden, W. (1997). *The practice of rational emotive behavior therapy* (2nd ed.). New York: Springer.

Ellis, A., & MacLaren, C. (1998). *Rational emotive behavior therapy: A therapist's guide.* Atascadero, CA: Impact.

Ellis, A., & Tafrate, R. C. (1997). *How to control your anger before it controls you.* New York: Kensington.

Ellis, A., & Wilde, J. (2001). *Case studies in rational emotive behavior therapy with children and adolescents.* Upper Saddle River, NJ: Prentice Hall.

Fryxell, D., & Smith, D. C. (2000). Personal, social, and family characteristics of angry students. *Professional School Counseling, 4*(2), 86–94.

Genest, M., & Turk, D. C. (1981). Think-Aloud approaches to cognitive assessment. In T. V. Merluzzi, C. R. Glass, & M. Genest, *Cognitive assessment.* New York: Guilford.

Gordon, T. (1970). *Parent effectiveness training: The tested way to raise responsible children.* New York: Peter H. Wyden.

Gordon, T. (2000). *Parent effectiveness training: The proven program for raising responsible children.* New York: Three Rivers Press.

Hauck, P. (1967). *The rational management of children.* New York: Libra.

Heide, K. M. (1999). *Young killers: The challenge of juvenile homicide.* Thousand Oaks, CA: Sage.

Jaffe, M. L. (1998). *Adolescence.* Danvers, MA: Wiley.

Kaplan, P. S. (2000). *A child's odyssey* (3rd ed.). Belmont, CA: Wadsworth.

Keat, D. L. (1979). *Multimodal therapy with children.* New York: Pergamon.

King, K. A., Price, J. H., Telljohann, S. K., & Wahl, J. (2000). Preventing adolescent suicide: Do high school counselors know the risk factors? *Professional School Counseling, 3*(4), 255–263.

Knaus, W. J. (1974). *Rational-emotive education: A manual for elementary school teachers.* New York: Institute for Rational Living.

Knaus, W. J. (2000). Overcoming procrastination. In M. E. Bernard & J. L. Wolfe (Eds.), *The REBT resource book for practitioners* (2nd ed., pp. 44–48). New York: Albert Ellis Institute.

Kwee, M., & Ellis, A. (1997). Can multimodal and rational emotive behavior therapy be reconciled? *Journal of Rational-Emotive and Cognitive-Behavior Therapy, 15*(2), 357–369.

Lazarus, A. A. (1976). *Multimodal behavior therapy.* New York: Springer.

Lockhart, E. J., & Keys, S. G. (1998). The mental health counseling role of school counselors. *Professional School Counseling, 1*(4), 3–6.

McDevitt, T. M., & Ormrod, J. E. (2002). *Child development and education.* Upper Saddle River, NJ: Pearson Education.

McWhirter, J. J., McWhirter, B. T., McWhirter, A. M., & McWhirter, E. H. (1998). *At risk youth: A comprehensive response* (2nd ed.). Pacific Grove, CA: Brooks/Cole.

Nelsen, J., & Lott, L. (1991). *I'm on your side.* Roseville, CA: Prima.

Nelsen, J., & Lott, L. (2000). *Positive discipline for teenagers: Empowering your teen and yourself through kind and firm parenting* (2nd ed.). Roseville, CA: Prima.

Newman, B. M., & Newman, P. R. (1991). *Development through life: A psychological approach.* Pacific Grove, CA: Brooks/Cole.

Owens, K. B. (2002). *Child and adolescent development: An integrated approach.* Belmont, CA: Wadsworth.

Piper, W. (1986). *Little engine that could.* New York: Platt and Munk.

Pipher, M. (1994). *Reviving Ophelia: Saving the selves of adolescent girls.* New York: Ballantine.

Pruitt, D. B. (Ed.). (1998). *Your child: What every parent needs to know about childhood development from birth to preadolescence.* New York: HarperCollins.

Ramsey, M. (1994). Student depression: General treatment dynamics and symptom specific interventions. *Elementary School Guidance and Counseling, 41,* 256–262.

Riley, P. L., & McDaniel, J. (2000). School violence prevention, intervention, and crisis response. *Professional School Counseling, 4*(2), 120–125.

Seifert, K. L., & Hoffnung, R. J. (1997). *Child and adolescent development* (4th ed.). Boston: Houghton Mifflin.

Seligman, M. E. (1995). *The optimistic child.* New York: HarperCollins.

Simon, S. (1975). Building students' self-concepts. In L. W. Howe & M. M. Howe (Eds.), *Personalizing education: Values clarification and beyond.* New York: Hart.

Smith, D. C., Furlong, M. E., Bates, M., & Laughlin, J. (1998). Development of the Multidimensional School Anger Inventory in males. *Psychology in the Schools, 35,* 1–15.

Vernon, A. (1980). *Help yourself to a healthier you: A handbook of emotional education exercises for children.* Washington, DC: University Press of America.

Vernon, A. (1989a). *Thinking, feeling, behaving: An emotional education curriculum for children* (Grades 1–6). Champaign, IL: Research Press.

Vernon, A. (1989b). *Thinking, feeling, behaving: An emotional education curriculum for adolescents* (Grades 7–12). Champaign, IL: Research Press.

Vernon, A. (1993). *Developmental assessment and intervention with children and adolescents.* Alexandria, VA: American Counseling Association.

Vernon, A. (1997). Applications of REBT with children and adolescents. In J. Yankura & W. Dryden (Eds.), *Special applications of REBT: A therapist's casebook* (pp. 11–37). New York: Springer.

Vernon, A. (1998a). *The Passport Program: A journey through emotional, social, cognitive, and self-development* (Grades 1–5). Champaign, IL: Research Press.

Vernon, A. (1998b). *The Passport Program: A journey through emotional, social, cognitive, and self-development* (Grades 6–8). Champaign, IL: Research Press.

Vernon, A. (1998c). *The Passport Program: A journey through emotional, social, cognitive, and self-development* (Grades 9–12). Champaign, IL: Research Press.

Vernon, A. (1999a). Applications of rational emotive behavior therapy with children and adolescents. In A. Vernon (Ed.), *Counseling children and adolescents* (2nd ed., pp. 140–157). Denver: Love Publishing.

Vernon, A. (1999b). Counseling children and adolescents: Developmental considerations. In A. Vernon (Ed.), *Counseling children and adolescents* (2nd ed., pp. 1–30). Denver: Love Publishing.

Vernon, A. (in press). Rational Emotive Behavior Therapy. In D. Capuzzi & D. R. Gross (Eds.), *Counseling and psychotherapy: Theories and interventions.* Upper Saddle River, NJ: Merrill Prentice Hall.

Vernon, A., & Al-Mabuk, R. (1995). *What growing up is all about: A parent's guide to child and adolescent development.* Champaign, IL: Research Press.

Walen, S. R., DiGiuseppe, R., & Dryden, W. (1992). *A practitioner's guide to rational-emotive therapy* (2nd ed.). New York: Oxford University Press.

Waters, V. (1979). *Color us rational.* New York: Institute for Rational Living.

Waters, V. (1980). *Rational stories for children.* New York: Institute for Rational Emotive Therapy.

Waters, V. (1981). The living school. *RET Work, 1,* 1–6.

Waters, V. (1982). Therapies for children: Rational-emotive therapy. In C. R. Reynolds & T. B. Gutkin (Eds.), *Handbook of school psychology* (pp. 37–57). New York: Wiley.

Weisfeld, G. (1999). *Evolutionary principles of human adolescence.* New York: Basic

Wilde, J. (1992). *Rational counseling with school-aged populations: A practical guide.* Muncie, IN: Accelerated Development.

Wilde, J. (1996). *Treating anger, anxiety, and depression in children and adolescents: A cognitive-behavioral perspective.* New York: Taylor and Francis.

Yankura, J. (1997). REBT and panic disorder with agoraphobia. In J. Yankura & W. Dryden (Eds.), *Using REBT with common psychological problems: A therapist's casebook* (pp. 112–157). New York: Springer.

Youngs, B. B. (1995). *Stress and your child: Helping kids cope with the strains and pressures of life.* New York: Ballantine.

About the Author

Ann Vernon, Ph.D., is a licensed mental health counselor and a nationally certified counselor. Dr. Vernon is professor and coordinator of counseling at the University of Northern Iowa, Cedar Falls, and a therapist in private practice, where she specializes in working with children, adolescents, and parents. In addition to these positions, Dr. Vernon is director of the Midwest Center for REBT and is currently the vice president of the Albert Ellis Board of Trustees.

Dr. Vernon has assumed numerous leadership positions within the counseling profession, including president of the Iowa Counseling Association and president of the North Central Association for Counselor Educators and Supervisors. She has written numerous books, chapters, and articles on applications of REBT for children and adolescents, as well as on other topics related to counseling children and adolescents. Her *Thinking, Feeling, Behaving* and *Passport* emotional education curricula are used extensively throughout the United States, Canada, and abroad to promote healthy development in young people. Dr. Vernon is also the author of *Counseling Children and Adolescents, What Growing Up Is All About: A Parent's Guide to Child and Adolescent Development,* and *Developmental Assessment and Intervention with Children and Adolescents.*

In addition to teaching, writing, and counseling, Dr. Vernon consults with schools and mental health agencies. She presents workshops throughout the world on topics pertaining to school counseling, emotional education, and counseling children and adolescents.

Other Research Press Publications by Ann Vernon

Thinking, Feeling, Behaving
An Emotional Education Curriculum

▷ **Grades 1–6**
   90 activities arranged by grade level

▷ **Grades 7–12**
   90 activities arranged by grade level

These two volumes are designed to help students learn to overcome irrational beliefs, negative feelings and attitudes, and the negative consequences that may result. For use in classroom or small-group settings.

The PASSPORT Program
A Journey through Emotional, Social, Cognitive, and Self-Development

▷ **Grades 1–5**
   80 learning activities and
   54 reproducible student handouts

▷ **Grades 6–8**
   60 learning activities and
   56 reproducible student handouts

▷ **Grades 9–12**
   64 learning activities and
   60 reproducible student handouts

This three-volume curriculum is based on developmental theory and the principles of rational emotive behavior therapy. Designed to help students learn what is normal for their age group and to help them learn effective strategies for dealing with the challenges and problems of growing up. For use in classroom or small-group settings.

What Growing Up Is All About
A Parent's Guide to Child and Adolescent Development

Discusses physical, intellectual, social, emotional, and self-development from ages 2 through 18. Examples of typical parenting problems and issues are accompanied by effective communication and discipline strategies.

Research Press   www.researchpress.com   800-519-2707